THIS WORLD IS WHITE NO LONGER

Herausgegeben von Edited by Thorsten Sadowsky

Für die Sammlung Generali Foundation – Dauerleihgabe am Museum der Moderne Salzburg
For the Generali Foundation Collection—Permanent Loan to the Museum der Moderne Salzburg

Verlag für moderne Kunst

GENERALI FOUNDATION

Museum der Moderne Salzburg

THIS WORLD IS WHITE NO LONGER

INHALT
CONTENTS

THIS WORLD IS WHITE NO LONGER
Ansichten einer dezentrierten Welt

THIS WORLD IS WHITE NO LONGER
Views of a Decentered World

PART I

INHALT
CONTENTS

ZUM GELEIT

Die Generali Foundation wurde 1988 von der Generali Gruppe Österreich als gemeinnütziger Verein mit dem Ziel der Förderung zeitgenössischer bildender Kunst gegründet. Der konsequente Aufbau einer Kunstsammlung sowie deren wissenschaftliche Erforschung, Dokumentation, Präsentation und Vermittlung gehören zu ihren zentralen Aufgaben. Auf der Basis einer mutigen Ankaufsstrategie und dank eines bedingungslosen gesellschaftskritischen Ausstellungsprogramms mit bisher rund hundert Ausstellungen und fast ebenso vielen Publikationen konnte die Generali Foundation diesen Anspruch auf erfolgreiche und vorbildhafte Weise verwirklichen. Entsprechend hoch ist das Ansehen, das die Sammlung international genießt.

Im Jahr 2014 gingen die Generali Foundation und das Museum der Moderne Salzburg eine umfassende Partnerschaft ein. Die Sammlung ist seither als Dauerleihgabe in Salzburg in einem exzellenten musealen Kontext verortet. Mit einigen der international bedeutendsten künstlerischen Positionen seit den 1960er-Jahren und ihrem unverwechselbaren Profil bereichert sie die vorhandenen Bestände ab der Moderne. Die Generali Foundation entwickelt die Sammlung nunmehr in diesem Umfeld kontinuierlich weiter und realisiert dazu ein ambitioniertes Ausstellungsprogramm, in dessen Rahmen die wachsenden Werkbestände in wechselnden Ausstellungen gezeigt werden. Ergänzt werden die Aktivitäten durch das Generali Foundation Studienzentrum, das seit 2016 im Rupertinum untergebracht und dort öffentlich zugänglich ist. Mit dem freien Zugang zu Bibliothek, Archiv und Mediathek der Sammlung erfüllt die Generali Foundation zudem einen Bildungsauftrag.

Ich freue mich, dass dieser Katalog den kritischen künstlerischen Diskurs zu grundlegenden Fragestellungen von Rassismus, Xenophobie und Postkolonialismus dokumentiert und fortsetzt, den die Generali Foundation am Museum der Moderne Salzburg mit der zweiteiligen Ausstellung *This World Is White No Longer* initiiert hat. Ziel dieser Ausstellungen sowie der Publikation ist es, nicht nur tief verwurzelte, teils unbewusste rassistische Denk- und Verhaltensmuster zu reflektieren, sondern auch den Perspektivenwechsel als Methode zu untersuchen, um die Deutungshoheit des eigenen Weltbildes zu hinterfragen.

OPENING REMARKS

The Generali Foundation was established in 1988 by the Generali Group Austria as a nonprofit association for the purpose of supporting the visual arts of our contemporary era. The foundation's central tasks include the concerted buildup of an art collection as well as its scholarly investigation, documentation, presentation, and public profile through educational programs. The Generali Foundation has been able to accomplish this undertaking in a successful, exemplary manner on the basis of a strategy of bold acquisitions and a socially critical, hence unconditional program featuring up to now around one hundred exhibitions along with almost as many publications. Today the collection enjoys a significant international reputation.

In 2014 the Generali Foundation and the Museum der Moderne Salzburg entered into a comprehensive partnership. The collection is located at the Museum der Moderne Salzburg as a permanent loan within an excellent museum context. It enriches the museum's other artworks with some of the internationally most significant artistic positions since the 1960s as well as with its striking profile. In this context, the Generali Foundation continues to ceaselessly develop the collection further, and it realizes an ambitious exhibition program, in the context of which the growing stock of works is shown in changing exhibitions. The activities are complemented by the Generali Foundation Study Center, which is open to the public and has been located since 2016 at the Rupertinum. With free access to the collection's library, archive, and media center, the Generali Foundation also fulfills an educational mission.

I am pleased that this catalog documents and continues the critical artistic discourse on fundamental issues of racism, xenophobia, and postcolonialism that the Generali Foundation initiated at the Museum der Moderne Salzburg with the two-part exhibition *This World Is White No Longer*. The aim of these exhibitions as well as the publication is not only to reflect on deeply rooted, partly unconscious racist patterns of thought and behavior, but also to examine the change of perspective as a method to question the claim of one's own worldview to interpretative sovereignty.

Ein zentrales Werk in diesem Zusammenhang ist die Installation *Black Box / White Box* von Adrian Piper, die im Jahr 2003 von der Generali Foundation erstmals in einer Ausstellung in Wien gezeigt und anschließend für die Sammlung erworben wurde. In dieser 1992 entstandenen Arbeit skizziert Piper zwei Perspektiven auf die Misshandlung des schwarzen US-Bürgers Rodney King durch Polizeibeamte und die anschließende Unterstützung der Täter durch den damaligen Präsidenten George Bush sen. – eine schwarze und eine weiße Perspektive. Die beiden Räume der Installation ermöglichen es den Besucher:innen, in zwei unterschiedliche Realitäten einzutauchen und vom jeweils eigenen Standpunkt aus einen Blickwechsel vorzunehmen. Während Betroffene eine Bestätigung ihrer Lebenswelt erfahren, werden alle anderen dafür sensibilisiert, was es heißt, unter Rassismus zu leiden. Pipers Werk ist ein Schlüsselwerk der jüngeren Kunstgeschichte. Wie kaum ein anderes Werk schließt es das Problem von Rassismus und Xenophobie mit dem Erkenntnispotenzial eines empathischen Perspektivenwechsels kurz.

Die beiden Teile der Ausstellung *This World Is White No Longer* und die vorliegende Publikation stellen signifikante künstlerische Positionen zur Diskussion, die verschiedene Orientierungs- und Ansatzpunkte für eine tiefgreifende Auseinandersetzung mit Fragen von Rassismus, Xenophobie und sozialer Ausgrenzung bieten. Dazu gehören auch die jungen Künstler:innen der Klasse für Fotografie und Neue Medien der Universität Mozarteum, die für die Ausstellung im Generali Foundation Studienzentrum eigene neue Arbeiten entwickelt haben. Ich bedanke mich bei allen beteiligten Künstler:innen, bei Thorsten Sadowsky, Direktor des Museum der Moderne Salzburg, und dem gesamten Team des Museums sowie dem Team der Generali Foundation mit der Sammlungsleiterin Doris Leutgeb und Kurator Jürgen Tabor und wünsche allen weiterhin eine produktive und fruchtbare Zusammenarbeit.

Dietrich Karner
Präsident, Generali Foundation

A central work in this context is the installation *Black Box / White Box* by Adrian Piper, which was first shown in an exhibition in Vienna by the Generali Foundation in 2003 and subsequently acquired for the collection. In this work, created in 1992, Piper outlines two perspectives on the mistreatment of Black U.S. citizen Rodney King by police officers and the subsequent support of the perpetrators by then-President George Bush Sr.—a black perspective and a white perspective. The two rooms of the installation allow visitors to immerse themselves in two different realities and to change their point of view. While those affected experience an affirmation of their lifeworld, everyone else is sensitized to what it means to suffer from racism. Piper's work is a key work in recent art history. Like hardly any other work, it short-circuits the problem of racism and xenophobia with the insight potential of an empathic change of perspective.

The two parts of the exhibition *This World Is White No Longer* and the present publication put up for discussion significant artistic positions that offer various points of orientation for a profound examination of issues of racism, xenophobia, and social exclusion. This also includes the young artists of the photography and new media class at the Mozarteum University, who have developed their own new works for the exhibition at the Generali Foundation Study Center. I offer my heartfelt thanks to all the artists involved, Thorsten Sadowsky, director of the Museum der Moderne Salzburg, along with the entire team of the museum, as well as the Generali Foundation team with its head of collection Doris Leutgeb and curator Jürgen Tabor, and I wish all participants a collaboration that will continue to be productive and fruitful.

Dietrich Karner
President, Generali Foundation

EINFÜHRUNG

Thorsten Sadowsky

"[...] See, the road to hell is paved with good intentions
Can't you tell the way they have to mention
How they helped you out, you're such a hopeless victim
Please don't do me any favors, Mr. Intentional
All their talk is seasoned to perfection
The road they walk, commanding your affection
They need to be needed, deceived by motivation
An opportunity, to further situation
Why they're so important is without explanation
Please don't patronize me, Mr. Intentional [...]"
Lauryn Hill, *Mr. Intentional*, MTV Unplugged No. 2.0, 2002

Gute Absichten zeitigen nicht unbedingt auch gute Ergebnisse. Gut gemeint bedeutet noch lange nicht gut gemacht. In seinem berühmten Essay *Politik als Beruf* von 1919 hat der Soziologe Max Weber die noch heute bedeutsame Unterscheidung zwischen Gesinnungsethik und Verantwortungsethik getroffen. Mit Gesinnungsethik wird ein Handeln bezeichnet, dessen ethisch reines Motiv höher bewertet wird als das Resultat. Seit geraumer Zeit ist es in Mode gekommen, den abwertenden deutschen Begriff des „Gutmenschen" mit Gesinnungsethik in Verbindung zu bringen. Der ehrenwerte und ethisch unbedingt gerechtfertigte Anspruch, ein guter Mensch sein zu wollen, wird in der Beschimpfung „Gutmensch" ins Negative gekehrt und mit Naivität, Weltfremdheit und moralischem Imperialismus in Verbindung gebracht. „Gutmensch" wurde 2015 in Deutschland, wo Sprachwissenschaftler:innen alljährlich das „Unwort des Jahres" küren, ebendieser Titel verliehen. „Gutmensch" ist die Steigerung von Political Correctness, da der Begriff ausschließlich diffamierend verwendet wird und Mitmenschlichkeit als Verantwortungslosigkeit diskreditiert. Gute Menschen haben es zurzeit schwer in Europa und der Welt.

Max Weber hatte übrigens durchaus Verständnis für die Gesinnungsethik, doch empfahl er dem Politiker eine Verantwortungsethik, die sich auf ein Handeln bezieht, bei dem das Ergebnis wichtiger ist als das Motiv. Der Politiker würde

INTRODUCTION

Thorsten Sadowsky

"[...] See, the road to hell is paved with good intentions
Can't you tell the way they have to mention
How they helped you out, you're such a hopeless victim
Please don't do me any favors, Mr. Intentional
All their talk is seasoned to perfection
The road they walk, commanding your affection
They need to be needed, deceived by motivation
An opportunity, to further situation
Why they're so important is without explanation
Please don't patronize me, Mr. Intentional [...]"
Lauryn Hill, *Mr. Intentional*, MTV Unplugged No. 2.0, 2002

Good intentions do not always produce good results. Well-meant is often far from well done. In his famous essay of 1919, *Politics as a Vocation*, sociologist Max Weber made the distinction between an ethics of moral conviction and an ethics of responsibility. The ethics of moral conviction stands for actions whose pure ethical motivation are appreciated more than their results. For a while now, it has been fashionable to link the deprecatory German concept of the "Gutmensch" (the good person) with an ethics of moral conviction. The honorable and certainly justified wish to be a good person is inverted in the insult "Gutmensch" and associated with naivety, unworldliness, and moral imperialism. In 2015, the word "Gutmensch" was selected by linguists in Germany as their annual "ugliest word of the year." "Gutmensch" is the superlative of political correctness, as the term is used exclusively in a defamatory sense and discredits humane behavior as a lack of responsibility. At present, good people are having a hard time in Europe and the world.

Max Weber certainly appreciated the value of an ethics of conviction, but he recommended politicians to pursue an ethics of responsibility, focused on action in which the result is more important than the motivation. Politicians, he argued, are judged by their deeds and not their good intentions. But the fact is that the schematic contraposition of the terror of an ethics of conviction, on the one hand, and responsible pragmatism on the other that is so current

an seinen Taten und nicht an seinen guten Absichten gemessen werden. Tatsächlich aber ist die heute übliche schablonenhafte Gegenüberstellung von Gesinnungsterror einerseits und verantwortungsvollem Pragmatismus andererseits ein zu grobes Strickmuster, um die Komplexität politischen Handelns zu beschreiben. Denn es sind ja gerade die sogenannten besorgten Bürger, die mit vorauseilenden Urteilen die Abgrenzung gegenüber anderen Gruppen betreiben und insbesondere die Flüchtlingsfrage für die eigene Identitätsbildung in Stellung bringen. Die apodiktische Festlegung, wer dazugehört und wer draußen bleiben soll, gehört zum Kerngeschäft von Vorurteilen.

In diesem Zusammenhang muss auf das Unwort des Jahres 2021 hingewiesen werden. Dazu wurde der aus dem Englischen stammenden Begriff „Pushback“ gewählt, mit dem der menschenverachtende Prozess des Zurückdrängens von Flüchtenden an den europäischen Außengrenzen beschönigt wird. Noch zu Beginn des Jahres 2022 konnte die Weltöffentlichkeit miterleben, wie Tausende von Geflüchteten aus Afghanistan und dem Nahen Osten an der belarussisch-polnischen Grenze zum Spielball eines neu aufflackernden Ost-West-Konflikts wurden. Das Scheitern der Europäischen Union an ihren eigenen Ansprüchen als einer auf Freiheit, Demokratie, Rechtsstaatlichkeit und Menschenrechten basierenden Wertegemeinschaft wurde in seinem ganzen Ausmaß offenkundig. Mit dem Angriffskrieg Russlands gegen die Ukraine kam es zu einer erneuten Flüchtlingswelle gen Westen, allerdings konnten die Flüchtenden dieses Mal mit einem Höchstmaß an europäischer Solidarität und Empathie rechnen. Das Bild wurde aber schon frühzeitig durch unschöne Szenen an der polnischen Grenze getrübt, als aus der Ukraine geflüchtete internationale Studierende aus den Maghreb-Staaten, dem subsaharischen Afrika und Indien sich von polnischen Rechtsradikalen beschimpfen lassen mussten. Es blieb erneut der Eindruck hängen, dass europäische Willkommenskultur für Menschen in Not eben nicht ohne Ansehen der Person stattfindet.

Wie kann ein österreichisches Kunstmuseum, das sich zu einer diversen und inklusiven Gesellschaft bekennt, in kritischer und angemessener Weise mit Phänomenen wie Rassismus und Xenophobie umgehen? Wie können aktuelle Themen wie physische und strukturelle Gewalt, kulturelle Identität und soziale Exklusion in den Blick genommen und eine Dekolonisierung des Denkens befördert werden? Und sind privilegierte weiße Kurator:innen überhaupt dazu

today is far too roughly hewn to be useful as a description of the complexity of political action. For it is precisely those so-called concerned citizens whose rushed judgments lead to the exclusion of other groups and in particular utilize the issue of refugees in forming their own identity. The apodictic definition of who belongs and who must stay outside is a fundamental component in the formation of prejudice.

It is necessary in this context to note the "ugliest word" of 2021—the English word "pushback" that is used in German as a softening euphemism to denote the misanthropic process of repelling refugees at Europe's exterior borders. Even in early 2022, the world was able to witness how thousands of refugees from Afghanistan and the Middle East were instrumentalized in an East-West conflict rekindled at the Belarussian-Polish border. The extent of the failure of the European Union to live up to its own ideals of a value-oriented community based on freedom, democracy, the rule of law, and human rights has become so very apparent. Russia's war of aggression against Ukraine has caused a new wave of refugees heading west, but with the difference that this time those fleeing were able to expect high degrees of European solidarity and empathy. This picture darkened quickly, with unpleasant scenes on the Polish border when international students from states in the Maghreb region, sub-Saharan Africa, and India who had fled Ukraine were insulted by Polish right-wing radicals. What again remained was the impression that a European culture of welcome for people in need does not operate without being selective in terms of what those people actually look like.

How can an Austrian art museum that has stated its support of a diverse and inclusive society take a critical and appropriate view of phenomena like racism and xenophobia? How can it look at current issues such as physical and structural violence, cultural identity, and social exclusion, and also promote the decolonization of thinking? And are privileged white curators even the right people to speak about racism, which they have never had to experience for themselves? Key points of reference here are self-criticism and the deconstruction of the white gaze onto the world, which had always been wrong and one-sided, but whose validity has only been challenged in recent decades. So that endeavors go beyond mere good intentions, the museum's exhibition program must truly implement declarations on decentering thinking and actually

berufen, über Rassismus zu sprechen, wenn sie diese Erfahrung am eigenen Leib nie machen mussten? Wesentliche Ansatzpunkte sind dabei die Selbstkritik und die Dekonstruktion des weißen Blicks auf die Welt, der immer schon falsch und einseitig war, aber dessen Gültigkeit erst in den letzten Jahrzehnten ins Wanken geraten ist. Damit es nicht bei den guten Absichten bleibt, muss das Ausstellungsprogramm die annoncierte Dezentrierung des Denkens tatsächlich umsetzen und außereuropäische bzw. diverse Perspektiven einbeziehen. Die Zeiten, in denen Weltkunst vornehmlich als weiße Kunst verstanden wurde, während andere Positionen und damit verbundene Wertvorstellungen und ästhetische Konzepte aus dem Olymp des White Cube ausgeschlossen blieben, sind vorbei. Einen neutralen europäischen Blick gibt es nicht, deshalb geht es um die kritische Auseinandersetzung mit der „cultural construction of whiteness" (Kobena Mercer) und darum, das Denken in Hautfarben zu überwinden. Diversität und Inklusion bedeuten in diesem Zusammenhang zudem ein Programm für die gesamte Bevölkerung und nicht allein für die weiße europäische Mehrheitsgesellschaft. Diversität umfasst auch die Aufgabe eigener Privilegien und die Repräsentanz kultureller Minderheiten in den Schaltzentralen der Museen, um Rollenmodelle für eine offene und dynamische Gesellschaft zu schaffen. Hier stehen wir leider erst am Anfang.

„Diese Welt ist nicht mehr weiß und wird es nie mehr sein", stellte der US-amerikanische Schriftsteller James Baldwin 1953 in seinem Essay *Stranger in the Village* fest. Baldwins prophetischer Satz steht für eine entschiedene Kritik am weißen, westlichen Denken und zugleich für einen Aufruf zu einem universellen Humanismus. Selbstverständlich war die Welt nie weiß, aber die weiße Weltsicht wurde seit dem Beginn der europäischen Kolonisierung der Welt zum Maß aller Dinge, und es ist gerade dieser unreflektierte Ethnozentrismus und Machtanspruch, den Baldwin für beendet erklärt. Doch der Weg war und ist noch weit, und wer Raoul Pecks Dokumentarfilm *I Am Not Your Negro* (2017) über die Biografie James Baldwins und die Situation der People of Color in den USA in der zweiten Hälfte des 20. Jahrhunderts sieht, der bekommt einen erschreckenden Eindruck vom exzessiven rassistischen „Othering", mit dem die afroamerikanische Bevölkerung abgewertet und diffamiert wurde. Die 2013 gegründete internationale Bewegung Black Lives Matter hat den Mangel an Chancengleichheit, die rassistische Polizeigewalt und die Kritik am Denken in

include diverse perspectives, including those from outside Europe. The days are over when world art was primarily understood as white art, while other positions and appertaining worldviews and aesthetic concepts were excluded from the echelons of the white cube. There is no neutral European gaze, and therefore what matters is a critical approach to the "cultural construction of whiteness" (Kobena Mercer) and overcoming thinking in colors of the skin. Diversity and inclusion in this context also mean a museum program for the entire population and not just for the white European majority society. Diversity also includes giving up own privileges and representing cultural minorities in the control rooms of museums, in order to create role models for an open and dynamic society. Here we really are only just beginning.

"This world is white no longer, and it will never be white again," wrote the US-American author James Baldwin in 1953 in his essay *Stranger in the Village*. Baldwin's prophetic sentence stands for decisive critique of white Western thinking and also a call for universal humanism. Of course, the world was never white, but since the onset of European colonialization the white view of the world was taken as the measure of all things, and it is exactly this unreflected ethnocentrism and claim to power that Baldwin declares to be over. But the path was and still is long—watching Raoul Peck's documentary film *I Am Not Your Negro* (2017) about James Baldwin's life and the situation of people of color in the USA in the second half of the twentieth century gives you a shocking idea of the excessive racist othering that devalues and defames Afro-Americans. The international Black Lives Matter movement founded in 2013 once again and to great effect drew attention to the lack of equal opportunities and racist police violence, while critiquing thinking in terms of skin color. The public killing of George Floyd on May 25, 2020, then became a symbol for inhuman police violence, triggering protests all over the world.

This publication documents two exhibition projects that were presented by the Generali Foundation Collection in 2021 at the Museum der Moderne Salzburg in the Rupertinum, and which were closely related to each other. *This World Is White No Longer. Views of a Decentered World* brought together works by Karo Akpokiere, Lothar Baumgarten, Danica Dakić, Forensic Architecture, Samuel Fosso, Charlotte Haslund-Christensen, Alfredo Jaar, Voluspa Jarpa, Belinda Kazeem-Kamiński, Adrian Piper, Lisl Ponger, and Kara Walker. The exhibition

Hautfarben erneut wirkungsmächtig ins Bewusstsein gerufen. Die öffentliche Tötung von George Floyd am 25. Mai 2020 wurde schließlich zu einem Symbol für menschenverachtende Polizeigewalt und löste weltweite Proteste aus.

Die vorliegende Publikation dokumentiert zwei Ausstellungsprojekte, die 2021 am Standort Rupertinum des Museum der Moderne Salzburg von der Sammlung Generali Foundation präsentiert wurden und eng miteinander verknüpft waren. Unter dem Titel *This World Is White No Longer. Ansichten einer dezentrierten Welt* wurden Werke von Karo Akpokiere, Lothar Baumgarten, Danica Dakić, Forensic Architecture, Samuel Fosso, Charlotte Haslund-Christensen, Alfredo Jaar, Voluspa Jarpa, Belinda Kazeem-Kamiński, Adrian Piper, Lisl Ponger und Kara Walker versammelt. Die Ausstellung zeigte ausgehend von zentralen Werken der Sammlung Generali Foundation – hier ist insbesondere die Multimedia-Installation *Black Box / White Box* der Künstlerin und Philosophin Adrian Piper zu nennen – eine Auswahl signifikanter Positionen von Künstlerinnen und Künstlern, die sich auf jeweils spezifische Weise mit der Dezentrierung und Dekolonisierung des Denkens und mit der Bewegung zwischen unterschiedlichen Identitäten und Lebenswirklichkeiten befassen. Das kuratorische Anliegen, wichtige Beispiele multiperspektivischer Globalität sowie kultureller Hybridität und künstlerischer Aneignung zu versammeln, stiftete die inhaltliche Klammer.

Gleichzeitig präsentierte die Klasse für Fotografie und Neue Medien der Universität Mozarteum die Projektausstellung *This World Is White No Longer*, die aus einer intensiven mehrmonatigen Beschäftigung mit unterschiedlichen Ausprägungen von Rassismus entstanden war. Mit einer Vielfalt an Zugängen reflektierten die Studierenden alltäglichen und strukturellen Rassismus, hinterfragten Identitätszuschreibungen und untersuchten Möglichkeiten von Machtkritik und Selbstermächtigung. Sie stellten Verbindungen zu anderen Diskriminierungsformen her und thematisierten die Mechanismen sozialer Medien ebenso wie neokolonialistische Praktiken des Tourismus. In insgesamt drei Ausstellungsperioden – Akte genannt – wurden die Arbeiten der folgenden Studierenden gezeigt: Alba Malika Belhadj Merzoug, Melanie Forsthuber, Pia Geisreiter, Magdalena Heller, Hannah Imhoff, Agnes Elena Kern, Vera Kern, Kevin Klinger, Leonie Mirjam Lindinger, Charlotte Pann, Sabine Reisenbüchler,

was based on key works in the Generali Foundation Collection, with a particular focus on the multimedia installation *Black Box / White Box* by artist and philosopher Adrian Piper, and presented a selection of significant positions by artists who in their own different ways address the decentering and decolonizing of thinking as well as the theme of operating between different identities and lived realities. The basic underlying curatorial aim was to combine important examples of multi-perspectivist globality as well as cultural hybridity and artistic appropriation. At the same time, the photography and new media class at the Mozarteum University presented their project exhibition *This World Is White No Longer*, which was based on their intensive exploration of various forms of racism over several months. The students took diverse approaches to everyday and structural racism, challenged ascriptions of identity, and investigated opportunities for a critique of power and for self-empowerment. They established connections to other forms of discrimination and addressed the mechanisms of the social media and also neo-colonialist practices in tourism. In a total of three different exhibition periods, which were called "acts," the works of the following students were shown: Alba Malika Belhadj Merzoug, Melanie Forsthuber, Pia Geisreiter, Magdalena Heller, Hannah Imhoff, Agnes Elena Kern, Vera Kern, Kevin Klinger, Leonie Mirjam Lindinger, Charlotte Pann, Sabine Reisenbüchler, Eva-Maria Schitter, Sculpting Feminism Reading Group, this world is Ego No longer, Angelika Wienerroither, Judith Zaunschirm, and Marija Živojinović.

I would like to warmly thank all those who contributed to the two exhibitions. I especially thank the artists and their gallery partners and all loaners of works for their trust and their readiness to support this ambitious project with important works. Belinda Kazeem-Kamiński created new works specifically for this exhibition and supported the project in many ways, and I express our appreciation and sincerely thank her also on behalf of the curators. I thank Gregor Neuerer, Sigrid Langrehr, Michael Mauracher, and Peter Schreiner, the teachers at the Mozarteum University who supervised this project, for their outstanding and collegial cooperation, and I thank the students for their remarkable commitment and artistically sensitive and ambitious works. I would particularly like to thank Jürgen Tabor, curator at the Generali Foundation Collection, who took charge of the superb development and implementation of the exhibition and this publication. Together with Stefanie Grünangerl, he

Eva-Maria Schitter, Sculpting Feminism Reading Group, this world is Ego No longer, Angelika Wienerroither, Judith Zaunschirm und Marija Živojinović.

Es ist mir ein großes Anliegen, allen an den beiden Ausstellungen beteiligten Akteur:innen sehr herzlich zu danken. Mein besonderer Dank geht an die Künstlerinnen und Künstler und ihre Galeriepartner:innen sowie an die Leihgeber:innen für ihr Vertrauen und die Bereitschaft, das ambitionierte Projekt mit wichtigen Werken zu unterstützen. Belinda Kazeem-Kamiński hat eigens neue Werke für die Ausstellung geschaffen und das gesamte Projekt in vielfältiger Weise unterstützt, wofür ich ihr im Namen der Kurator:innen unsere große Wertschätzung und unseren aufrichtigen Dank aussprechen möchte. Den verantwortlichen Lehrenden an der Universität Mozarteum Gregor Neuerer, Sigrid Langrehr, Michael Mauracher und Peter Schreiner danke ich für die hervorragende kollegiale Zusammenarbeit und den Studierenden für ihr großes Engagement und ihre reflektierten und künstlerisch anspruchsvollen Positionierungen. Besonders hervorheben möchte ich Jürgen Tabor, der in seiner Funktion als Kurator der Sammlung Generali Foundation für die sehr gelungene Entwicklung und Umsetzung der Ausstellung und Publikation maßgeblich verantwortlich gewesen ist. Zusammen mit Stefanie Grünangerl hat er auch die Projektausstellung der Studierenden kuratiert; für den großen Arbeitseinsatz und das souveräne Projektmanagement gebührt beiden mein großer Dank. Die Publikation enthält Beiträge von Stefanie Grünangerl, Gregor Neuerer und Jürgen Tabor, ein Interview mit Belinda Kazeem-Kamiński, das Stefanie Grünangerl und Jürgen Tabor geführt haben, sowie Statements von sämtlichen Studierenden. Mein Dank gilt den Autor:innen ebenso wie Annja Krautgasser für die gelungene Gestaltung des Katalogs und dem Verlag für moderne Kunst Wien für die angenehme Zusammenarbeit. Und schließlich gilt mein herzlicher Dank dem Team des Museum der Moderne Salzburg und der Sammlung Generali Foundation für den engagierten und professionellen Einsatz.

also curated the students' project exhibition, and I thank both warmly for all their work and their excellent project management. This publication contains contributions by Stefanie Grünangerl, Gregor Neuerer, and Jürgen Tabor, an interview with Belinda Kazeem-Kamiński, which was conducted by Stefanie Grünangerl and Jürgen Tabor, and statements by all the participating students. I thank all the authors and also Annja Krautgasser for the excellent catalogue design, and the publishing house Verlag für moderne Kunst Wien for their cooperation with us. Finally, I would like to warmly thank the team of the Museum der Moderne Salzburg and the Generali Foundation Collection for all their committed and professional work.

KÜNSTLER:INNEN / ARTISTS

Texte / Texts: Jürgen Tabor, Künstler:innen / Artists

KARO AKPOKIERE

1981 Lagos, NG – Lagos, NG und Hamburg, DE

Die Zeichnungen von Karo Akpokiere, der in Lagos, der größten Stadt Nigerias, aufgewachsen ist, zeichnen sich durch eine enge Verbindung von Bild und Text sowie durch eine von urbanem Graffiti und Schriftkultur inspirierte Formensprache aus. Darüber hinaus zeugen seine Arbeiten von einer scharfen Beobachtung der gesellschaftlichen Verhältnisse. Akpokiere studierte Grafikdesign am Yaba College of Technology in Lagos und interessierte sich schon früh dafür, die Möglichkeiten des Designs nicht nur für kommerzielle Zwecke, sondern auch für die Vermittlung sozialer und politischer Botschaften zu nutzen. Die Millionenstadt Lagos mit ihrem multikulturellen Mix aus Bildern und Texten, Mustern aller Art, Comics, Design, lokaler und internationaler Musik spielte eine große Rolle bei der Entwicklung seiner künstlerischen Identität. In seinen Werken verknüpft er traditionelle und digitale Zeichentechniken und lässt die Grenzen zwischen Grafik, bildender Kunst, Comics, Illustration und Typografie verschwimmen.

Akpokiere beschreibt seine Serie von Zeichnungen *Zwischen Lagos und Berlin* als einen „Spaziergang" durch die Städte, eine Art „visuelles Tagebuch" der sozialen, politischen und persönlichen Erfahrungen und Beobachtungen, die er in den beiden Metropolen gemacht hat, während er dort arbeitete. Die Zeichnungen erzählen vom Leben auf verschiedenen Kontinenten, vom Wechsel zwischen den Kulturen und den damit verbundenen politischen und sozialen Fragen: Mobilität, Migration, Stereotypen, Religion, die Trennung zwischen Arm und Reich. (JT)

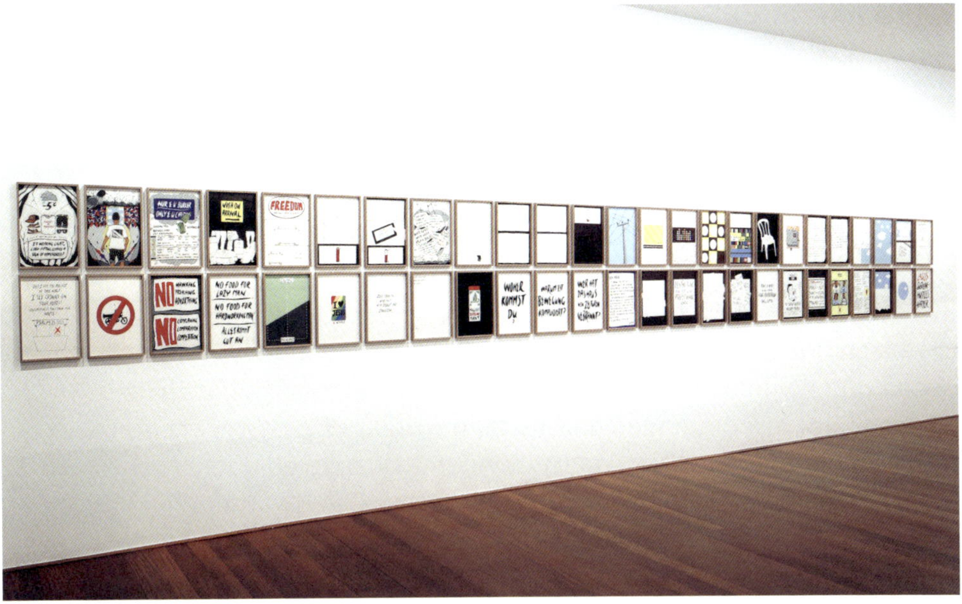

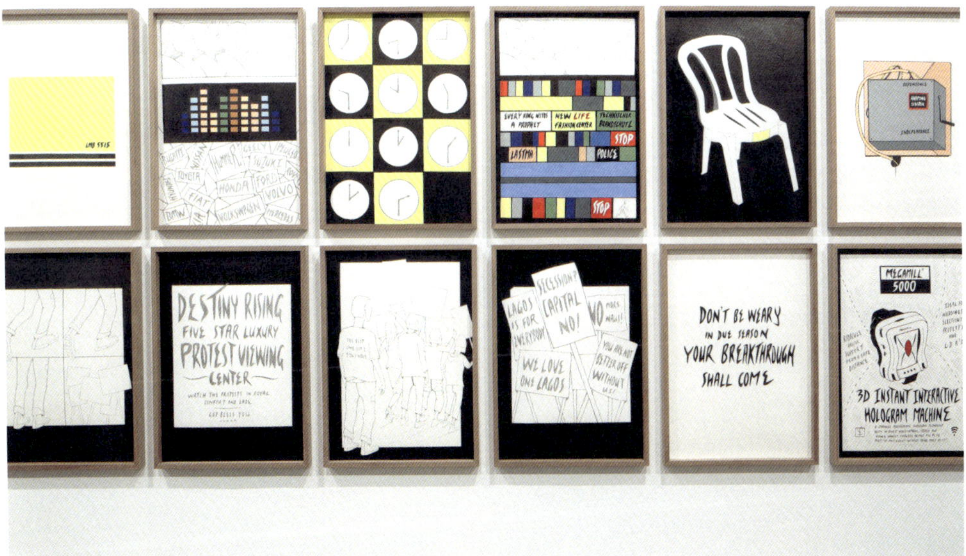

Zwischen Lagos und Berlin, 2015

KARO AKPOKIERE

1981 Lagos, NG—Lagos, NG and Hamburg, DE

The drawings of Karo Akpokiere, who grew up in Lagos, Nigeria's largest city, are characterized by a close connection between image and text, a formal idiom inspired by urban graffiti and writing culture and a keen power of observation of social conditions. Akpokiere studied graphic design at the Yaba College of Technology in Lagos, and became interested early on in using the possibilities of design not only for commercial purposes but also to convey social and political messages. The megacity Lagos itself, with its multicultural mix of images and texts, a myriad of patterns, comics, design, and local and international music, played a key role in Akpokiere's development of a visual identity. In his works he combines traditional and digital drawing techniques and blurs the borders between graphic design, fine art, comics, illustration, and typography.

Akpokiere calls the series *Zwischen Lagos und Berlin* [Between Lagos and Berlin] a "walk through the cities," and a kind of "visual diary" on the social, political, and personal experiences and observations he made in the two metropolises while working there. The drawings tell of life on different continents, of the shift between the cultures, and of political and social issues that are linked to this: mobility, migration, stereotypes, religion, and the divisions between the rich and the poor. (JT)

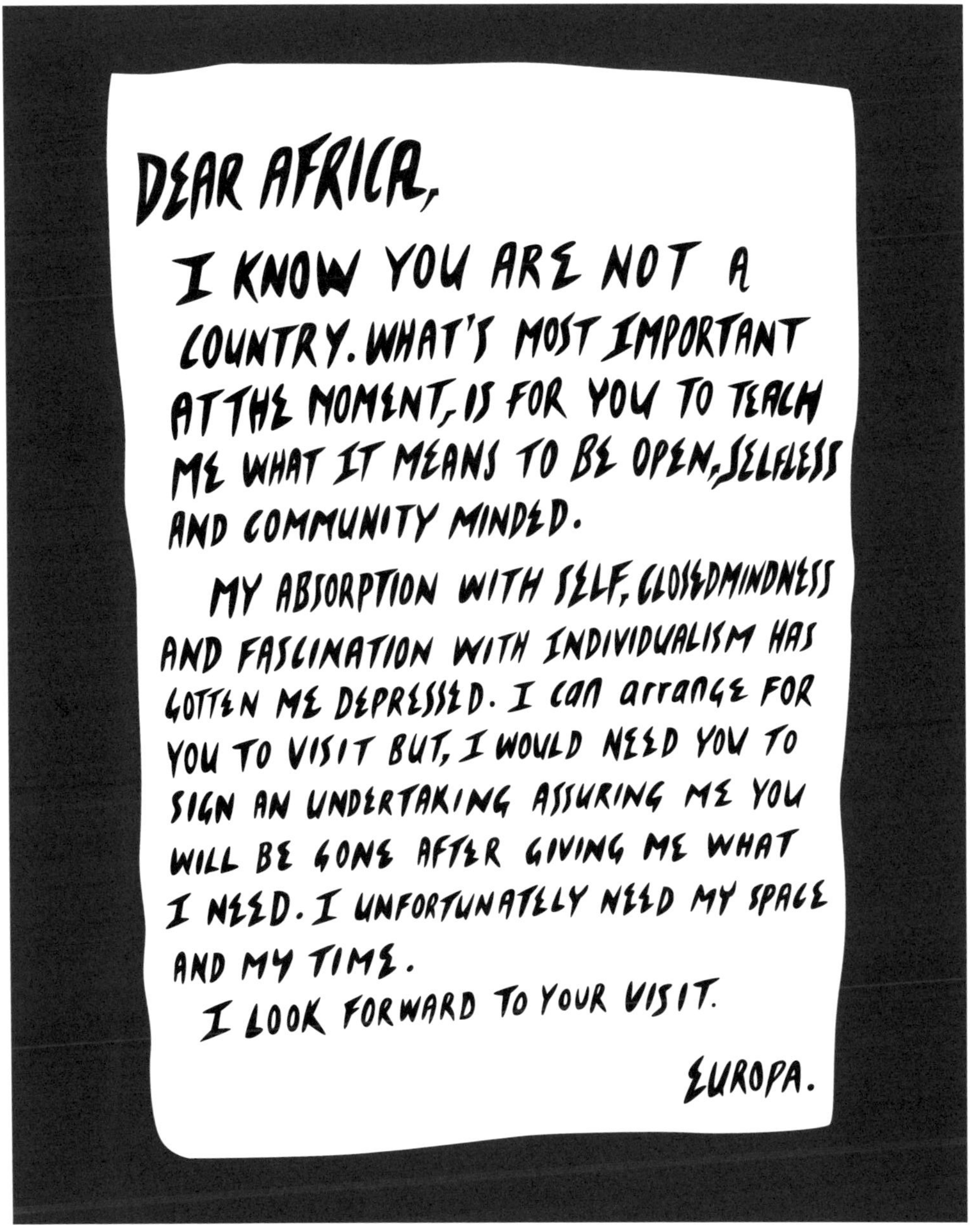
DEAR AFRICA,

I KNOW YOU ARE NOT A COUNTRY. WHAT'S MOST IMPORTANT ATTHE MOMENT, IS FOR YOU TO TEACH ME WHAT IT MEANS TO BE OPEN, SELFLESS AND COMMUNITY MINDED.

MY ABSORPTION WITH SELF, CLOSEDMINDNESS AND FASCINATION WITH INDIVIDUALISM HAS GOTTEN ME DEPRESSED. I can arrange FOR YOU TO VISIT BUT, I WOULD NEED YOU TO SIGN AN UNDERTAKING ASSURING ME YOU WILL BE GONE AFTER GIVING ME WHAT I NEED. I UNFORTUNATELY NEED MY SPACE AND MY TIME.

I LOOK FORWARD TO YOUR VISIT.

EUROPA.

Zwischen Lagos und Berlin (Detail / detail), 2015

LOTHAR BAUMGARTEN

1944 Rheinsberg, DE – 2018 Berlin, DE

Lothar Baumgarten war ein Protagonist der institutions- und ideologiekritischen Kunst ab den 1960er-Jahren. In seinen Werken hinterfragte er den eurozentrischen Blick auf andere Kulturen und die damit verbundene Kolonisierung des Fremden. Er beschäftigte sich intensiv mit den Schriften des Anthropologen und Ethnologen Claude Lévi-Strauss und lebte wie dieser lange Zeit in Südamerika.

Von 1968 bis 1969 schuf Baumgarten eine fotografische Studie, die zeigt, wie sich der Wunsch nach Unterwerfung, Kontrolle, Aneignung und Anpassung des Fremden in der inzwischen historischen museologischen Praxis vieler ethnografischer Museen in Europa manifestierte. In der Lichtbildprojektion *Unsettled Objects* veranschaulicht er das kolonialistisch geprägte Geschichts- und Kulturverständnis des Pitt Rivers Museum in Oxford, eines anthropologischen Museums des späten 19. Jahrhunderts. In 80 Dias, in denen Baumgarten seine eigenen fotografischen Perspektiven auf die Sammlung mit Begriffen der museologischen Praxis überlagert, zeigt er die Vielzahl von Aktivitäten, durch die ethnografische Artefakte organisiert werden. In seinen Ordnungs- und Präsentationskriterien folgt das Museum den evolutionistischen Ideen seines Gründers, des britischen Offiziers Augustus Pitt Rivers. Aus ihren ursprünglichen Kontexten herausgelöst, auf ihren ästhetischen Wert reduziert und zu musealen Fetischen stilisiert, werden ethnografische Artefakte in künstliche Vergleichszusammenhänge gestellt, um ein eurozentrisches Verständnis soziokultureller Evolution zu propagieren. (JT)

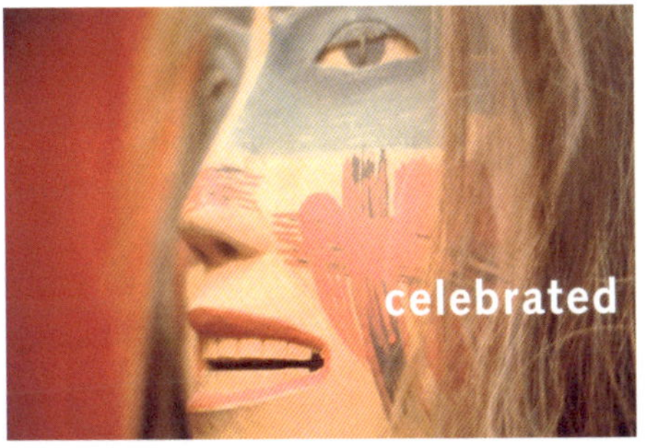

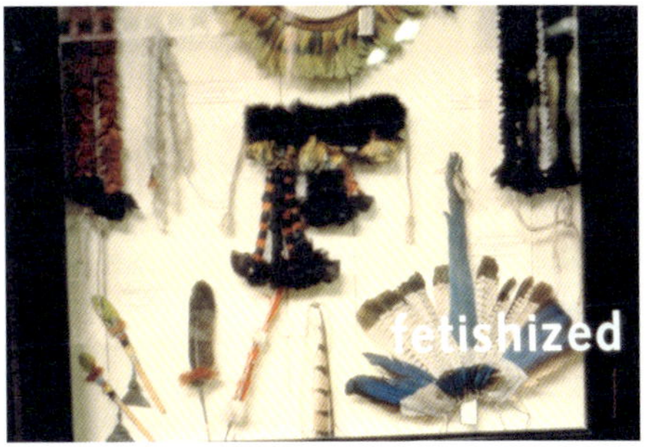

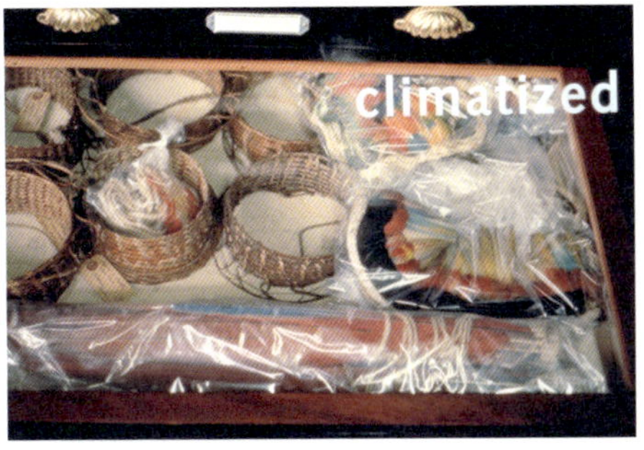

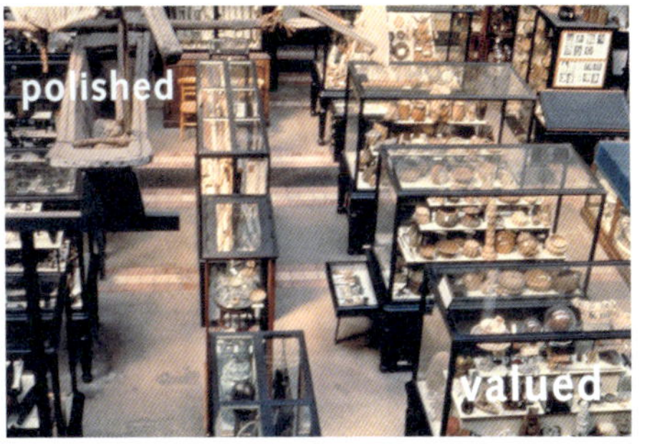

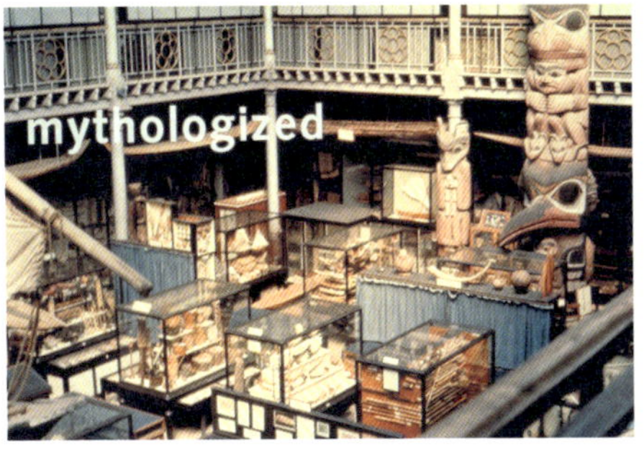

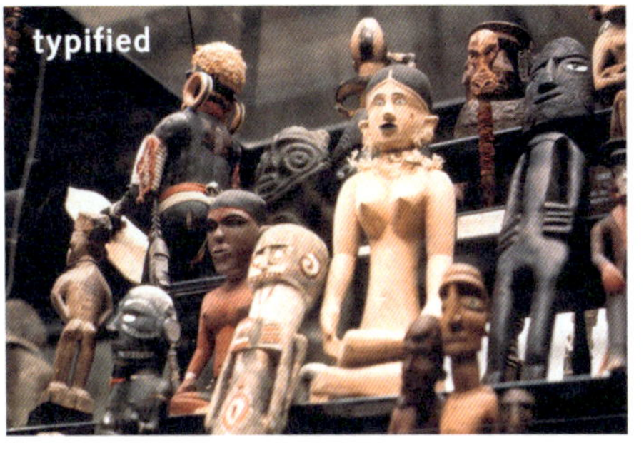

Unsettled Objects, Pitt Rivers Museum, Oxford, 1968/69

LOTHAR BAUMGARTEN

1944 Rheinsberg, DE—2018 Berlin, DE

Lothar Baumgarten was a protagonist of the movement in art that began to take a critical look at institutions and ideologies in the 1960s. In his work, he challenged the Eurocentric perspective on other cultures and the appertaining colonialization of the foreign. In doing this, he intensively studied the writings of the anthropologist and ethnologist Claude Lévi-Strauss, and, like him, he lived for a long period in South America.

From 1968 to 1969, Baumgarten created a photographic study that shows how the desire for subjugation, control, appropriation, and adaptation of the foreign manifested itself in the now historical museological practice of many ethnographic museums in Europe. In the slide projection *Unsettled Objects*, he illustrates the colonialist-influenced understanding of history and culture at the Pitt Rivers Museum in Oxford, an anthropological museum of the late nineteenth century. In eighty slides in which Baumgarten overlays his own photographic perspectives on the collection with notions of museological practice, he shows the multiplicity of activities through which ethnographic artifacts are organized. In its criteria of order and presentation, the museum follows the evolutionist ideas of its founder, the British officer Augustus Pitt Rivers. Removed from their original contexts, reduced to their aesthetic value, and stylized into museum fetishes, ethnographic artifacts are placed in artificial comparative contexts in order to propagate a Eurocentric understanding of sociocultural evolution. (JT)

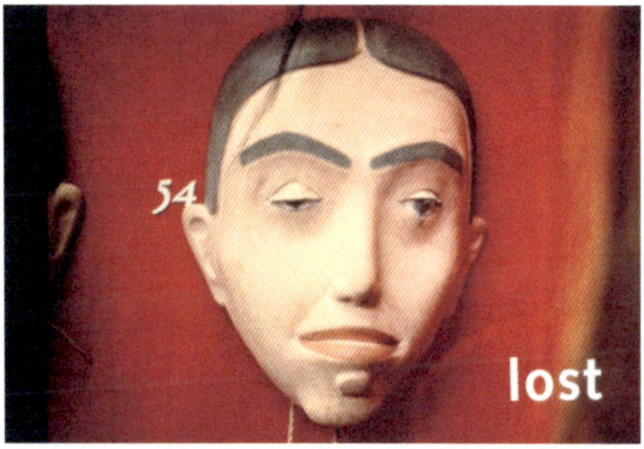

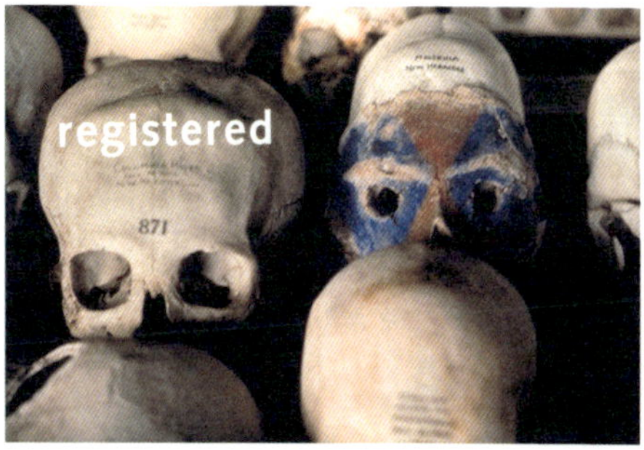

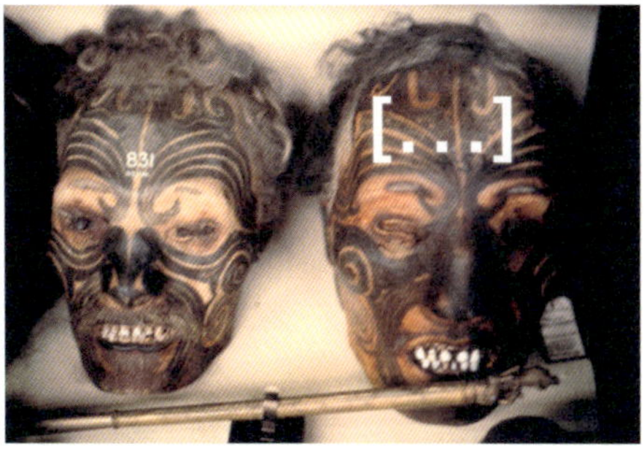

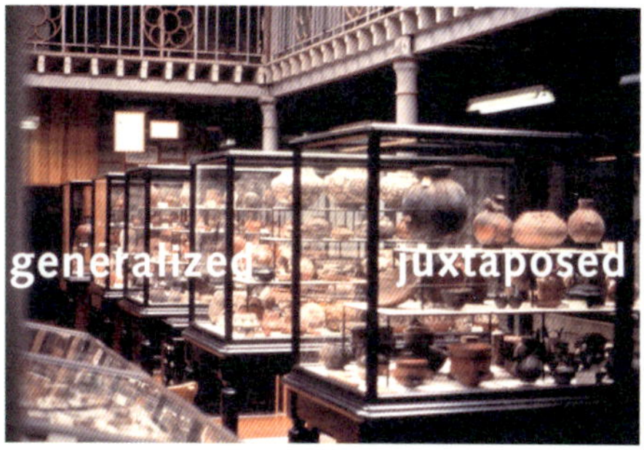

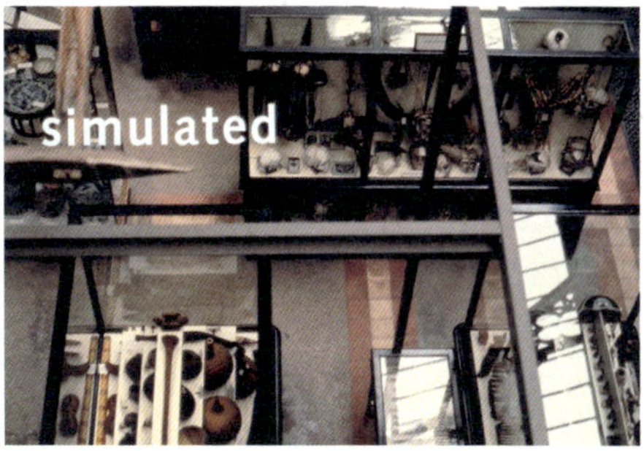

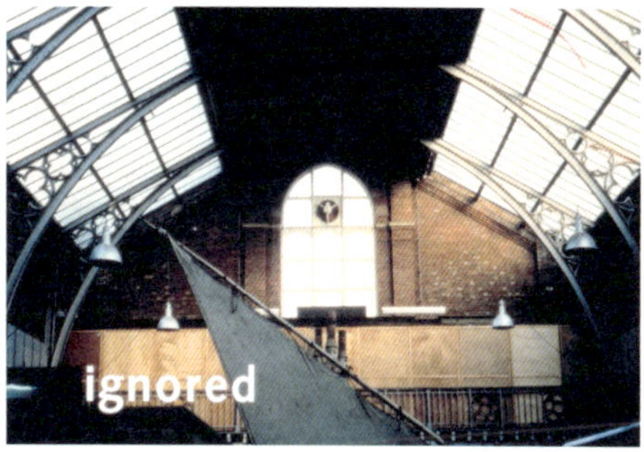

Unsettled Objects, Pitt Rivers Museum, Oxford, 1968/69

DANICA DAKIĆ

1962 Sarajevo, BA – Düsseldorf, DE

Die Legende von El Dorado, einem Goldenen Land inmitten des dichten Urwalds von Südamerika, hat seit dem 17. Jahrhundert die Fantasie europäischer Eroberer beflügelt. El Dorado wurde zu einem Sinnbild für die Suche nach einer paradiesischen Welt und steht zugleich für die Kolonisierung Südamerikas durch spanische und portugiesische Eroberer, die dort unermessliche Schätze zu finden hofften.

Die monumentale Panoramatapete *Eldorado*, die sich im Deutschen Tapetenmuseum in Kassel befindet, wurde 1859 in der Manufaktur Jean Zuber & Cie. in Rixheim im Elsass gedruckt. Auf einer Größe von 12 mal 2 Metern breitet sie eine globalisierte Interpretation des Mythos aus: Sie zeigt üppige Vegetationen mit architektonischen Motiven, die Afrika, Amerika, Asien und Europa repräsentieren. Die Tapete bringt die Welt, die exotische Fremde, in gezähmter und paradiesischer Form in die eigenen vier Wände.

Danica Dakić' *EL DORADO. Gießbergstraße* ist in Kassel verankert. Die Video- und Fotoinstallation entstand mit Jugendlichen, die in einem Wohnheim für minderjährige Flüchtlinge untergebracht waren. Die Panoramatapete und andere Orte im Museum dienten als Projektionsflächen, vor denen die Protagonist:innen ihre Lebenssituation, ihre Sehnsüchte und Vorstellungen von Glück und Zukunft zu szenischen Darstellungen formten. Die Räume des Tapetenmuseums wurden zum Bühnenbild und Handlungsraum für die Jugendlichen. „Es ging darum, vor dieser historischen Projektionsfolie von ‚El Dorado' die Umbrüche ihres Aufwachsens, ihrer Migration und ihrer Suche nach dem Paradies zu verhandeln. Für mich war es wichtig, diesen jungen Menschen zu begegnen, zu sehen, wie sie reagieren und was kommt, und dann von ihnen selbst zu erfahren, was sie denken, wie sie fühlen."[1] (JT)

1 Danica Dakić, „documenta 12: Traum und Trauma", Interview mit Johanna Hofleitner, in: *Die Presse*, 28.06.2007.

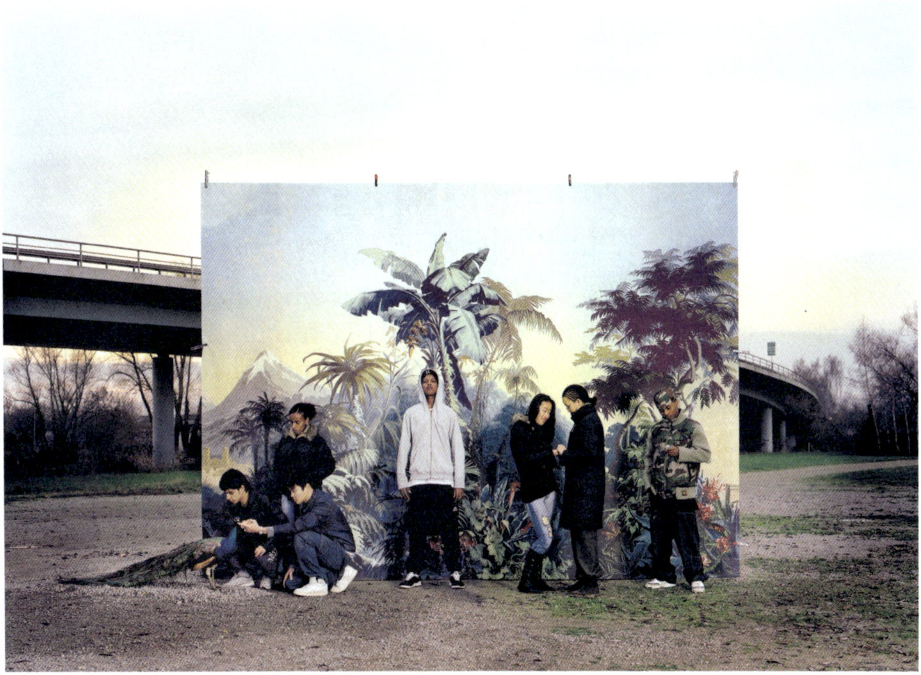

EL DORADO. Gießbergstraße, 2006/07

DANICA DAKIĆ

1962 Sarajevo, BA—Dusseldorf, DE

The legend of El Dorado, a golden land in the middle of a dense jungle in South America, has fired the imagination of European conquerors since the seventeenth century. El Dorado became a symbol of the quest for a paradise, but it also stands for the colonialization of South America by Spanish and Portuguese conquerors, who hoped to find great treasures there.

The monumental panoramic tapestry *Eldorado* in the German Wallpaper Museum in Kassel was printed in 1859 by Jean Zuber & Cie. in Rixheim in Alsace. It presents a global interpretation of the myth over a size of 12 by 2 meters, showing opulent vegetation and architectural motifs representing Africa, America, Asia, and Europe. This wallpaper brings the exotic and unknown world into our own four walls as a tamed paradise.

Danica Dakić's *EL DORADO. Gießbergstraße* is anchored in Kassel. She made this video and photo installation together with young people who were housed in a residential home for unaccompanied and underage refugees in Kassel. The panoramic wallpaper and other scenes from the museum are used as a projection surface, before which the protagonists shape their own personal situations, their desires, and visions of happiness and the future into theatrical performances. The galleries of the wallpaper museum served the young people as the stage sets and sphere of action. "The idea was for these youths to consider their difficult transition to adulthood, their migration, and their own quest for paradise before the backdrop of this historical vision of 'El Dorado.' It was important for me to meet these young people, to see how they reacted and what would come next, and to learn from them what they were thinking and feeling."[1] (JT)

1 Danica Dakić, "documenta 12: Traum und Trauma", interview with Johanna Hofleitner, in: *Die Presse*, June 28, 2007.

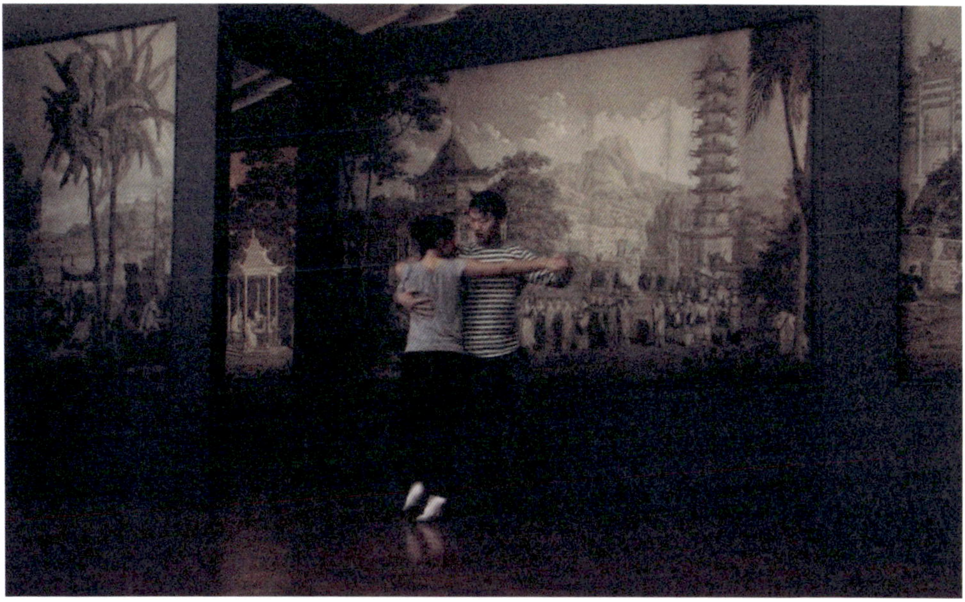

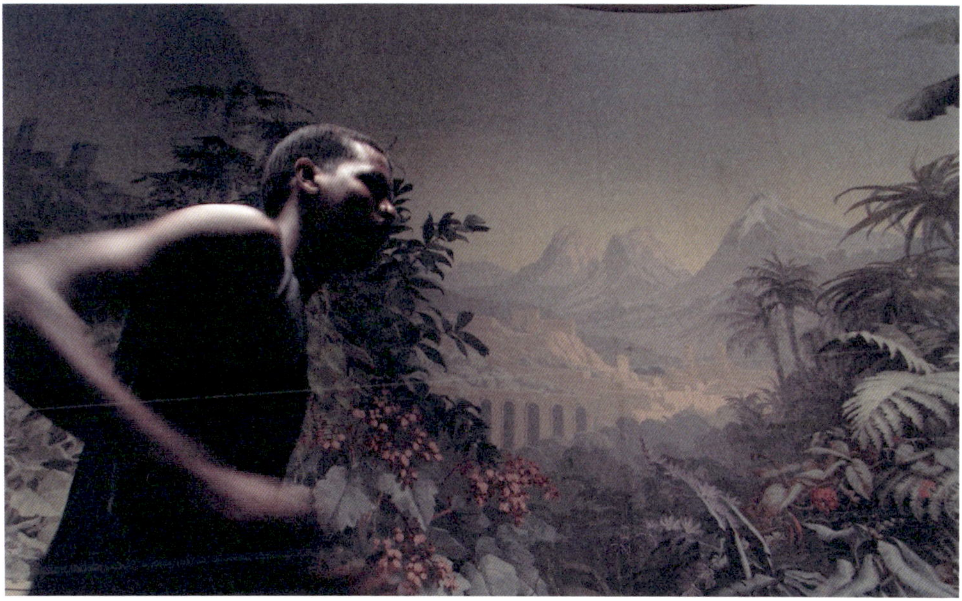

EL DORADO. Gießbergstraße, 2006/07

FORENSIC ARCHITECTURE

2011 gegründet am Centre for Research Architecture, Goldsmiths, University of London

Gewalt an der Grenze des Flusses Evros/Meriç: sechs Untersuchungen

Der Fluss Evros/Meriç markiert die einzige „Landgrenze" zwischen Griechenland und der Türkei. Von Bulgarien im Norden bis zum Ägäischen Meer im Süden ist diese sogenannte natürliche Grenze seit Langem in ein umfassenderes System zur Grenzverteidigung eingebunden.

Seit Jahren berichten Migrant:innen und Flüchtlinge, die den Fluss nach Griechenland überqueren, dass sie von unbekannten maskierten Männern nachts und ohne Zugang zu Asylverfahren festgehalten, misshandelt und über den Fluss in die Türkei „zurückgeschoben" werden. Im März 2020 geriet die verdeckte Gewalt in den Blick der Öffentlichkeit, als die türkische Regierung die Grenzen des Landes zu Griechenland öffnete und Tausende von Migrant:innen und Flüchtlinge in die Region strömen ließ. Die griechische Regierung deklarierte dies zu einer „hybriden Invasion" und entsandte Polizei und Militär in die Region. Infolgedessen wurden zwei Menschen erschossen und mindestens sechs weitere verwundet – durch Schüsse, die von der griechischen Seite der Grenze abgefeuert worden waren.

Bis zum heutigen Tag bezeichnen die griechischen Behörden diese Berichte über Schießereien und Abschiebungen als „Fake News" und verweigern jegliche Untersuchung. Diese Leugnung wird durch die komplexe militarisierte Geografie der Region begünstigt. Das Flussufer ist auf beiden Seiten durch eine „Pufferzone" gesichert, zu der Zivilist:innen, humanitäre Helfer:innen, Journalist:innen oder Beobachter:innen keinen Zutritt haben. In dieser Pufferzone befinden sich häufig Internierungseinrichtungen und Grenzschutzstationen, in denen diejenigen, die den Fluss

überqueren, isoliert werden – vor den Augen der Öffentlichkeit verborgen und ohne Zugang zu rechtlicher Unterstützung. Die Festgenommenen berichten, dass ihre Telefone, Dokumente und Besitztümer konfisziert und oft in den Fluss geworfen wurden, was auf eine Operation schließen lässt, die mit Bedacht darauf ausgelegt ist, ihre eigenen Spuren zu verwischen.

Insgesamt ist festzustellen, dass die örtlichen Umstände als Waffe eingesetzt werden, um diejenigen, die versuchen, den Fluss zu überqueren, abzuschrecken und die gegen sie verübte Gewalt zu verschleiern, ohne sich dazu zu bekennen. Unsere Untersuchungsergebnisse erhellen die obskuren Umstände: Sie zeigen auf, dass derartige „Pushbacks" am Fluss Evros/Meriç methodisch und in großem Umfang praktiziert werden, und belegen den Tod von zwei Asylsuchenden durch Schüsse im März 2020. Sie rekonstruieren die Fälle von Fady, einem syrischen Mann, der in Deutschland als Flüchtling anerkannt, in Griechenland aber verhaftet und kurzerhand über den Fluss abgeschoben wurde; von Ayşe Erdoğan, einer türkischen Lehrerin, die in Griechenland Asyl beantragte, jedoch in die Türkei „zurückgeschoben" und dort anschließend inhaftiert wurde; von Kuzey, einem türkischen Mann, der festgenommen, gefoltert und über den Fluss zurückgewiesen wurde, und zwar fünfmal in einem Zeitraum von neun Tagen; sowie vom „Pushback" einer Gruppe, der mit einer versteckten Kamera aufgezeichnet wurde, und die Ermordung von Muhammad al-Arab und Muhammad Gulzar. (FA)

FORENSIC ARCHITECTURE

Founded in 2011 at the Centre for Research Architecture, Goldsmiths, University of London

Border Violence Across the Evros/Meriç River: Six Investigations

The Evros/Meriç river delineates the only "land" border between Greece and Turkey. From Bulgaria in the north to the Aegean Sea in the south, this so-called "natural" border has long been incorporated into a wider system of border defense.

For years, migrants and refugees crossing the river into Greece have testified to being detained, beaten, and "pushed back" across the river to Turkey, by unidentified masked men, at night, and without access to asylum procedures. In March 2020, this covert violence erupted into view when the Turkish government opened its borders with Greece, funneling thousands of migrants and refugees to the region. The Greek government declared this a "hybrid invasion," and deployed police and its military to the region. As a result, two people were shot dead and at least six more wounded, by bullets fired from the Greek side of the border.

To this day, Greek authorities denounce these reports of shootings and pushbacks as "fake news," and refuse to investigate. These denials are enabled by the complex, militarized geography of the region. A "buffer zone" skirts both banks of the river, prohibiting access to civilians, humanitarian workers, researchers, and monitors. Detention sites and border guard stations are often located within this buffer zone, keeping those who cross the river isolated, out of sight, and without access to legal support. Those detained describe having their phones, documents, and possessions confiscated and often thrown into the river, suggesting an operation that is carefully designed to cover its own tracks.

Overall, the river's natural processes have been weaponized to deter those who attempt to cross, to obscure the violence perpetrated against them, and to deflect responsibility. Our investigations penetrate that veil of obscurity, demonstrating that "pushbacks" at Evros/Meriç are methodical and widespread, and verifying the deaths by gunfire of two asylum seekers in March 2020. They reconstruct the cases of Fady, a Syrian man recognized as a refugee in Germany but arrested in Greece and summarily expelled across the river; Ayşe Erdoğan, a Turkish teacher who sought asylum in Greece only to be "pushed back" and subsequently imprisoned in Turkey; Kuzey, a Turkish man who was detained, tortured, and "pushed back" across the river five times in the space of nine days; a group "pushback" that was recorded with a concealed camera; and the killings of Muhammad al-Arab and Muhammad Gulzar. (FA)

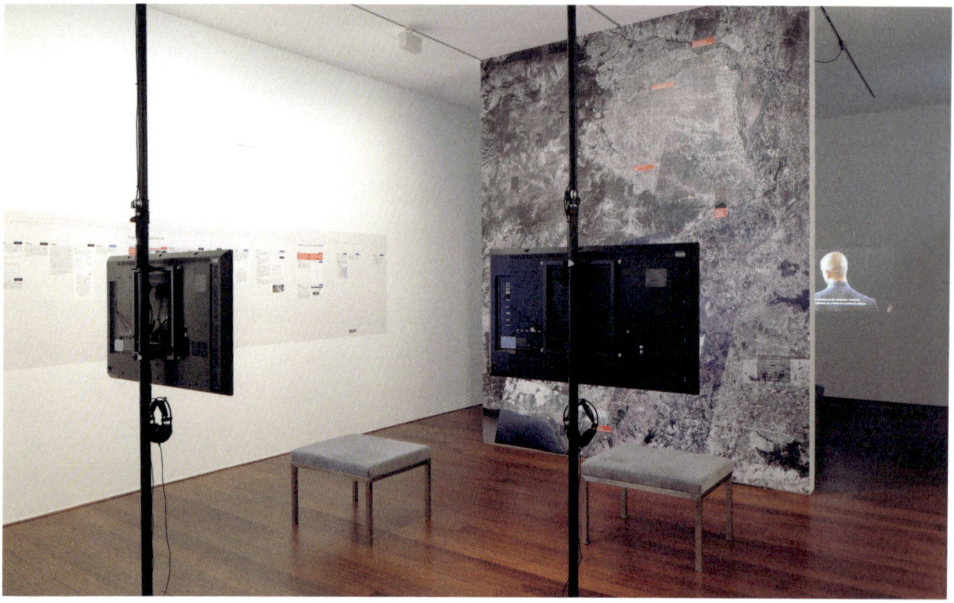

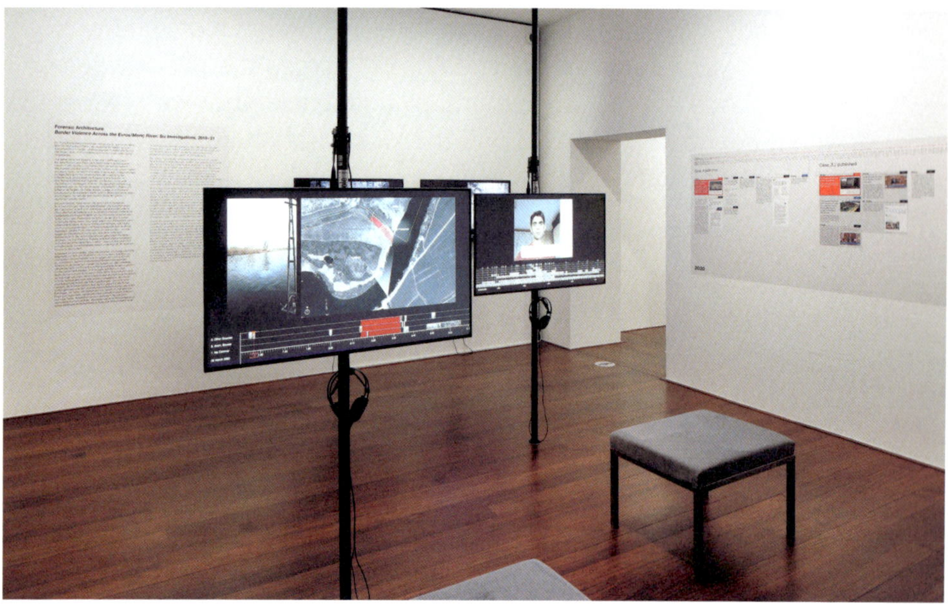
Forensic Architecture
Border Violence Across the Evros/Meriç River: Six Investigations, 2019–21

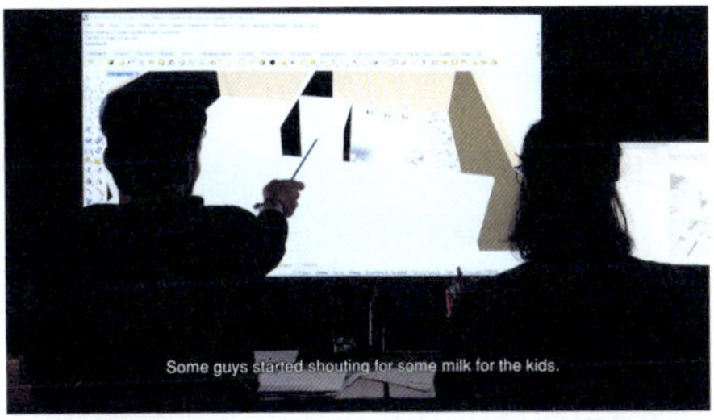

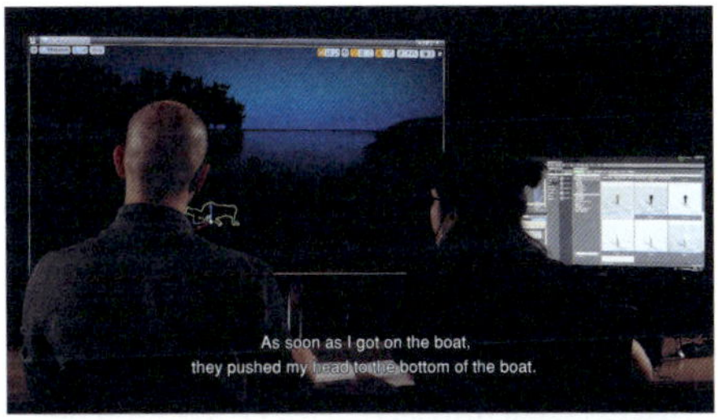

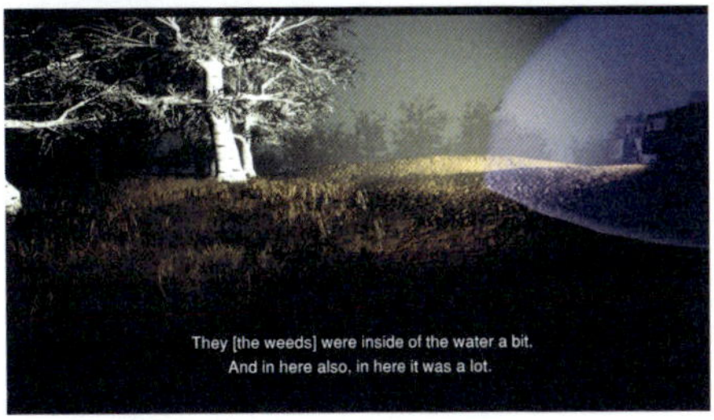

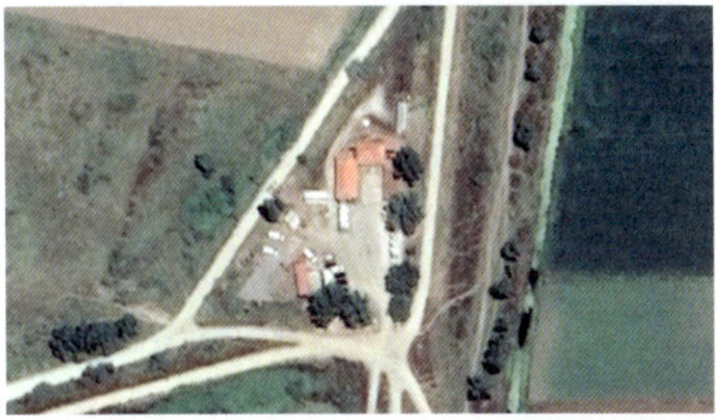

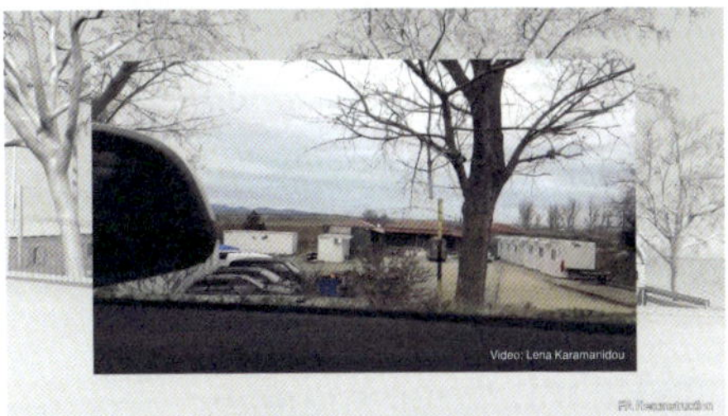

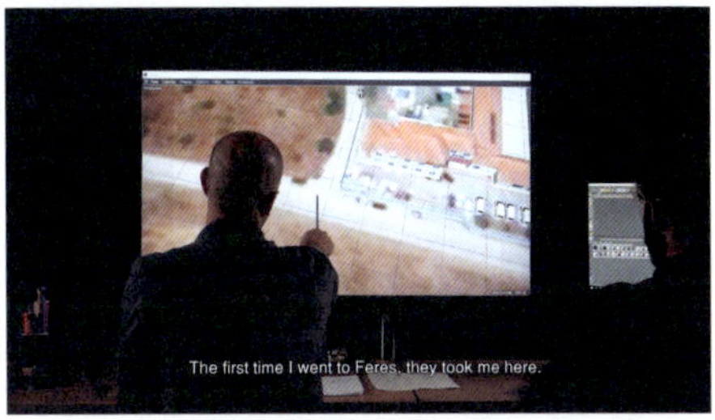

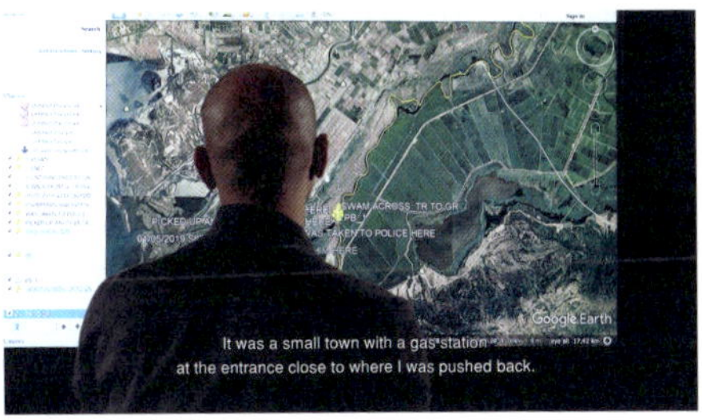

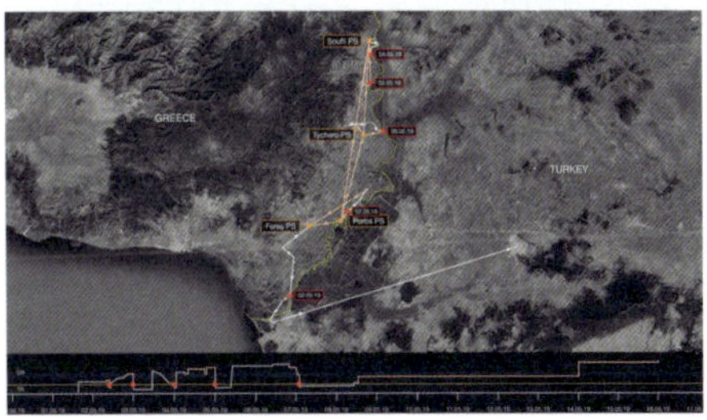

Border Violence Across the Evros/Meriç River: Six Investigations, 2019–21

SAMUEL FOSSO

1962 Kumba, CM – Bangui, CF und Paris, FR

Samuel Fosso zählt zu den renommiertesten Fotokünstlern Afrikas. In seinen seit Mitte der 1970er-Jahre entstandenen Werken verbindet er Fotografie und Performance zu höchst theatralischen Selbstporträts. Mit kunstvollem Make-up und aufwendigen Kostümen, Requisiten und Kulissen schafft er autofiktionale Selbstporträts, in denen er in erster Linie nicht sich selbst darstellt, sondern eine Transformation seiner Person vollzieht. Er schlüpft in Rollen und leiht sich Identitäten – von historischen Schlüsselfiguren ebenso wie von gesellschaftlichen Archetypen, die im globalen Bildgedächtnis tief verankert sind. Seine Selbstporträts sind Ausdruck der Komplexität und Vielfalt afrikanischer Identitäten und eine Erkundung der Beziehungen Afrikas zum Osten und zum Westen in der Ära des Postkolonialismus und der Globalisierung.

1975, im Alter von 13 Jahren, eröffnete Fosso sein eigenes Studio für Porträtfotografie in Bangui, der Hauptstadt der Zentralafrikanischen Republik. Der Erfolg seines Studios beruhte auf seinem Sinn für Mode und Schönheit und seinem Talent, seine Kund:innen zu ermutigen, ihren persönlichen Stil zu zeigen. Tagsüber porträtierte er seine Kundschaft, abends jedoch stellte er sich selbst vor die Kamera und inszenierte sich, inspiriert von westafrikanischer und afroamerikanischer Musik, Jugendkultur und politischer Rebellion, in engen Hemden, extravaganten Schlaghosen und Plateauschuhen sowie ausgefallenen Requisiten in freien, ungezwungenen Posen. Auf diese Weise entstand Fossos frühe Fotoserie, die unter dem Titel *70's Lifestyle* (1974–78) bekannt wurde. Fosso entwirft darin ein alternatives Bild von Männlichkeit, in dem er spielerisch und selbstbewusst Konventionen der Darstellung von Körper, Geschlecht und Sexualität durchkreuzt.

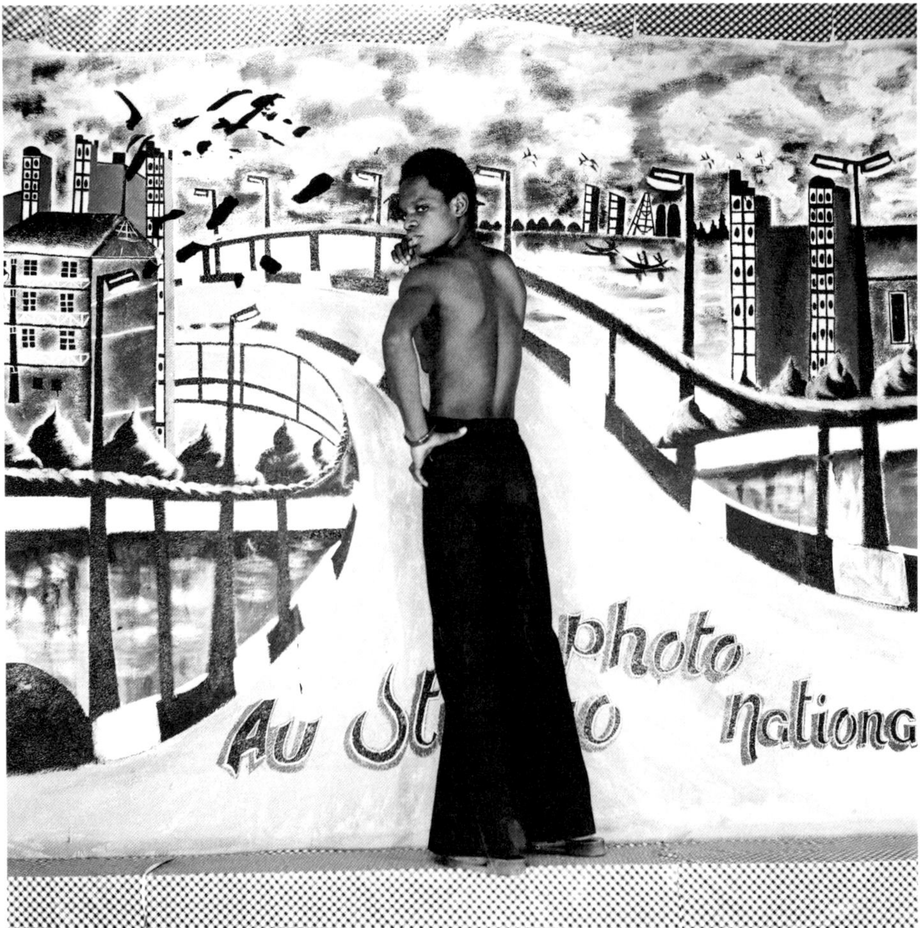

70's Lifestyle, 1974–78

In späteren Werkserien wie *African Spirits* (2008) und *Emperor of Africa* (2013) verleiht Fosso seinem Werk einen deutlichen politischen Zug. In *African Spirits* verkörpert er Protagonist:innen der panafrikanischen Unabhängigkeits- und Bürgerrechtsbewegung wie Angela Davis, Martin Luther King Jr., Malcolm X und Tommie Smith. Bei den Selbstporträts handelt es sich um Reinszenierungen, die auf historischen Bildern aus Magazinen und Zeitungen basieren. Der Prozess der Identifikation und Verkörperung wird hier von Fosso mit äußerster Präzision und Intensität ausgeführt. *African Spirits* verweist damit auf die zentrale Rolle der Kämpfer:innen für Bürgerrechte und postkoloniale Unabhängigkeit für die Entwicklung Schwarzer Identität.

In seiner Serie *Emperor of Africa* thematisiert Fosso die tiefgreifenden Machtverhältnisse zwischen China und Afrika. Dazu schlüpft er in die Rolle des umstrittenen chinesischen Revolutionärs und kommunistischen Parteiführers Mao Tse-tung. In seinen Reinszenierungen stellt Fosso Mao als ambivalentes Symbol eines modernen Imperialismus dar. Während die wachsende wirtschaftliche und kulturelle Präsenz Chinas von afrikanischen Führern zunächst begrüßt wurde, gibt die damit verbundene Machtausübung zunehmend Anlass zur Sorge.

In einer seiner jüngsten Serien, *Black Pope*, verkörpert Fosso auf überzeugende und zugleich herausfordernde Weise die zentrale Identifikationsfigur der katholischen Kirche, den Papst. Er entwirft die Vision eines schwarzen Papstes – hier ins Gebet vertieft – und stellt zugleich Fragen nach der Macht und Autorität, die mit den Attributen, Ausstattungen und Normen der Kirche verbunden sind, in diesem Fall mit dem ikonischen Weiß der Papstgewänder. (JT)

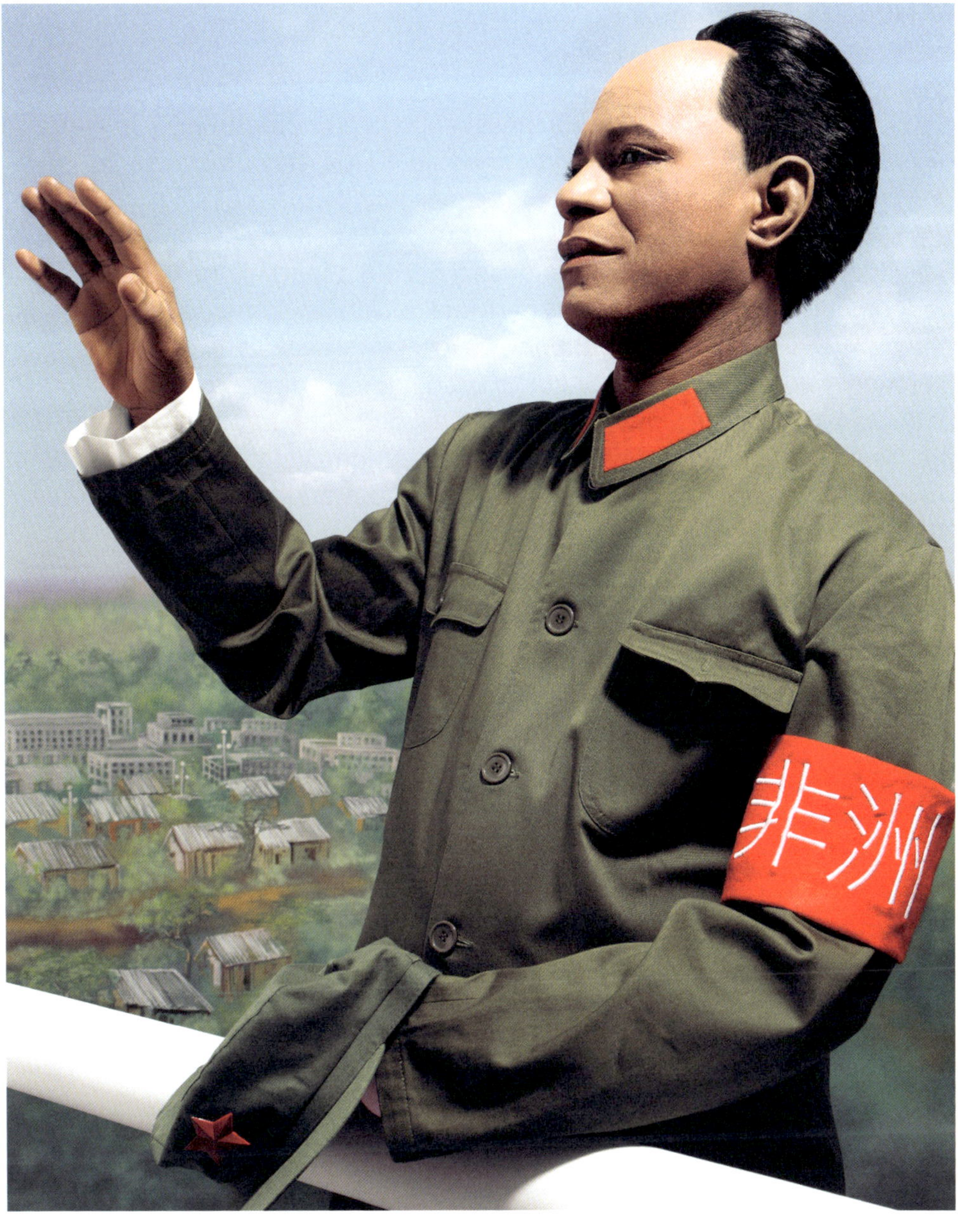

Emperor of Africa, 2013

SAMUEL FOSSO

1962 Kumba, CM—Bangui, CF and Paris, FR

Samuel Fosso is one of Africa's most renowned photographic artists. In his works, created since the mid-1970s, he combines photography and performance to create highly theatrical self-portraits. With skillful makeup and elaborate costumes, props, and backdrops, he creates autofictional self-portraits in which he does not primarily portray himself, but performs a transformation of his person. He slips into roles and borrows identities—identities of key historical figures as well as of social archetypes that are deeply anchored in global visual memory. His self-portraits are an expression of the complexity and diversity of African identities, and an exploration of Africa's relations with the East and the West in the era of postcolonialism and globalization.

In 1975, at the age of 13, Fosso opened his own portrait photography studio in Bangui, the capital of the Central African Republic. The success of his studio was based on his sense of fashion and beauty and his talent for encouraging clients to show their personal style. During the day he took portraits of his clients, but in the evenings he put himself in front of the camera and, inspired by West African and African-American music, youth culture, and political rebellion, staged himself in tight shirts, flamboyant bell-bottoms and platform shoes, and fancy props in free, informal poses. This is how Fosso's early photo series, which became known as *70's Lifestyle* (1974–78), was created. In it, Fosso presents an alternative image of masculinity in which he playfully and self-confidently thwarts conventions of the representation of the body, gender, and sexuality.

In later series of works such as *African Spirits* (2008) and *Emperor of Africa* (2013), Fosso infuses his work with a distinctly political streak. In *African Spirits*, he embodies protagonists of the Pan-African independence and civil rights movement such as Angela

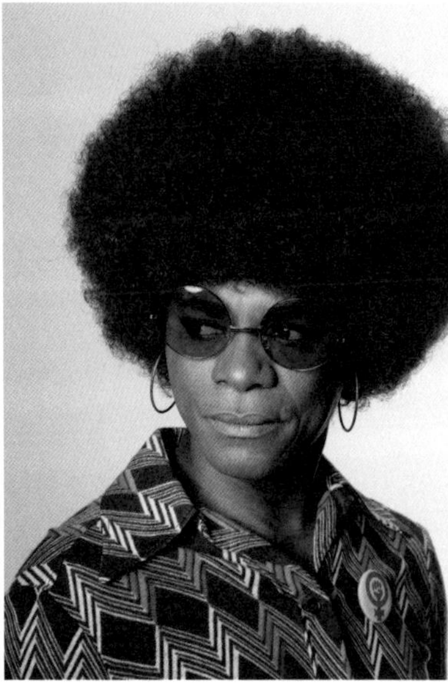

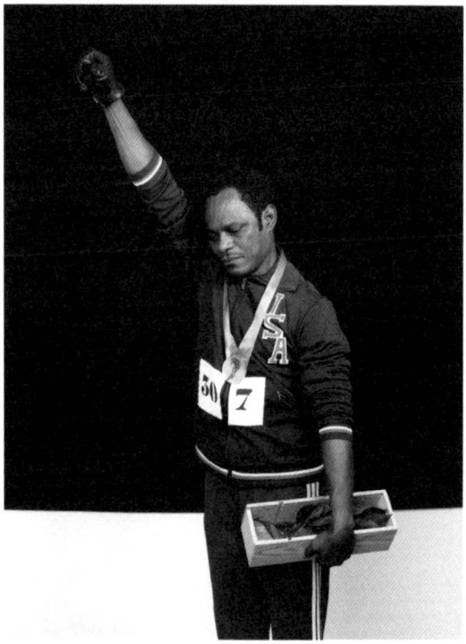

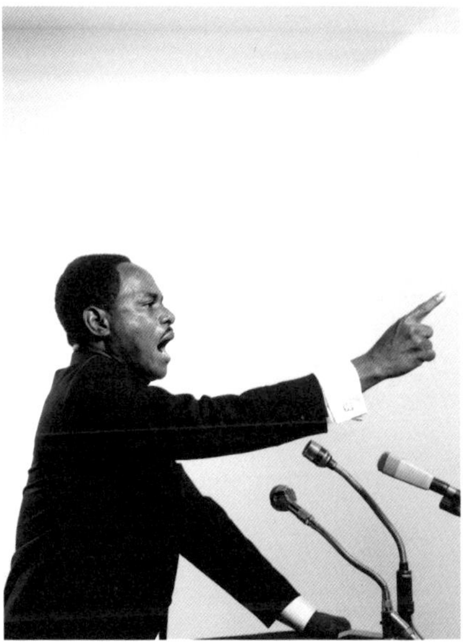

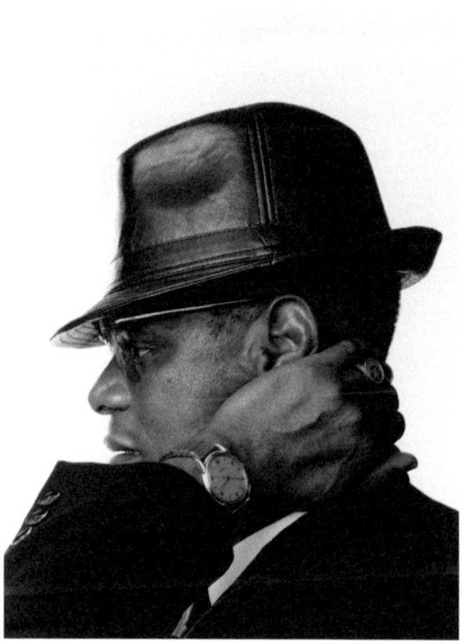

Self-Portrait (Angela Davis), aus der Serie / from the series: *African Spirits*, 2008
Self-Portrait (Tommie Smith), aus der Serie / from the series: *African Spirits*, 2008
Self-Portrait (Martin Luther King Jr.), aus der Serie / from the series: *African Spirits*, 2008
Self-Portrait (Malcolm X), aus der Serie / from the series: *African Spirits*, 2008

Davis, Martin Luther King Jr, Malcolm X, and Tommie Smith. The self-portraits are re-stagings based on historical images from magazines and newspapers. The process of identification and embodiment is executed here by Fosso with the utmost precision and intensity. *African Spirits* thus refers to the central role of the fighters for civil rights and postcolonial independence in the development of black identities.

In his series *Emperor of Africa*, Fosso addresses the profound power relations between China and Africa. To this end, he slips into the role of the controversial Chinese revolutionary and communist party leader Mao Tse-tung. In his reenactments, Fosso portrays Mao not as a liberator but as a symbol of modern imperialism. While China's growing economic and cultural presence was initially welcomed by African leaders, the exercise of power it entails is increasingly causing concern.

In one of his most recent series, *Black Pope*, Fosso convincingly yet challengingly embodies the Catholic Church's central figure of identification, the Pope. He raises the vision of a Black Pope, deep in prayer, while questioning the power and authority associated with the attributes, paraphernalia, and norms of the church, in this case the iconic white of the Pope's garments. (JT)

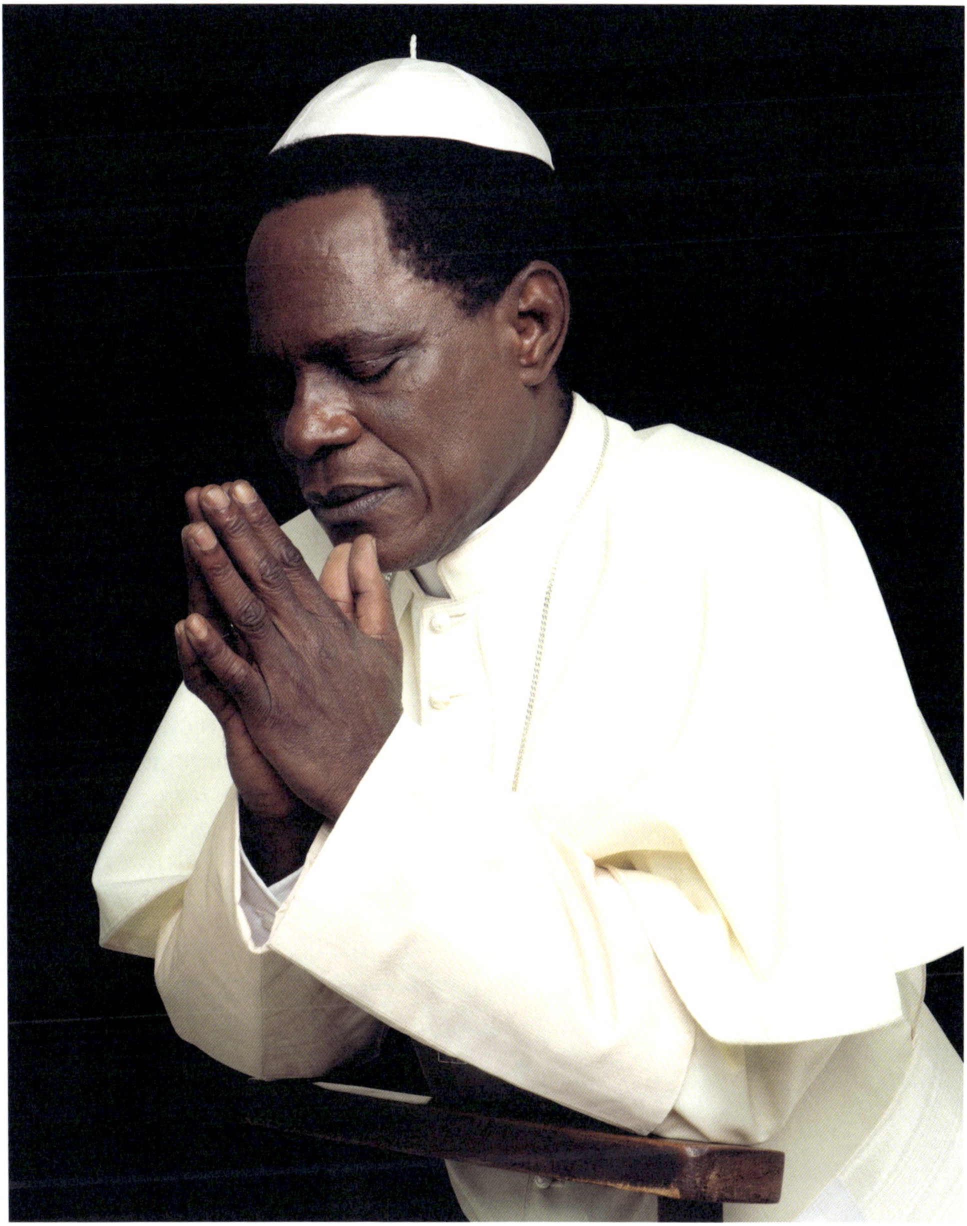

Black Pope, 2017

CHARLOTTE HASLUND-CHRISTENSEN

1963 Kopenhagen, DK – Kopenhagen, DK

Charlotte Haslund-Christensens Videoarbeit *HOPE & FEAR* richtet sich gegen ein wiederauflebendes Klima von Nationalismus, Isolation und Ausgrenzung. Ihr Langzeitprojekt ist ein Aufruf zu globaler Solidarität und gegenseitigem Respekt. Vier Jahre lang reiste sie in verschiedene Kontinente und stellte 250 Menschen die gleichen zwei Fragen: „Was ist Ihre größte Angst?“ und „Was ist Ihre größte Hoffnung?“. Das Video zeigt Menschen auf den Straßen von Peking, Buenos Aires, Kairo, Kopenhagen, Dar Es Salaam, New York und Ulan-Bator – Lehrer:innen, Straßenverkäufer:innen, Polizist:innen, Künstler:innen, Priester:innen, Schamanen und Imame, Kinder, Jugendliche, Eltern und Großeltern, die in ihrer jeweiligen Landessprache zu uns sprechen. Trotz der Vielfalt der Generationen und Kulturen drücken ihre tiefsten Ängste und Wünsche etwas Gemeinsames und Verbindendes aus.

„Die Antworten der Menschen waren ehrlich und bewegend. Was mich am meisten überrascht hat, war, dass die Antworten nicht so stark mit der Region oder der lokalen Situation zusammenhängen, wie ich erwartet hätte. Vielleicht ist der größte Faktor für unsere Ängste und Hoffnungen die Phase, in der wir uns in unserem Leben befinden. Kinder blicken in die Zukunft und haben große Träume. Sie wollen Erfinder, Weltmeister und Fußballstars werden! Teenager und junge Menschen können egozentrische Züge haben, aber wenn wir Menschen Kinder haben, verschiebt sich der Fokus plötzlich. Und wenn die Menschen älter werden, sehen sie ihr Leben als Möglichkeit, etwas weiterzugeben.“[1] (JT)

[1] Charlotte Haslund-Christensen, „HOPE & FEAR“, in: *Medium.com*, 28.10.2019, https://denmarkinnewyork.medium.com/hope-fear-an-exhibition-by-danish-artist-charlotte-haslund-christensen-44aa7cb216c1 (20.09.2022).

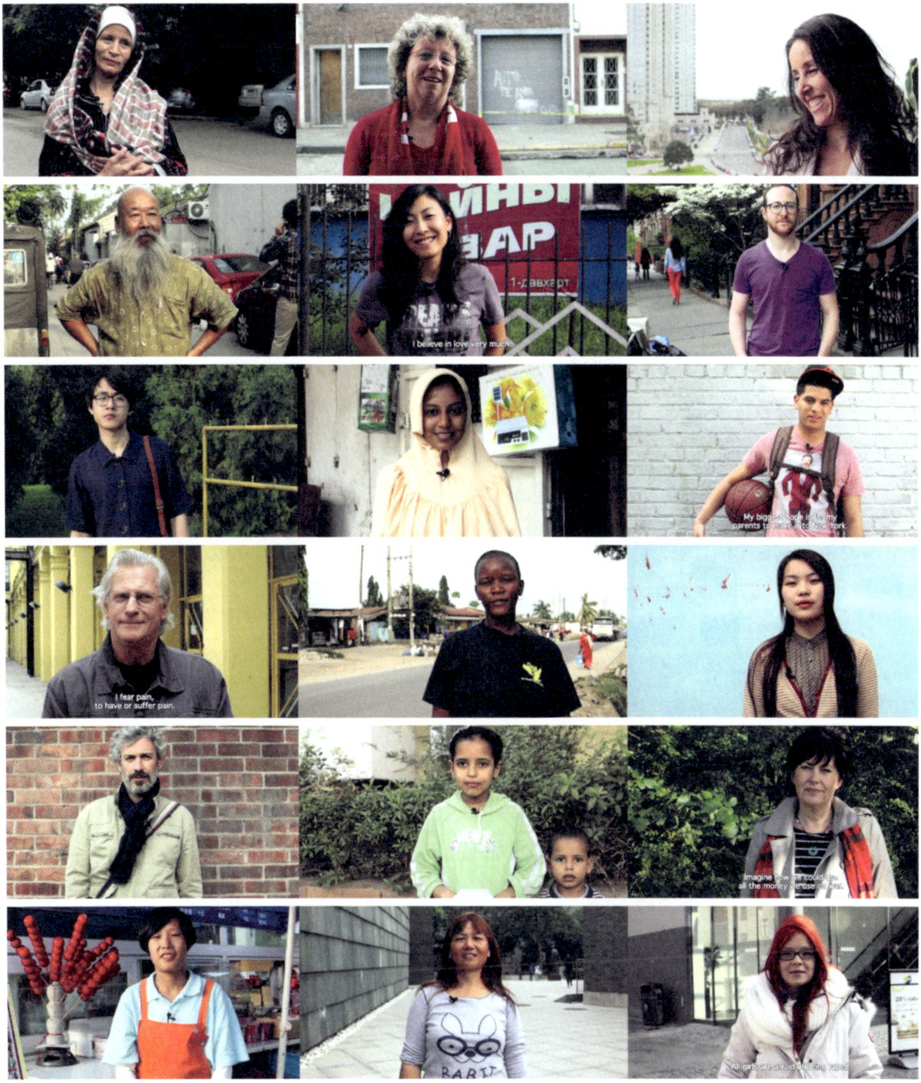

HOPE & FEAR, 2016

CHARLOTTE HASLUND-CHRISTENSEN

1963 Copenhagen, DK—Copenhagen, DK

In her video *HOPE & FEAR*, Charlotte Haslund-Christensen resists a resurgent climate of nationalism, isolationism, and exclusion. She sees her long-term project as a call for global solidarity and mutual respect. Over the course of four years, she traveled the continents of the world and spoke to 250 people, asking them two questions: "What is your greatest fear?" and "What is your greatest hope?" The video shows people on the streets of Beijing, Buenos Aires, Cairo, Copenhagen, Dar Es Salaam, New York, and Ulan-Bator—teachers, street traders, police officers, priests, shamans and imams, children, young adults, parents and grandparents, who all talk to us in their own languages. Among all the diversity of generations and cultures, their greatest fears and hopes all have something in common, something that we all share.

"People's answers were honest and moving. I think what surprised me most was that the answers weren't as related to region or the local situation as I might have expected. Maybe the biggest factor is the stage we're at in our lives. Children look to the future and have big dreams. They want to be inventors, world champions, and football stars! Teenagers and young people can be more self-centered, but when we people have kids, the focus suddenly shifts. And as people approach old age, they start to see their lives as an opportunity to pass something on." (JT)

1 Charlotte Haslund-Christensen, "HOPE & FEAR," in *Medium.com*, October 28, 2019, https://denmarkinnewyork.medium.com/hope-fear-an-exhibition-by-danish-artist-charlotte-haslund-christensen-44aa7cb216c1 (20.09.2022).

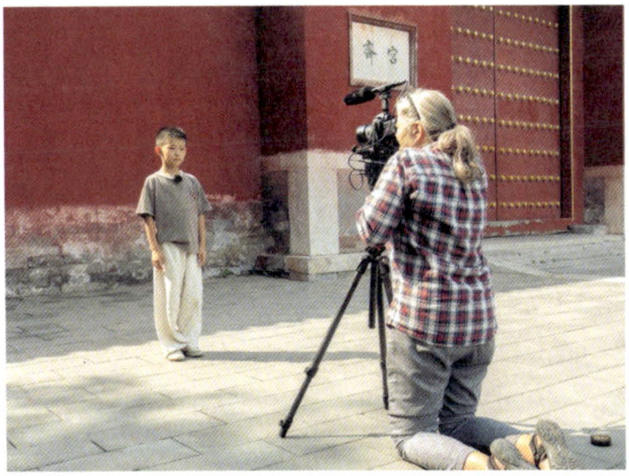

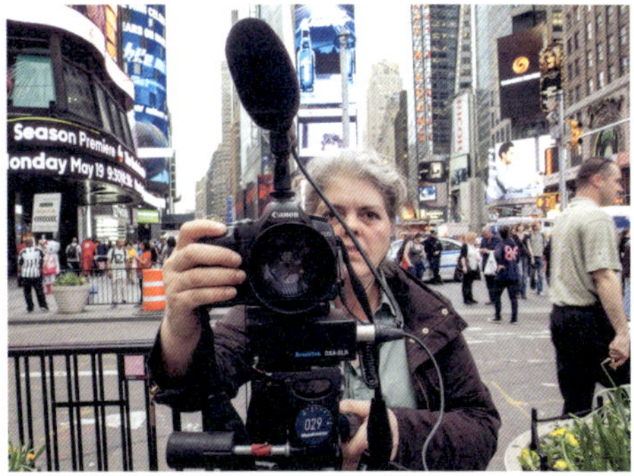

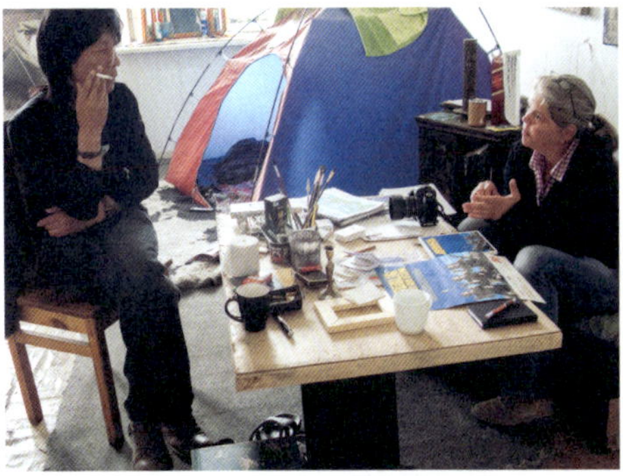

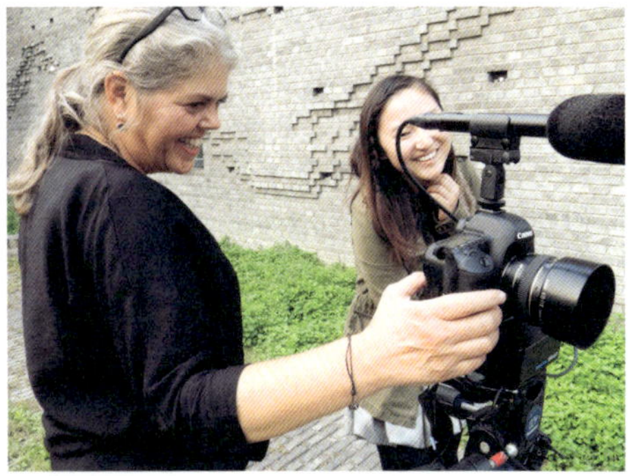

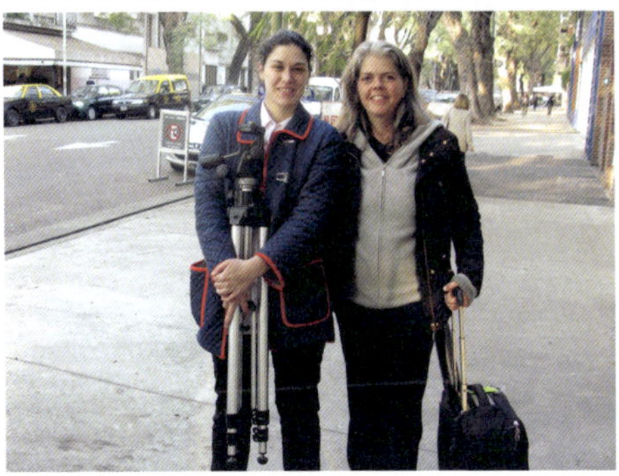

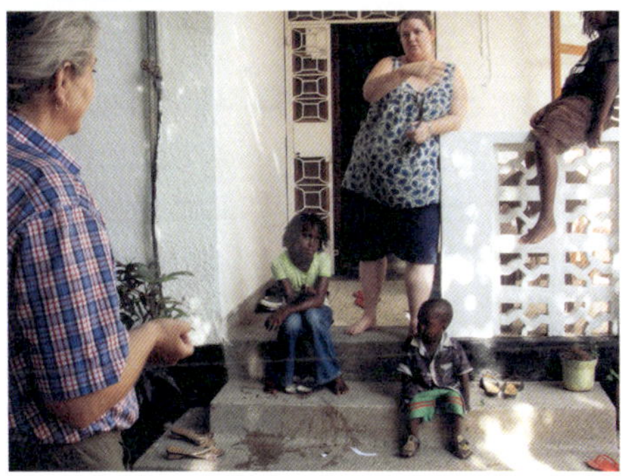

HOPE & FEAR, 2016

ALFREDO JAAR

1956 Santiago de Chile, CL – New York, NY, US

Alfredo Jaars Werke basieren auf einer kritischen Analyse ungleicher Machtverhältnisse in globalisierten Gesellschaften und widmen sich Fragen sozialer Gerechtigkeit. In seinen in der Mitte der 1990er-Jahre entstandenen Arbeiten *Untitled (Newsweek)* und *Searching for Africa in LIFE* untersucht er den strukturellen Rassismus in der inhaltlichen Schwerpunktsetzung einflussreicher US-amerikanischer Medien.

Jaar hat sich in mehreren Werken, die unter dem Titel *The Ruanda Project* (1994–2010) zusammengefasst sind, intensiv mit dem Völkermord in Ruanda beschäftigt. Der Genozid hat im Jahr 1994 bis zu einer Million Menschen das Leben gekostet. In knapp 100 Tagen töteten Angehörige der Hutu-Mehrheit etwa 75 Prozent der in Ruanda lebenden Minderheit der Tutsi sowie moderate Hutu, die sich dem Genozid widersetzten oder sich nicht daran beteiligten. Schockiert von der Gleichgültigkeit der Weltöffentlichkeit, reiste Jaar kurz nach den offensichtlichen Anfängen des Genozids selbst nach Ruanda, um die Ereignisse zu dokumentieren und über die Jahre wiederkehrend an die Öffentlichkeit zu bringen. Eine der frühesten Arbeiten, die in diesem Zusammenhang entstand, ist *Untitled (Newsweek)*. Die Bildreihe stellt eine textbasierte Chronik des Völkermords und des zögerlichen Eingreifens der internationalen Politik einer Abfolge von siebzehn Covern der Magazins *Newsweek* gegenüber. Nach dem Beginn der Gewalttaten im April 1994 dauerte es bis zum 1. August 1994, dass das Magazin das Thema auf den Umschlag brachte. Die Zeitschrift, die von sich behauptete, über die wichtigsten Ereignisse der Welt zu informieren und zu berichten, erwähnte den Genozid zuvor nur in knappster Form – eine „barbarische und kriminelle Gleichgültigkeit" gegenüber Afrika, wie Jaar formuliert.

Searching for Africa in LIFE versammelt in minimalistischer Rasterform alle 2.128 Cover des *LIFE*-Magazins, die zwischen

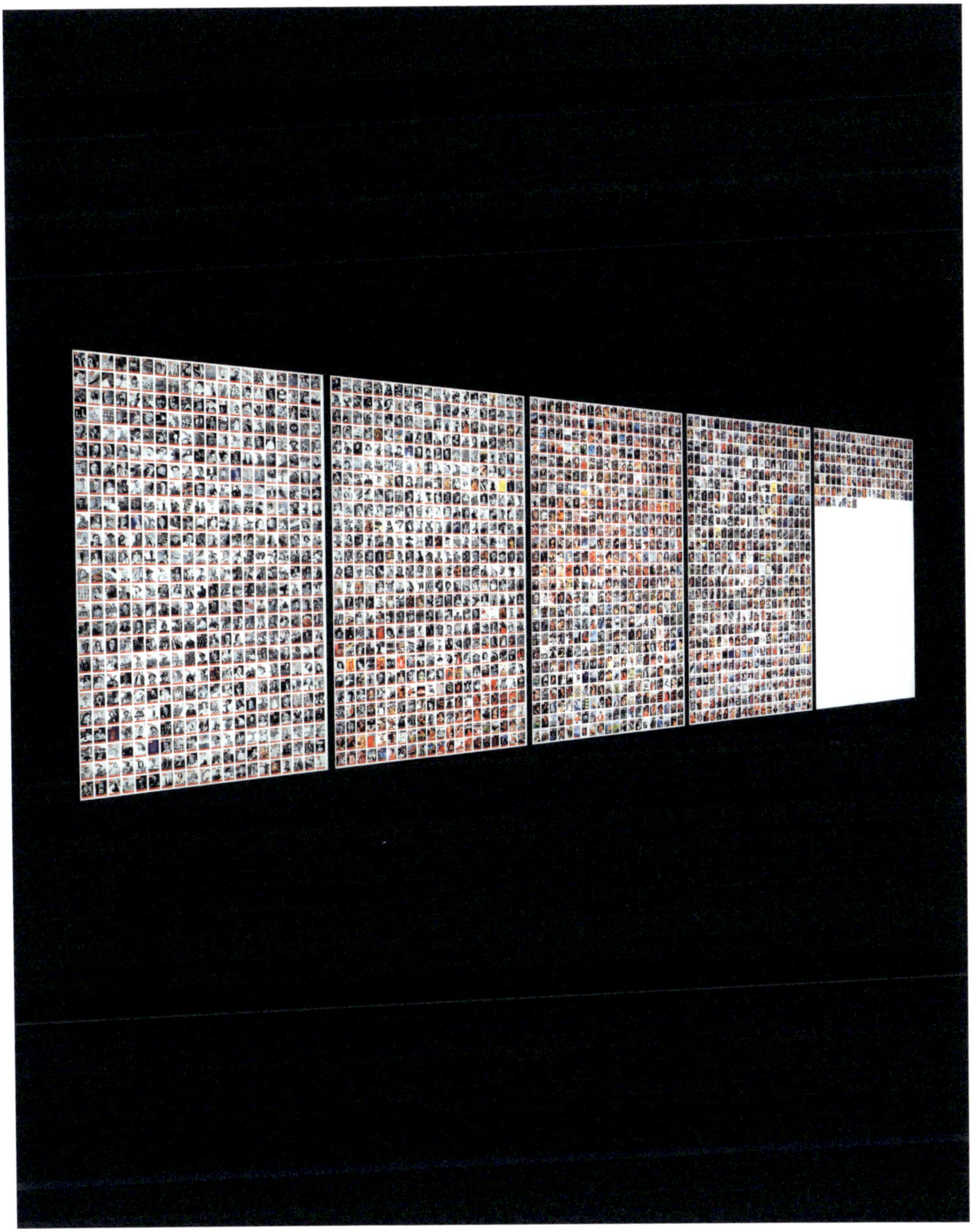

Searching for Africa in LIFE, 1996

1936 und 1996 veröffentlicht worden waren. „Für die Vereinigten Staaten war *LIFE* das erste und einflussreichste rein fotografische Nachrichtenmagazin. Mit mehr als dreizehn Millionen wöchentlichen Leser:innen in der Blütezeit bestand seine Mission darin, dem Land ein Fenster zur Welt zu öffnen. Als der Verleger von *LIFE*, Henry Luce, die Publikation ins Leben rief, war sein erklärtes Ziel, ‚das Leben zu sehen; die Welt zu sehen; die großen Ereignisse mitzuerleben …'. Dass in der sechzigjährigen Geschichte des Magazins nur so wenige Cover mit afrikanischen Themen erschienen, bietet jedoch die Gelegenheit, diesen Anspruch neu zu bewerten. *Searching for Africa in LIFE* spiegelt die historischen US-amerikanischen Einstellungen zu Kultur und Ethnizität wider – Einstellungen, die bis heute nachhallen."[1]

Die dreiteilige Fotoinstallation *LIFE Magazine, April 19, 1968* basiert auf der Reproduktion eines Fotos, das den Trauerzug für den ermordeten US-amerikanischen Bürgerrechtler und Pastor Martin Luther King Jr. zeigt. Jaar fügt dem reproduzierten Zeitungsfoto zwei weitere Bilder hinzu, in denen er die rassistischen Einstellungen der damaligen Zeit auf ebenso einfache wie eindrucksvolle Weise verdeutlicht. Auf dem einen Bild sind alle Afroamerikaner:innen, die an der Beerdigung teilnahmen, mit einem schwarzen Punkt markiert, auf dem anderen alle Weißen mit einem roten Punkt. Tausende von schwarzen Punkten stehen einzelnen roten Punkten gegenüber. Die Trauer über den Tod des schwarzen Bürgerrechtlers war außerordentlich ungleichmäßig verteilt. Während viele Schwarze befürchteten, dass jede:r von ihnen Opfer rassistischer Gewalt werden könnte, bedauerten die Weißen Kings Tod überwiegend nur wegen der erwarteten Proteste. (JT)

1 Alfredo Jaar

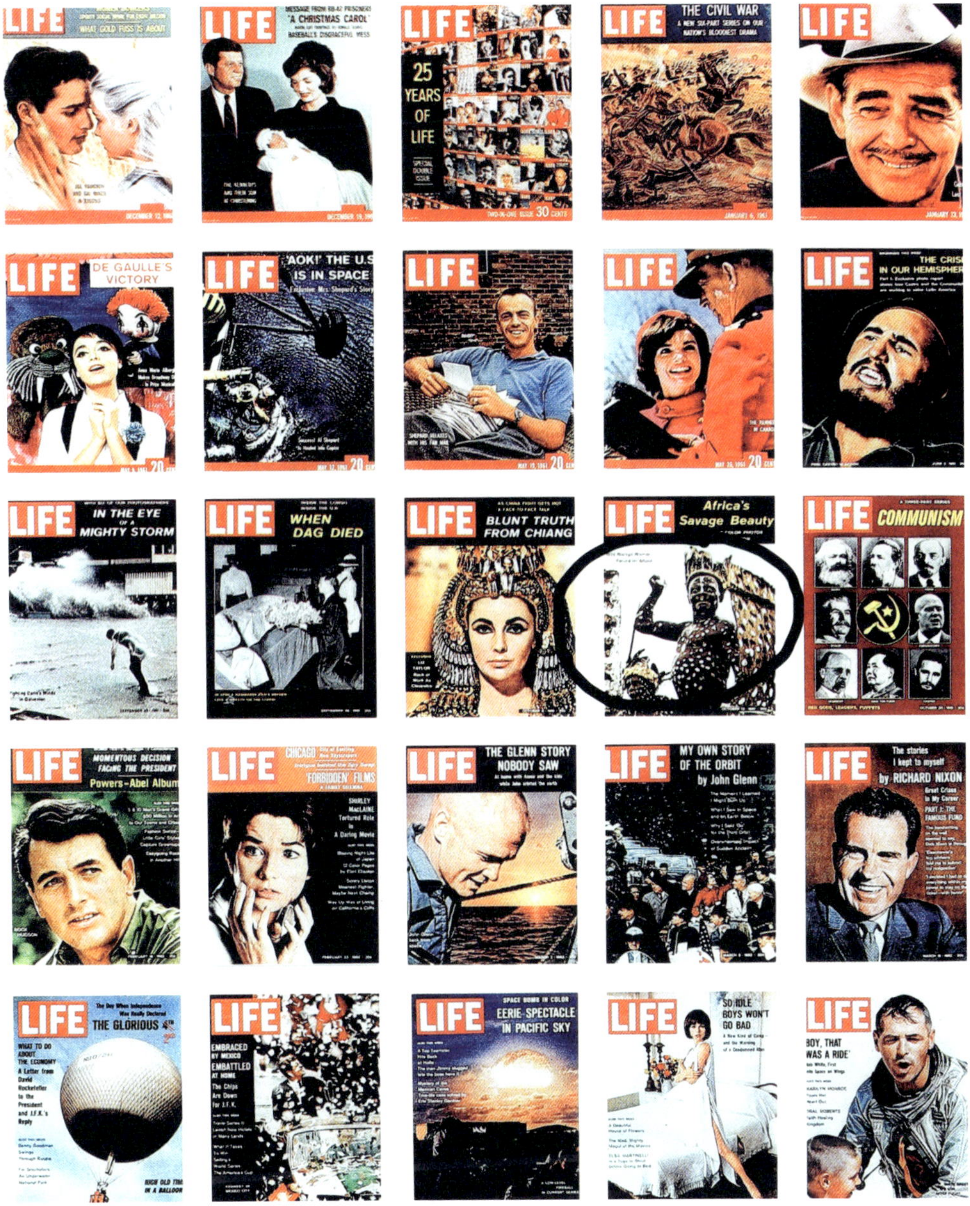

Searching for Africa in LIFE (Detail / detail), 1996

ALFREDO JAAR

1956 Santiago de Chile, CL—New York, NY, US

Alfredo Jaar's works are based on a critical analysis of unequal power relations in globalized societies and are dedicated to questions of social justice. In his mid-1990s works *Untitled (Newsweek)* and *Searching for Africa in LIFE*, he examines structural racism in the content focus of influential U.S. media.

In several works that were collected together under the title *The Rwanda Project* (1994—2010), Jaar addressed extensively the genocide in Rwanda, which cost up to a million lives in 1994. In just under a hundred days, members of the Hutu majority killed about 75 percent of the Tutsi minority in Rwanda and also moderate Hutus who protested against or did not participate in the genocide. Shocked by the indifference of the rest of the world, Jaar himself went to Rwanda shortly after the genocide had become apparent, in order to document events and to be able to make them public again and again over the following years. One of the earliest works that he created in this context is *Untitled (Newsweek)*. The series of images contrasts a text-based chronicle of the genocide and the reluctant intervention of international politics to get involved with a series of seventeen covers of Newsweek. It took from April 1994 to August 1, 1994, for the magazine to finally decide to put Rwanda on its cover. While the magazine claimed to be showing people the most important events around the world, the genocide was mentioned only very briefly—a "barbaric and criminal indifference" to Africa, as Jaar puts it.

Searching for Africa in LIFE assembles in minimalist grid form all 2,128 covers of *LIFE* from between 1936 and 1996. "For the United States, *LIFE* was the first and most influential all-photographic news magazine. With over thirteen million weekly readers at its peak, its mission was to provide the country with a window into the world. When *LIFE*'s publisher, Henry Luce, launched the publication, his stated purpose was 'To see life; to see the world; to

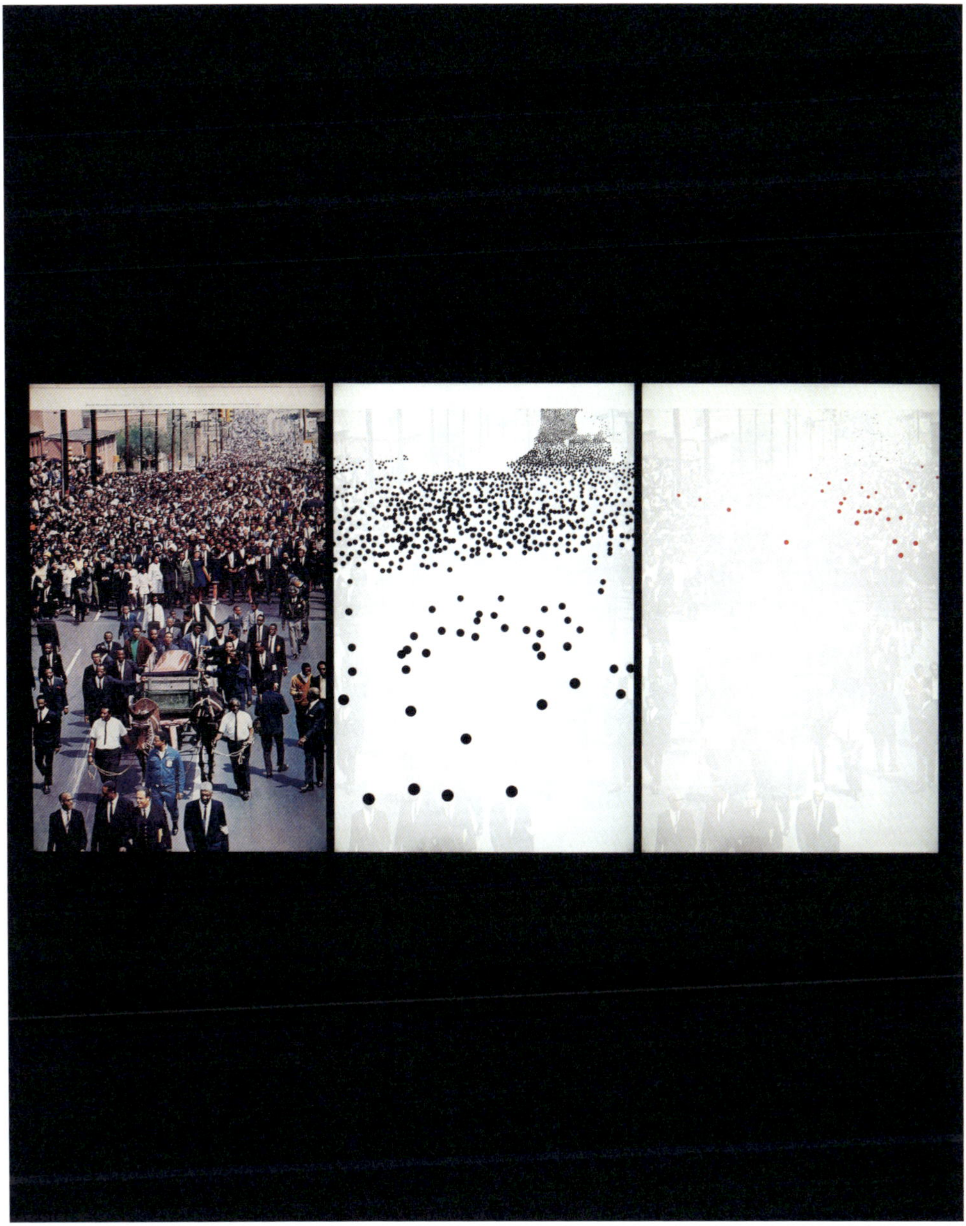

LIFE Magazine, April 19, 1968, 1995

eyewitness great events...' However, the scarcity of covers featuring African subjects throughout the magazine's sixty-year circulation provides an opportunity to reevaluate this claim. *Searching for Africa in LIFE* reflects historical American attitudes about culture and race—attitudes that continue to reverberate today."[1]

The three-part photo installation *LIFE Magazine, April 19, 1968* is based on the reproduction of a photograph depicting the funeral procession for assassinated U.S. civil rights activist and pastor Martin Luther King Jr. Jaar adds two further images in which he reveals the racist attitudes of the time in a simple and highly effective way. In one of them, all the Afro-Americans who attended the funeral are marked with a black dot; and in the other, all the white attendees are marked with a red dot. Thousands of black dots contrast with just a few red dots. Mourning for the death of the Black civil rights activist was extremely imbalanced. While many Black people were afraid that any one of them might become a victim of racist violence, whites regretted King's death mainly due to the protests they were expecting. (JT)

1 Alfredo Jaar

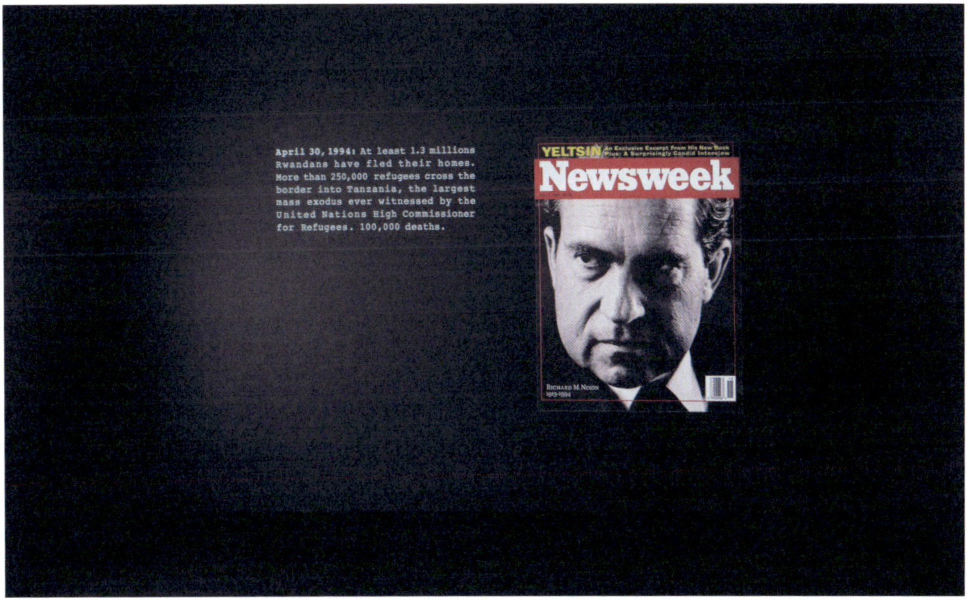

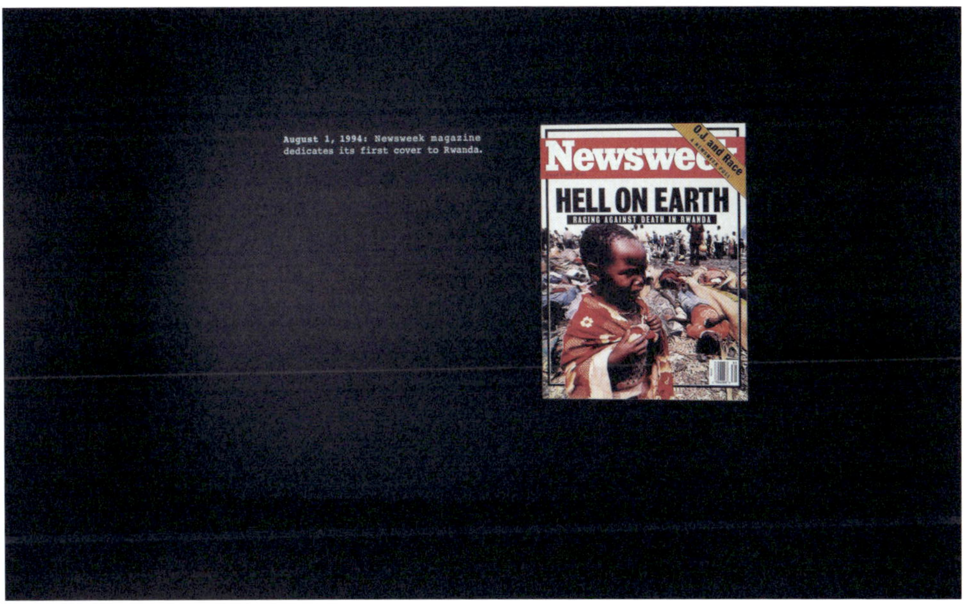

Untitled (Newsweek), 1994

VOLUSPA JARPA

1971 Rancagua, CL – Santiago de Chile, CL

Voluspa Jarpa gehört zur ersten Generation chilenischer Künstler:innen, die nach der Militärdiktatur von Augusto Pinochet (1973–90) unter demokratischen Bedingungen studieren konnten. In ihren Arbeiten setzt sie sich mit kolonialistischer und rassistischer Unterdrückung auseinander und verbindet diese mit feministischen Anliegen und dem Kampf um selbstbestimmte geschlechtliche und sexuelle Identitäten.

In *The Emancipating Opera* greift Jarpa die musikalische Form der Kantate auf und nutzt dieses aus der europäischen Musikgeschichte stammende Genre, um eine Erzählung über Macht und Emanzipation zu schaffen. In dem Stück treffen Stimmen aufeinander, die einerseits die hegemoniale Psyche der weißen, europäischen und später US-amerikanischen patriarchalischen Kolonisatoren und andererseits die subalterne Psyche marginalisierter Gesellschaftsschichten besingen. Im Video vermitteln zwei Protagonist:innen zwischen diesen Polen: zum einen der „arriero“, ein traditioneller chilenischer Maultiertreiber, und zum anderen die transsexuelle Sängerin und Schauspielerin Daniela Vega.

Die Wurzeln der „arriero“ liegen in der europäischen Kolonialisierung Chiles; andererseits sind sie auch Nachkommen indigener Gemeinschaften und eng mit der ungezähmten Natur und der frühen Kultur der Andenvölker verbunden. In Jarpas Video wird die indigene Kultur mit kolonialistischen Schriften kontrastiert, die mit ihrem Abwertungsdiskurs die Unterwerfung nicht-westlicher Kulturen zu legitimieren suchten. Die Sängerin Daniela Vega agiert als eine Figur der mehrfachen Rebellion: Sie widersetzt sich nicht nur der Kolonisierung von Natur, Kultur und Menschen, sondern auch der Einschränkung und Zähmung des Körpers. (JT)

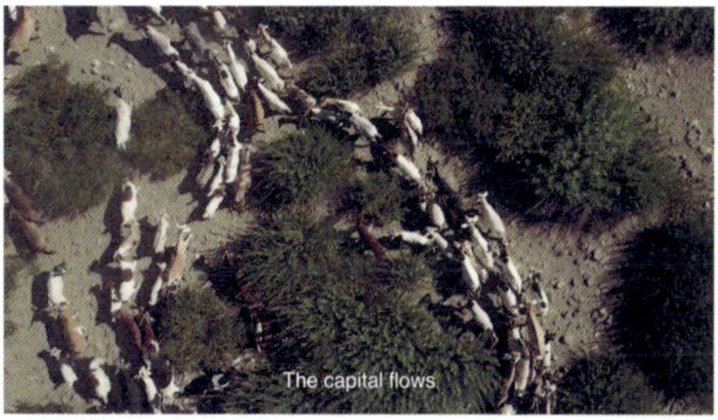

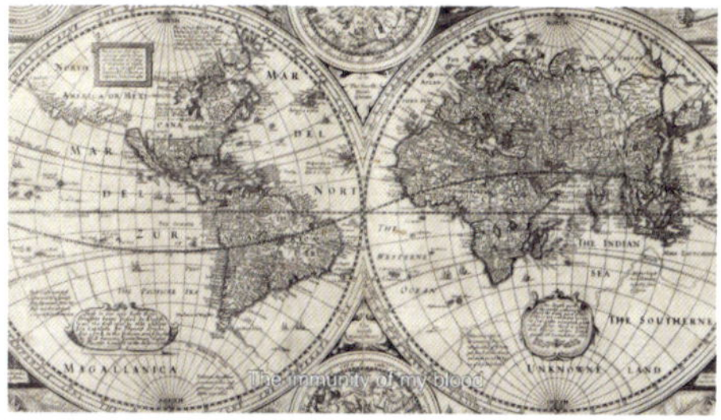

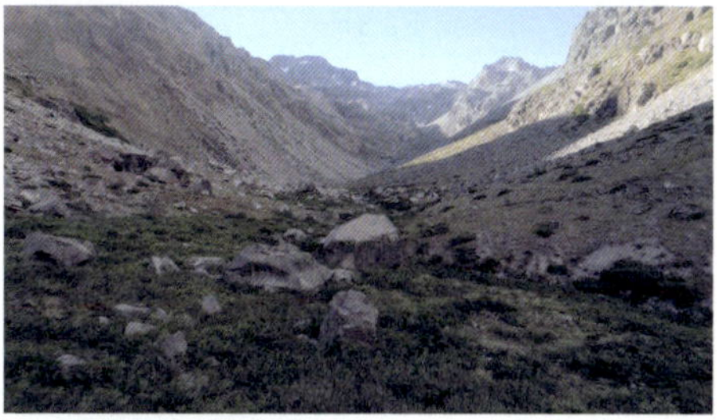

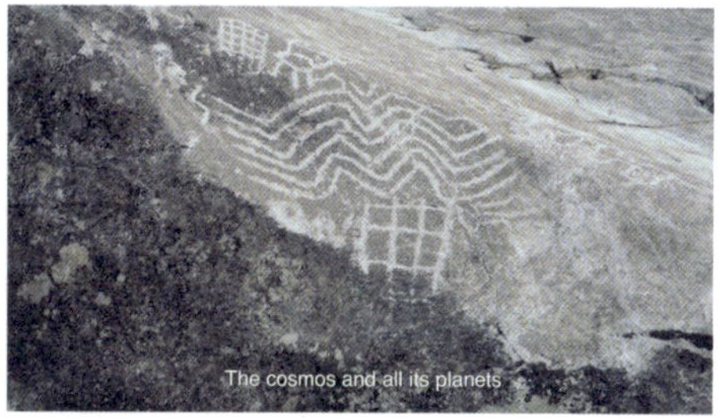

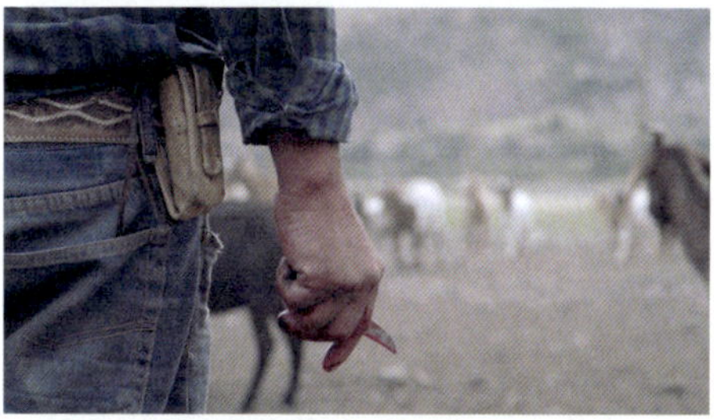

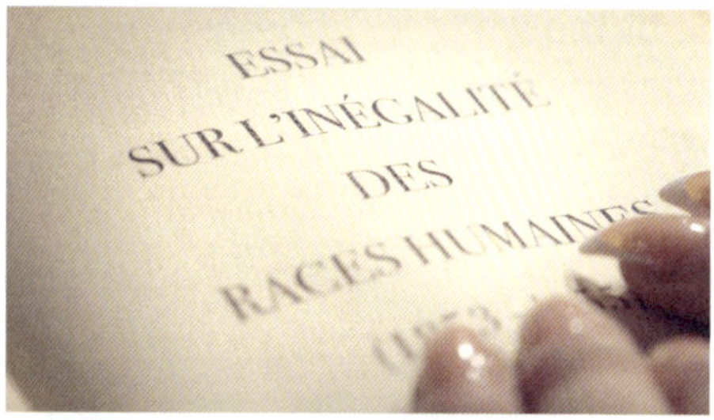

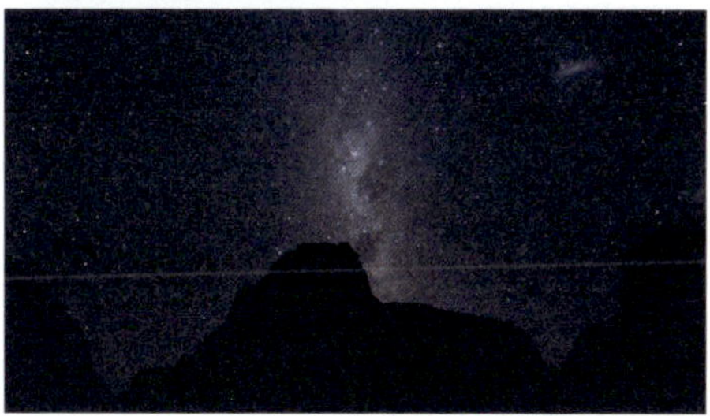

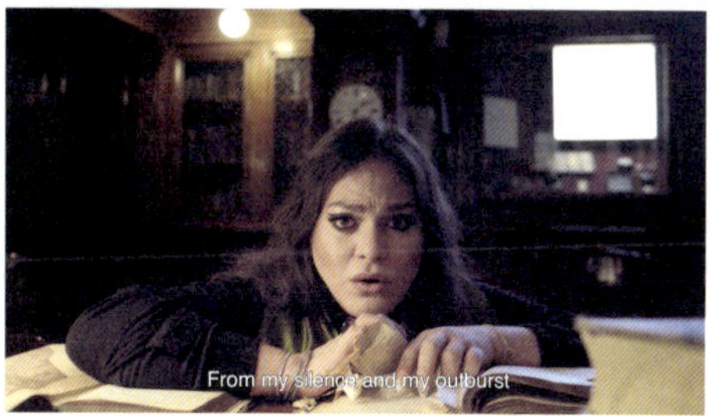

The Emancipating Opera, 2019

VOLUSPA JARPA

1971 Rancagua, CL—Santiago de Chile, CL

Voluspa Jarpa is among the first generation of Chilean artists able to study under democratic conditions after the end of Augusto Pinochet's military dictatorship (1973–90). In her works, she addresses colonialist and racist repression and links this with feminist concerns and the struggle for self-determined gender and sexual identities.

In *The Emancipating Opera* she draws on the musical form of the cantata, the sung piece, and uses this genre from European musical history in the form of a contemporary video cantata in order to unfold a narrative about power and emancipation. Voices come up against each other, singing of the hegemonial psyche (the psyche of the white, European, and later US-American patriarchal colonizers) and the subaltern psyche (the psyche of excluded elements of society). In the video, two protagonists mediate between these two poles: On the one hand the "arriero," a traditional Chilean mule driver, and on the other the trans singer and actress Daniela Vega.

The "arriero" traveling through the mountain landscape of the Andes brings together various origins. On the one hand his roots are in the European colonialization of Chile, and on the other the "arriero" is a descendant of indigenous communities and closely intertwined with the untamed nature and early culture of the early inhabitants of the Andes. In this video, Jarpa contrasts indigenous cultures with her exploration of colonialist and racist writings in which a discourse of devaluation attempted to legitimate the subjugation of non-Western cultures. The singer Daniela Vega here operates as a multiple figure of rebellion against repressive concepts of identity. She not only turns against the colonialization of nature, culture, and people, but also against the limitation and taming of the body. (JT)

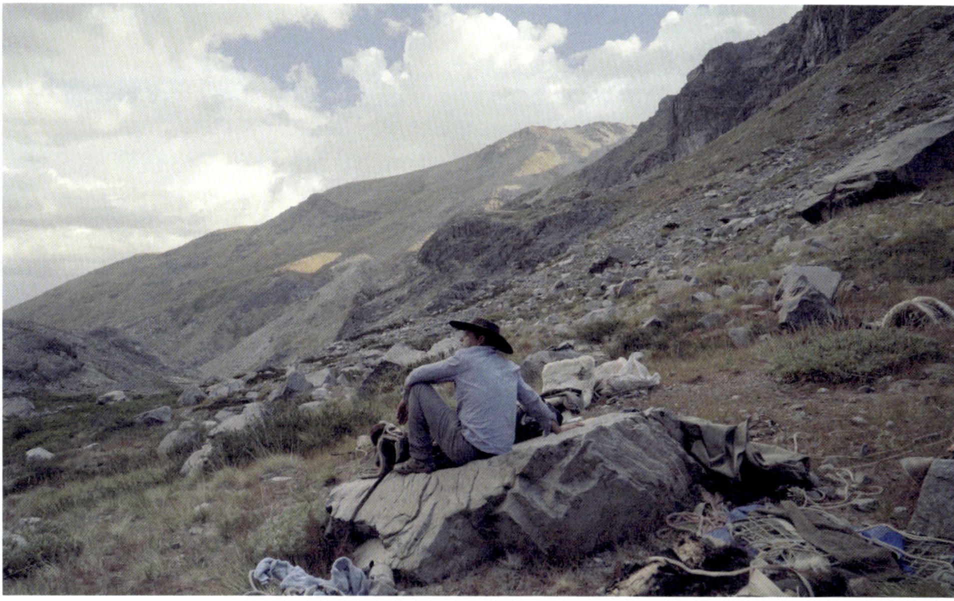

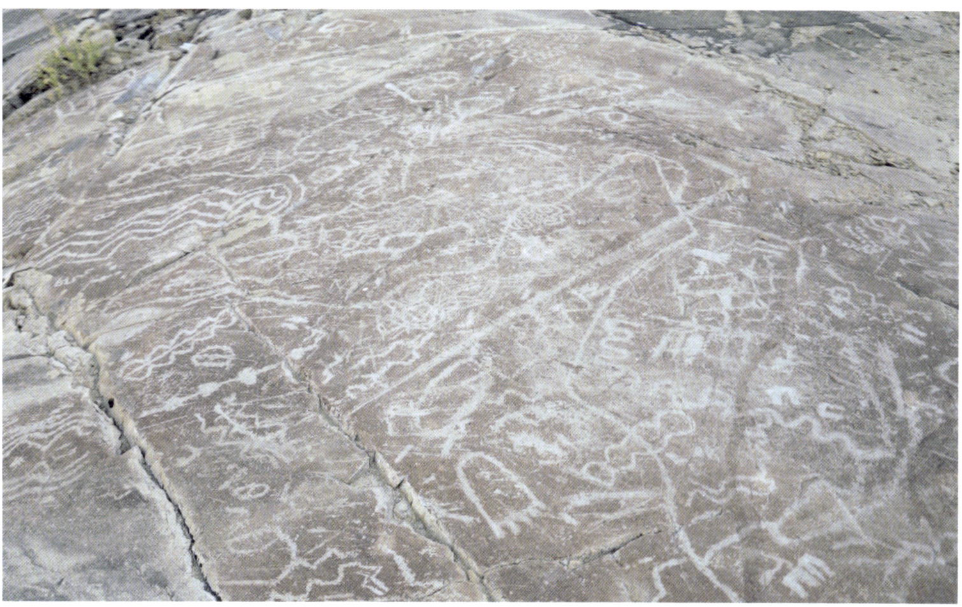

The Emancipating Opera, 2019

BELINDA KAZEEM-KAMIŃSKI

1980 Wien, AT – Wien, AT

Die Künstlerin, Autorin und Kulturtheoretikerin Belinda Kazeem-Kamiński ist in der Schwarzen feministischen Theorie und Praxis verwurzelt. Ihre Arbeiten basieren häufig auf Recherchen zu unterdrückten Geschichten und Sichtweisen Schwarzer Menschen, die sie in Archiven, Sammlungen und Bibliotheken in Europa vorfindet. Zugleich legt sie die *weißen* Perspektiven offen, die diesen Institutionen in Form von bestimmten Wissens- und Ordnungssystemen zugrunde liegen, und stellt ihnen oppositionelle Blicke gegenüber.

Die Fotoserie *In Search of Red, Black, and Green* wurde durch Kazeem-Kamińskis wiederholte Auseinandersetzung mit Christina Sharpes Buch *In the Wake: On Blackness and Being* (2016) inspiriert. Darin stellt Sharpe fest, dass Schwarzsein in dieser Welt nicht von den Erfahrungen von Versklavung, Polizeigewalt, Trauer und Schmerz, historischen und aktuellen Formen von Ungerechtigkeit und erlittenem Leid getrennt werden kann. Gleichzeitig betont Sharpe aber auch, dass Schwarzes Leben nicht auf diese Erfahrungen reduzierbar ist.

Die Protagonistin in Kazeem-Kamińskis Fotografien blickt fokussiert auf das, was vor ihr liegt. Sie scheint darüber nachzudenken, was die Farben Rot, Schwarz und Grün für sie bedeuten. Viele Menschen der afrikanisch-diasporischen Gemeinschaft assoziieren diese Farben mit Befreiung und Freiheit. „Die Antwort auf die Frage, was Black Freedom in einer Welt, die von *weißer* Vorherrschaft geprägt ist, bedeuten kann, oder eine Antwort auf die Tatsache, dass Black Freedom ein ‚noch unvollendetes Projekt' (Saidiya Hartman) ist, müssen Schwarze Menschen in der Diaspora für sich selbst und in Gemeinschaft finden. Wir sind noch immer nicht angekommen, und es ist fraglich, ob wir bei der Art und Weise, wie diese Welt beschaffen ist, ankommen werden. Dennoch ist es wichtig, weiter nach Befreiung und Freiheit zu

streben und somit die starren Grenzen dieser Welt allmählich zu durchbrechen."[1]

Library of Requests (LoR) ist ein fortlaufendes, partizipatives Projekt. Ausgangspunkt ist die Auseinandersetzung mit Bibliotheken als Wissensspeicher und den damit verbundenen Ein- und Ausschlüssen. Mithilfe von Expert:innen sammelt Kazeem-Kamiński mehrsprachige Bücher, Zines, Zeitschriften, Filme etc. zu einem ausgewählten Thema, zum Beispiel zum Empowerment Schwarzer Kinder und Jugendlicher (LoR #4), um sie den Besucher:innen von Ausstellungen und Bibliotheken zugänglich zu machen. Oft finden auch gemeinsame Lesungen, Read-ins oder Diskussionsrunden statt.

„Bei *Library of Requests #7 (solo edition)* habe ich ohne Expert:innen gearbeitet und mir die Freiheit genommen, eine Sammlung von Büchern und Texten zusammenzustellen, die ich gerne schon früher gehabt hätte: eine Sammlung von Texten überwiegend Schwarzer, feministischer Frauen aus dem deutschsprachigen Raum, die sich aus einer selbstbestimmten Perspektive mit Schwarzsein in diesem Raum auseinandersetzen. Die Sammlung erhebt nicht den Anspruch, vollständig zu sein, vielmehr soll sie dazu anregen, ausgehend von diesen Texten noch mehr Texte zu sammeln. Die Aufmerksamkeit für die Theorie und Praxis Schwarzer Frauen im deutschsprachigen Raum will der hier gerne angewandten Strategie Einhalt gebieten, Diskriminierung Schwarzer Menschen, aber auch den Widerstand dagegen, nicht im eigenen Land, sondern in den USA, Frankreich oder Großbritannien zu verorten."[2] (JT)

1 Belinda Kazeem-Kamiński, E-Mail an den Autor, 09.04.2021.

2 Belinda Kazeem-Kamiński, ebd.

BELINDA KAZEEM-KAMIŃSKI

1980 Vienna, AT—Vienna, AT

The artist, author, and cultural theorist Belinda Kazeem-Kamiński is rooted in Black feminist theory and practice. Her works are often based on research on the repressed histories and perspectives of Black people, which she finds in archives, collections, and libraries in Europe. At the same time, she exposes the *white* perspectives that underlie these institutions in the form of particular systems of knowledge and order, and juxtaposes them with oppositional views.

The photo series *In Search of Red, Black, and Green* was inspired by Kazeem-Kamiński's repeated explorations of Christina Sharpe's book *In the Wake: On Blackness and Being* (2016). Sharpe ascertains that being Black in this world cannot be separated from experiences of slavery, police violence, mourning and pain, and historical and contemporary forms of injustice and lived suffering. At the same time, however, Sharpe also emphasizes that Black lives are not reducible to these experiences.

The protagonist in Kazeem-Kamiński's photographs is taking a concentrated look at what is before her. She seems to be thinking about what the colors red, black, and green mean for her. Many people in the African diaspora community associate these colors with liberation and freedom. "Black people in the diaspora must find their own personal and collective answers to the question as to what Black Freedom is in a world shaped by white dominance, and also to how to deal with the fact that Black Freedom is a 'still unfinished project' (Saidiya Hartman). We have still not arrived, and it is not sure if we will ever arrive, given the state of this world. Nonetheless, it is important to continue to strive for liberation and freedom and thus to gradually break down the rigid borders of this world."[1]

Library of Requests (LoR) is an ongoing participatory project. The starting point is an investigation of libraries as stores of

knowledge and the appertaining processes of inclusion and exclusion. With assistance from experts, Kazeem-Kamiński collects multilingual books, zines, magazines, films, etc., on themes such as the empowerment of Black children and youths (LoR #4), so as to make these accessible for visitors to exhibitions and libraries. There are also frequently shared readings, read-ins, and discussion groups.

"For *Library of Requests #7 (solo edition)* I worked without experts and took the liberty of compiling a book collection that I would have liked to have had earlier: A collection of texts by predominantly Black feminist women from the German-speaking world, who take a self-determined approach to being Black in this region. The collection makes no claims to be complete or exhaustive, rather it should inspire people looking at these texts to search for more. Drawing attention to the theory and practice of Black women in the German-speaking world is intended to counter the popular strategy of situating the discrimination of Black people in the USA, France, or the United Kingdom, but not in your own country."[2] (JT)

1 Belinda Kazeem-Kamiński, e-mail to author, April 9, 2021.

2 Belinda Kazeem-Kamiński, ibid.

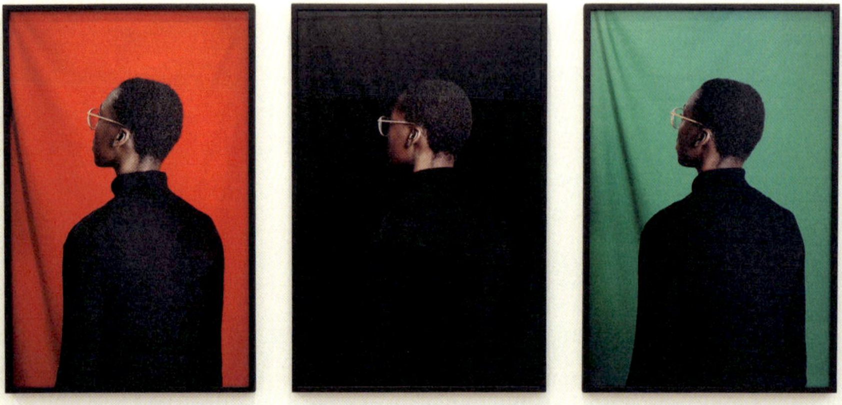

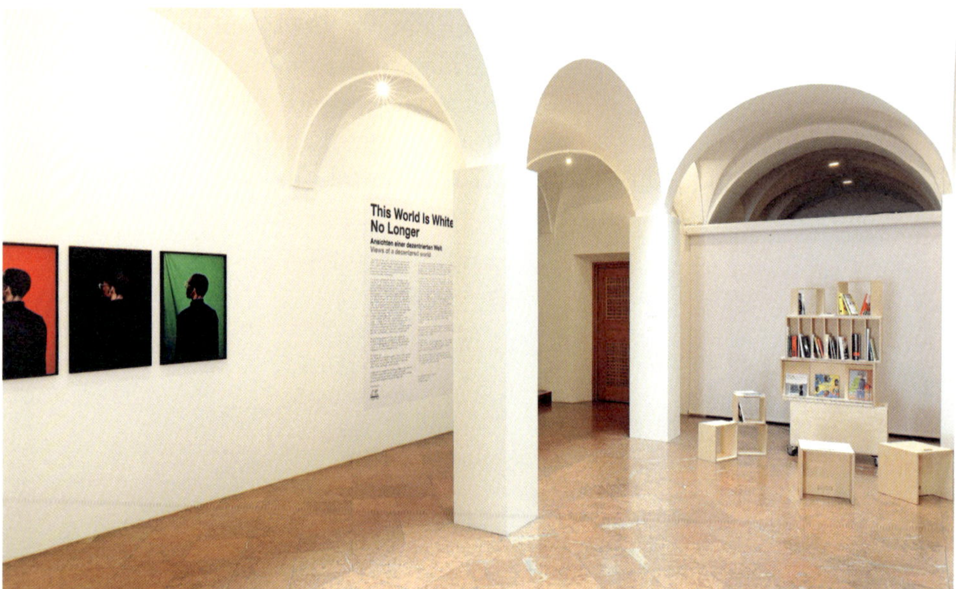

In Search of Red, Black, and Green, 2021
Library of Requests #7 (solo edition), 2021

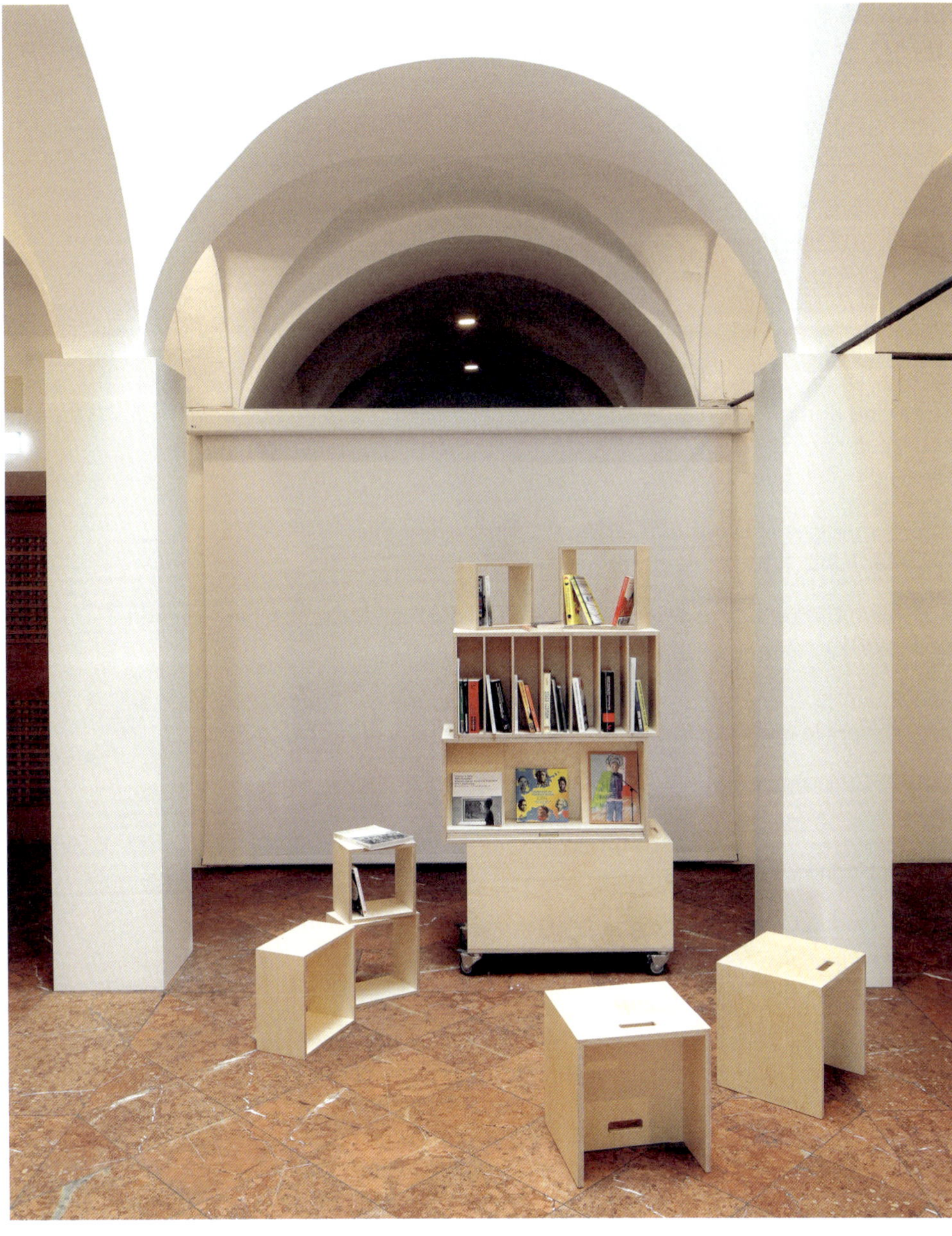

Library of Requests #7 (solo edition), 2021

BELINDA KAZEEM-KAMIŃSKI
Library of Requests #7 (solo edition), 2021

Susan Arndt et al., Hg. / eds., *Mythen, Masken und Subjekte. Kritische Weißseinsforschung in Deutschland*, 4. Aufl. / 4th ed., Münster: Unrast, 2020.

Susan Arndt, Nadja Ofuatey-Alazard, Hg. / eds., *Wie Rassismus aus Wörtern spricht. (K)Erben des Kolonialismus im Wissensarchiv deutsche Sprache. Ein kritisches Nachschlagewerk*, 3. Aufl. / 3rd ed., Münster: Unrast, 2019.

Lilly Axster et al., *Ein bisschen wie Du / A little like you*, Wien / Vienna: Zaglossus, 2018.

May Ayim, Katharina Oguntoye, Dagmar Schultz, Hg. / eds., *Farbe bekennen. Afro-deutsche Frauen auf den Spuren ihrer Geschichte*, Neuausgabe / new ed., Berlin: Orlanda, 2020.

May Ayim, *Blues in Black and White. A Collection of Essays, Poetry, and Conversations*, Trenton, Asmara: Africa World Press, 2003.

May Ayim, *Grenzenlos und unverschämt*, Frankfurt am Main: Fischer Taschenbuch, 2002.

Tina Campt, *Other Germans. Black Germans and the Politics of Race, Gender, and Memory in the Third Reich*, Ann Arbor: University of Michigan Press, 2004.

Anne Chebu, *Anleitung zum Schwarz sein*, 4. Aufl. / 4th ed., Münster: Unrast, 2020.

Sharon Dodua Otoo, *Adas Raum*, Frankfurt am Main: S. Fischer, 2021.

Sharon Dodua Otoo, *die dinge, die ich denke, während ich höflich lächle … und Synchronicity*, 3. Aufl. / 3rd ed., Frankfurt am Main: Fischer Taschenbuch, 2019.

Fatima El-Tayeb, *European Others. Queering Ethnicity in Postnational Europe*, Minneapolis, London: University of Minnesota Press, 2011.

Fatima El-Tayeb, *Schwarze Deutsche. Der Diskurs um „Rasse“ und nationale Identität 1890-1933*, Frankfurt am Main, New York: Campus, 2001.

Kien Nghi Ha, Nicola Lauré al-Samarai, Sheila Mysorekar, Hg. / eds., *re/visionen. Postkoloniale Perspektiven von People of Color auf Rassismus, Kulturpolitik und Widerstand in Deutschland*, 2. Aufl. / 2nd ed., Münster: Unrast, 2016.

Initiative Schwarze Menschen in Deutschland e. V., Hg. / ed., *Homestory Deutschland. Schwarze Biografien in Geschichte und Gegenwart*, Frankfurt am Main: Initiative Schwarze Menschen in Deutschland e. V., 2006.

Njideka Iroh, *Expectations?*, 2020.

Njideka Iroh, *Sojourner Truth Is in My Corner*, 2013.

Njideka Iroh, *Partner in Crime*, 2012.

Araba-Evelyn Johnston-Arthur, „Jenseits von Integration ... Überlegungen zur Dekolonisierung des österreichischen Klassenzimmers", in: *Class works. Weitere Beiträge zu vermittelnder, künstlerischer und forschender Praxis*, Hg. / eds. Eva Egerman, Anna Pritz. Wien / Vienna: Löcker, 2009, S. / pp. 113–138.

Belinda Kazeem, Nicola Lauré al-Samarai, Peggy Piesche, „Museum. Space. History. New Sites of Political Tectonics. A Virtual Exchange between Belinda Kazeem, Nicola Lauré al-Samarai, and Peggy Piesche", in: *transversal: Postcolonial displays*, Juni / June 2008, https://transversal.at/transversal/0708/kazeem-piesche/en (03.12.2021).

Belinda Kazeem, Nicola Lauré al-Samarai, Peggy Piesche, „Museum. Raum. Geschichte: Neue Orte politischer Tektonik. Ein virtueller Gedankenaustausch zwischen Belinda Kazeem, Nicola Lauré al-Samarai und Peggy Piesche", in: *transversal: Postcolonial displays*, Juni / June 2008, https://transversal.at/transversal/0708/kazeem-piesche/de (03.12.2021).

Natasha A. Kelly, Hg. / ed., *Schwarzer Feminismus. Grundlagentexte,* Münster: Unrast, 2019.

Natasha A. Kelly, *Millis Erwachen. Schwarze Frauen, Kunst und Widerstand / Milli's Awakening. Black Women, Art, and Resistance*, Berlin: Orlanda, 2018.

Natasha A. Kelly, Hg. / ed., *Sisters and Souls. Inspirationen durch May Ayim*, 2. Aufl. / 2nd ed., Berlin: Orlanda, 2018.

Grada Kilomba, *Plantation Memories. Episodes of Everyday Racism*, 6. Aufl. / 6th ed., Münster: Unrast, 2020.

Marion Kraft, Rukshana Shamim Ashraf Khan, Hg. / eds., *Schwarze Frauen der Welt. Europa und Migration*, Berlin: Orlanda, 1994.

Nicola Lauré al-Samarai, „Inspirited Topography. Über/Lebensräume, Heim-Suchungen und die Verortung der Erfahrung in Schwarzen deutschen Kultur- und Wissenstraditionen“, in: *Mythen, Masken und Subjekte. Kritische Weißseinsforschung in Deutschland*, Hg. / eds. Susan Arndt et al., 4. Aufl. / 4th ed., Münster: Unrast, 2020, S. / pp. 118–134.

Nkechi Madubuko, *Empowerment als Erziehungsaufgabe*, 3. Aufl. / 3rd ed., Münster: Unrast, 2020.

Tupoka Ogette, *Exit Racism. Rassismuskritisch denken lernen*, 9. Aufl. / 9th ed., Münster: Unrast, 2020.

Katharina Oguntoye, *Schwarze Wurzeln. Afro-deutsche Familiengeschichten von 1884 bis 1950*, Berlin: Orlanda, 2020.

Pädagogisches Zentrum Aachen e. V. (PÄZ), Hg. / ed., *Schwarzes Europa. Legenden die uns verborgen blieben. Schwarze Jugendliche auf den Spuren ihrer Geschichte*, Münster: edition assemblage, 2017.

Projekt Lern- und Erinnerungsort Afrikanisches Viertel (Leo) beim Amt für Weiterbildung und Kultur des Bezirksamtes Mitte von Berlin, Elina Marmer, Hg. / eds., *Rassismuskritischer Leitfaden zur Reflexion bestehender und Erstellung neuer didaktischer Lehr- und Lernmaterialien für die schulische und außerschulische Bildungsarbeit zu Schwarzsein, Afrika und afrikanischer Diaspora*, Hamburg, Berlin: o. V. / n. p., 2015, https://www.elina-marmer.com/wp-content/uploads/2015/03/IMAFREDU-Rassismuskritischer-Leitfaden_Web_barrierefrei-NEU.pdf (03.12.2021).

SFC Schwarze Frauen Community Austria, *Meine Traum-Familie. Familienbilder jenseits von Stereotypen*, Wien / Vienna: SFC Schwarze Frauen Community Austria, 2014.

Christina Sharpe, *In the Wake. On Blackness and Being*, Durham, London: Duke University Press, 2016.

Noah Sow, *Deutschland Schwarz Weiß. Der alltägliche Rassismus*, aktual. Aufl. / rev. ed., Norderstedt: BoD-Books on Demand, 2018.

Hito Steyerl, Encarnación Gutiérrez Rodríguez, Hg. / eds., *Spricht die Subalterne deutsch? Migration und postkoloniale Kritik*, Münster: Unrast, 2003.

Claudia Unterweger, *Talking Back. Strategien Schwarzer österreichischer Geschichtsschreibung*, Wien / Vienna: Zaglossus, 2016.

Marie von dem Berge, Yvonn Barth, Hg. / eds., *Wie erkläre ich Kindern Rassismus? Eine Anleitung für Eltern und Erwachsene*, 2. Aufl. / 2nd ed., Berlin: Familiar Faces, 2021.

Niko Wahl, Philipp Rohrbach, Tal Adler, *SchwarzÖsterreich. Die Kinder afroamerikanischer Besatzungssoldaten*, Ausst.-Kat. / exh. cat., Wien / Vienna: Volkskundemuseum, Wien / Vienna: Löcker, 2016.

Olivia Wenzel, *1000 Serpentinen Angst*, 5. Aufl. / 5th ed., Frankfurt am Main: S. Fischer, 2020.

ADRIAN PIPER

1948 New York, NY, US – Berlin, DE

Die US-amerikanische Künstlerin Adrian Piper, die seit 2005 in Berlin lebt, gehört zur ersten Generation der Conceptual Art und ist emeritierte Professorin für analytische Philosophie. In den 1970er-Jahren führte sie die Auseinandersetzung mit Xenophobie, Rassismus und Gender in das Vokabular der Konzeptkunst ein und verfolgte diese Themenstränge über mehrere Jahrzehnte. Dabei ging sie von ihren eigenen sozialen Erfahrungen als „US-amerikanische Frau mit afrikanischer Abstammung“ aus. Sie setzte sich konsequent mit identitätspolitischen Fragen auseinander und entwickelte dafür eine künstlerische Sprache, mit der die Betrachter:innen auf allgemein verständliche, direkte und emotionale Weise angesprochen werden sollen, um Veränderungen zu bewirken.

Die Multimedia-Installation *Black Box / White Box* ist eines von Pipers zentralen Werken. Sie schafft darin zwei Perspektiven auf den bekannten rassistischen Vorfall, bei dem der schwarze US-Bürger Rodney King 1991 in Los Angeles von Polizisten brutal zusammengeschlagen wurde. Wie 2020, nach der Ermordung des Afroamerikaners George Floyd durch einen Polizeibeamten, kam es 1992 zu schweren Unruhen, nachdem die Täter zunächst freigesprochen wurden. Der damalige Präsident George Bush sen. ließ den vor allem von der afroamerikanischen Bevölkerung getragenen Aufstand gegen den institutionell verankerten Rassismus durch Streitkräfte niederschlagen – eine historische Parallele zum Vorgehen der Trump-Administration, die im Mai 2020 mit Polizeieinsätzen auf die Proteste der „Black Lives Matter“-Bewegung reagierte.

Pipers Installation ermöglicht es uns, in zwei verschiedene Perspektiven – eine schwarze und eine weiße – einzutauchen und einen Blickwechsel vorzunehmen. Im schwarzen Raum nehmen wir gegenüber einem Porträt Platz, das den misshandelten Rodney King zeigt. 30 Sekunden lang erscheint das Bild seines verletzten

Gesichts, während seine brüchige Stimme zu hören ist, mit der er kurz nach dem Vorfall dazu aufrief, einander trotz aller Konflikte die Hand zu reichen. Im weißen Raum werden wir mit der bekannten Amateuraufnahme konfrontiert, auf der die Polizisten zu sehen sind, die King brutal zusammenschlagen. Piper hat das Video mit Ausschnitten aus einer Ansprache des ehemaligen Präsidenten Bush sowie mit Soul-Nummern als Soundtrack unterlegt, darunter *What's Going On* von Marvin Gaye. Piper setzt Empathie in dieser Arbeit als zentrales Mittel ein. Während die vom Rassismus Betroffenen eine traurige Bestätigung ihrer Situation erfahren, wird für die anderen fast körperlich spürbar, was es bedeutet, rassistische Diskriminierung und Gewalt zu erleben. (JT)

ADRIAN PIPER

1948 New York, NY, US—Berlin, DE

The US-American artist Adrian Piper, who has been living in Berlin since 2005, belongs to the first generation of conceptual artists and is a retired professor for analytical philosophy. In the 1970s, she introduced a critical approach to xenophobia, racism, and gender into the idioms of conceptual art, an approach that she herself pursued over several decades. In this, she drew in many ways on her own social experience as a "US-American woman with African roots." She consistently addressed issues of identity politics and developed an artistic language for this, attempting to directly address beholders in ways that everyone can understand. Her works present situations in which people are touched emotionally and are surprised by their own impulses and reactions. The aim is to provoke some change in the beholder.

The multimedia installation *Black Box / White Box* is one of Piper's key works. In it she develops two perspectives on the well-known racist incident when the US citizen Rodney King was brutally beaten in 1991 by police in Los Angeles. As in the year 2020 after the murder of the Afro-American George Floyd by a policeman, in 1992 there was serious unrest, after the perpetrators had been acquitted. The president at the time, George Bush senior, used the military to repress the protests against institutional racism, which came mainly from the Afro-American population—a historical parallel to the actions of the Trump administration, which in May 2020 reacted to the protests of the emergent Black Lives Matter movement by deploying the police.

Piper's installation makes it possible to immerse yourself into two different perspectives—a black and a white—and to undertake a perspective shift. In the black room we are placed in front of a portrait showing the mistreated Rodney King. For thirty seconds we see his injured face, while his broken voice can be heard saying just shortly after the incident that people should take steps

toward each other in spite of all their conflicts. In the white room we are confronted with the well-known amateur film showing the police brutally beating King. Piper added excerpts from a speech by former President Bush and used soul songs as a soundtrack, including Marvin Gaye's 1971 hit *What's Going On*. Here Piper is deploying empathy as her main strategy. While people affected by racism experience a sad confirmation of their situation, for others what it means to experience racist discrimination and violence becomes almost physically tangible. (JT)

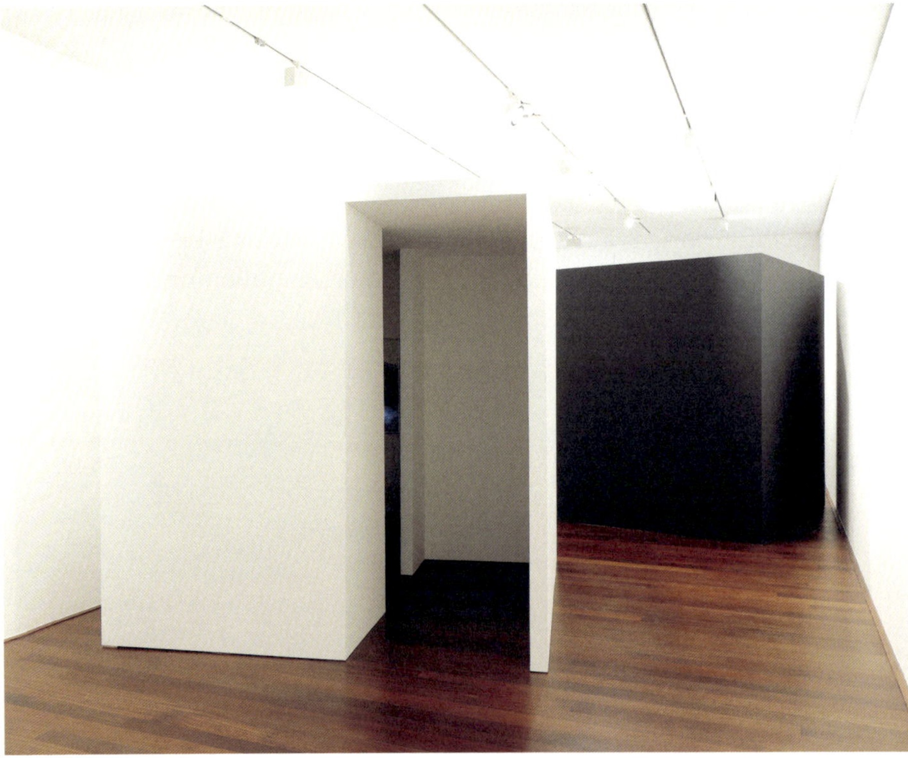

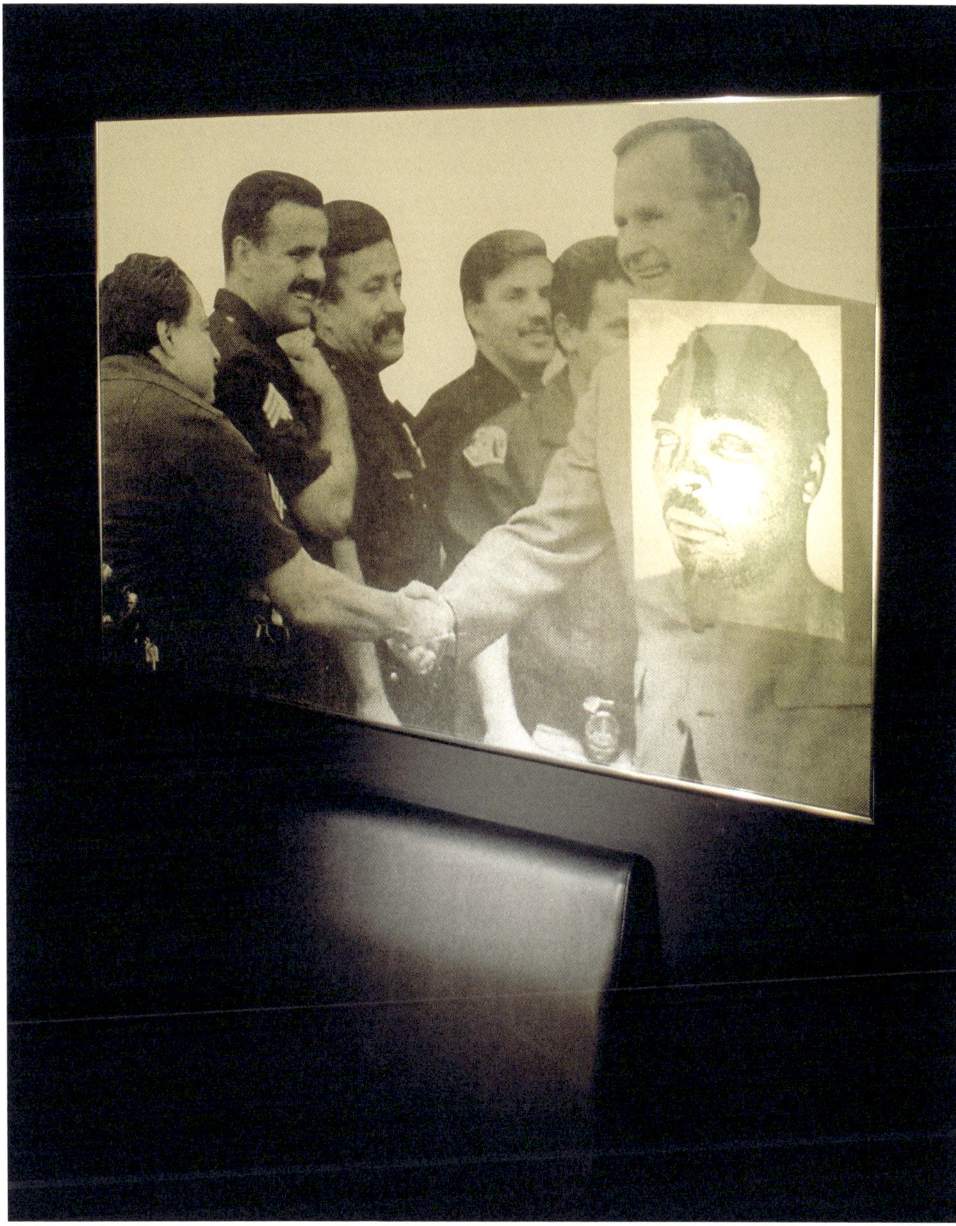

Black Box / White Box, 1992

LISL PONGER

1947 Nürnberg, DE – Wien, AT

Lisl Ponger beschäftigt sich seit vielen Jahren mit der Frage, wie der europäische Blick das sogenannte Andere und Fremde durch kolonialistische und rassistische Wahrnehmungsstereotype hervorbringt. Zugleich zeigen ihre Arbeiten oftmals Strategien auf, mit denen dieser Blick kritisch auf sich selbst zurückgeworfen werden kann. Pongers bevorzugte Untersuchungsfelder sind die Ethnologie und die Anthropologie, die sich lange Zeit der Erforschung und (Mit-)Konstruktion des „Fremden" widmeten, bevor die Denkmuster und Lebensweisen des „Eigenen" in ihr Blickfeld rückten.

Pongers Selbstporträt mit dem Titel *Teilnehmende Beobachterin* zeigt die Künstlerin bei der Betrachtung ihres Spiegelbildes. Ausgestattet mit ihrer Kamera und anderen sorgsam arrangierten Requisiten, in denen sich das Motiv des beobachtenden Auges schier endlos wiederholt, erscheint sie als doppelsinnige Allegorie der Feldforschungsmethode, die im 20. Jahrhundert zeitweilig als ethnologische Königsdisziplin galt. Die Künstlerin begegnet sich in der Rolle der teilnehmenden Beobachterin selbst und lässt uns an dieser Begegnung teilhaben. Die programmatische Arbeit lässt im Spiegelbild Alterität und Identität konvergieren – sie steht für den paradoxen Versuch, sich selbst mit den Augen der anderen zu sehen. Der Blick in den Spiegel ist damit nicht länger ein Instrument der Selbstbestätigung, sondern wird durch das theatralische Setting im gleichwohl prosaischen Interieur zu einer Kritik des Sehens. Ponger macht auf diese Weise die Begegnung mit Fremdheit für das Nachdenken über das Eigene, Gewohnte und möglicherweise Begrenzte fruchtbar. (JT / ThS)

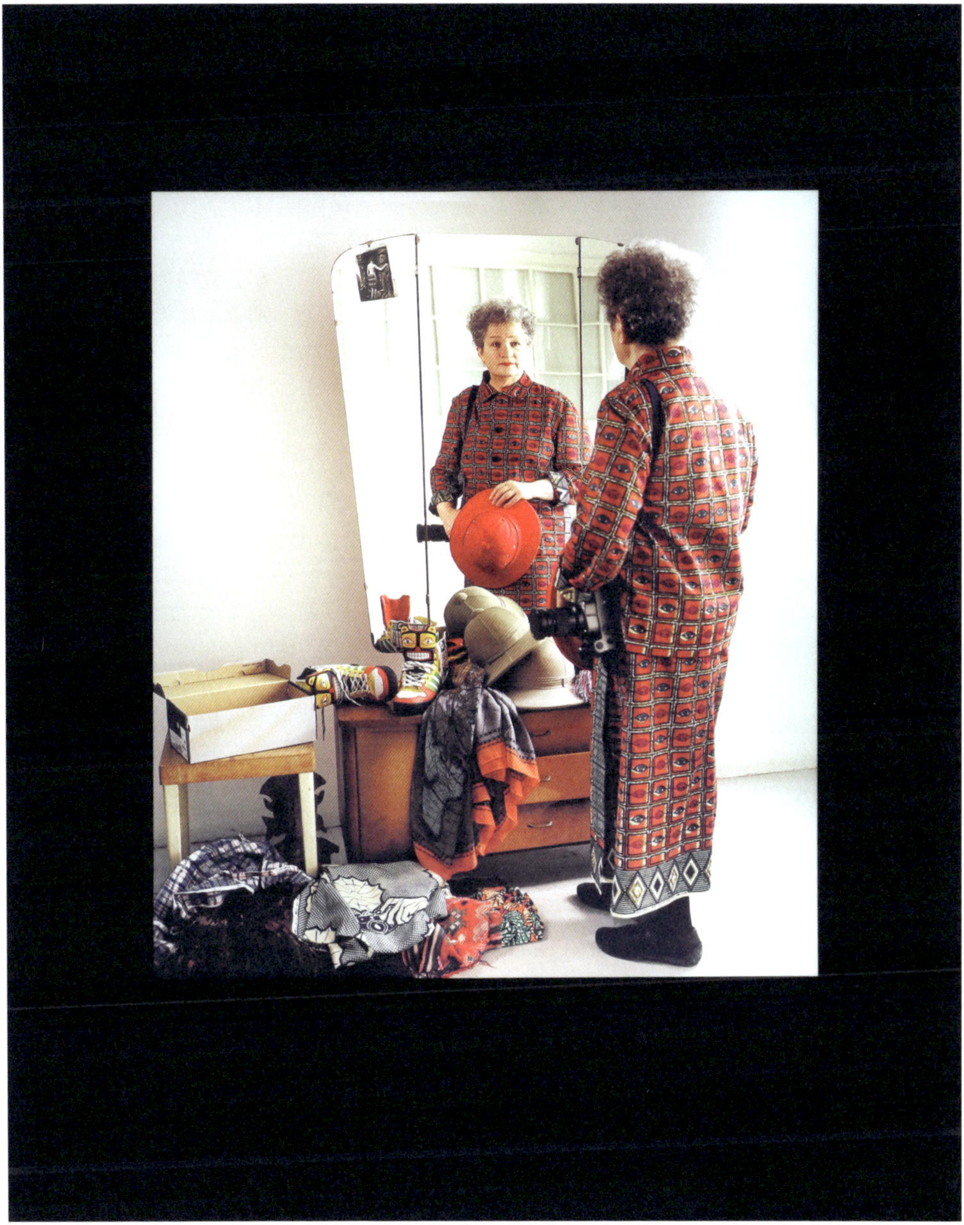

Teilnehmende Beobachterin / Participant Observer, 2016

LISL PONGER

1947 Nuremberg, DE—Vienna, AT

For many years now, Lisl Ponger has been addressing the question as to how a European gaze produces its own other by means of perceptions based on colonialist and racist stereotypes. At the same time her works often present strategies to critically direct this gaze upon ourselves. Ponger's preferred fields of exploration are the disciplines of ethnology and anthropology, which for a long time were devoted to the research and (co-)construction of the "foreign," before the patterns of thought and ways of life of the "own" became objects of investigation.

Ponger's self-portrait entitled *Participating Observer* shows the artist looking at her own mirror image. Equipped with her camera and a number of further carefully placed props, in which the motif of the observing eye is repeated almost endlessly, she appears as an ambivalent allegory of the methods of field research that for much of the twentieth century were seen as the supreme discipline of ethnological studies. The artist Ponger encounters herself in the role of the participating observer, and she allows us to take part in this encounter. This programmatic work converges alterity and identity in the mirror image by showing the paradoxical attempt to see yourself with the eyes of others. The gaze into the mirror thus seems no longer an instrument of self-assertion, but due to its theatrical setting in a very much prosaic interior it leads to a critique of seeing. Ponger makes the encounter with the other fruitful for a critical approach to the self, the customary, and the potentially restricted. (JT / ThS)

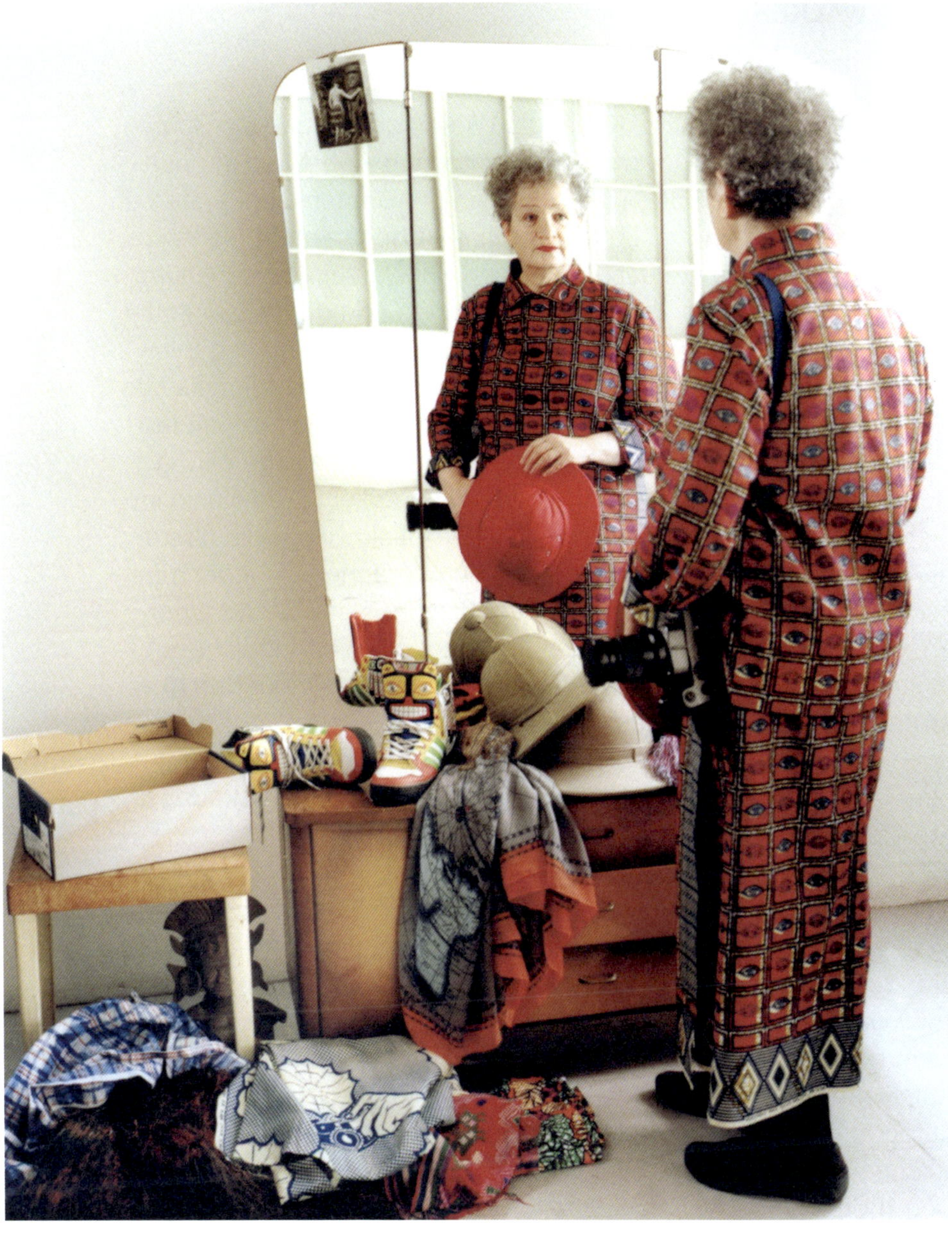

Teilnehmende Beobachterin / Participant Observer, 2016

KARA WALKER

1969 Stockton, CA, US – New York, NY, US

Kara Walker definiert ihre Kunst als Widerstand gegen die Spuren, die Kolonialismus, Sklaverei, Rassismus und Apartheid in unserem alltäglichen Verhalten und unseren gewohnten Denksystemen hinterlassen haben. Im Mittelpunkt ihrer Arbeiten steht die lange und dunkle Geschichte der Repression Schwarzer Menschen im amerikanischen Süden vor dem Bürgerkrieg und der verzweifelte Kampf der Unterdrückten um ihre Freiheit. In detailreichen Bildgeschichten, für die sie meist die Technik und Formensprache des Scherenschnitts verwendet, setzt sie sich insbesondere mit Motiven auseinander, die zur Stigmatisierung und Unterdrückung Schwarzer Menschen geschaffen wurden. Walkers Werke sind immer auch visuelle Fallen. Auf den ersten Blick wirken die filigranen Scherenschnitte verspielt, inhaltlich sprechen sie jedoch mit scharfer Ironie all jene rassistischen Klischees und Stereotypen an, die unsere Gesellschaft über Jahrhunderte verinnerlicht hat. In ihren Kurzfilmen verwendet Walker aus Papiersilhouetten geformte Puppen, die sie selbst von Hand führt. Sie bezieht sich dabei unter anderem auf die deutsche Silhouetten-Animationsfilmerin Lotte Reiniger, die in den 1920er-Jahren mit Trickfilm zu arbeiten begann.

Der Film *National Archives Microfilm M999 Roll 34: Bureau of Refugees, Freedmen and Abandoned Lands: Lucy of Pulaski* entstand aus Walkers Recherchen in den Archiven eines Büros, das 1865 gegründet wurde, um ehemaligen Sklaven und Sklavinnen beim Übergang in die Freiheit zu helfen. Das Büro führte genaue Aufzeichnungen über die Gewalt, der sie während des Wiederaufbaus nach dem Bürgerkrieg ausgesetzt waren. Walkers Film zeichnet einen konkreten Vorfall von Rassenunruhen nach, der sich 1868 in Pulaski, Tennessee, ereignete. Die Niederschrift des Büros über diesen Fall schildert detailliert, wie es zu der gewalttätigen Konfrontation kam, und zeigt dabei selbst eine tief verwurzelte männlich-sexistische rassistische Sichtweise. Beschrieben

wird das Stereotyp einer Schwarzen Frau, deren angeblich lockere Moral den Aufruhr ausgelöst haben soll.

Miss Merrimac and the Monitor ist eine farbige Licht-Schatten-Projektion, die auf einfachsten technischen Mitteln beruht. Mithilfe einer transparenten Folie und eines Overheadprojektors wird die Silhouette einer kriechenden Frauengestalt in Südstaatengewand und mit einem Schwert in der Hand auf die Wand projiziert. Über ihr schwebt eine Mischung von Wolkengebilde und Ungeheuer, in und auf ihr balancieren vier kleine Figuren in Form von schwarzen Miniaturscherenschnitten. „Miss Mary Mack" ist ein in den USA bekanntes Klatschspiel. Der Titel des Werks bezieht sich auch auf die berühmte Seeschlacht von Hampton Roads im amerikanischen Bürgerkrieg, der sich an der Frage der Sklaverei entzündet hatte. Süd- und Nordstaaten standen sich in dieser Schlacht mit den Panzerschiffen Virginia (gebaut aus dem Rumpf des versenkten Kriegsschiffes Merrimack) und Monitor gegenüber. (JT)

KARA WALKER

1969 Stockton, CA, US—New York, NY, US

Kara Walker defines her art as resistance against the traces that colonialism, slavery, racism, and apartheid have left in our everyday behavior and habitual systems of thought. Her work focuses on the long and dark history of repression of Black people in the American South before the Civil War and the desperate struggle of the oppressed for their freedom. In richly detailed pictorial stories, for which she usually uses the technique and formal language of paper cuts, she particularly looks at images and motifs that were created to stigmatize and repress Black people. Walker's works are always visual tricks. At first glance, the delicate paper cuts appear playful, but in terms of content they address with sharp irony all those racist clichés and stereotypes that our society has internalized over centuries. In her short films, Walker uses puppets formed from paper silhouettes, which she guides by hand herself. She references, among others, the German silhouette animator Lotte Reiniger, who began working with animation in the 1920s.

The film *National Archives Microfilm M999 Roll 34: Bureau of Refugees, Freedmen and Abandoned Lands: Lucy of Pulaski* grew out of Walker's research in the archives of an office founded in 1865 with the aim of supporting former slaves in their transition to freedom. Here, very exact record was kept of the gratuitous violence that former slaves suffered during the time of reconstruction after the Civil War. Walker's film retells the story of a specific case of racial unrest, which took place in 1868 in Pulaski, Tennessee. The written report of the office on this incident gives a detailed account of how the violent conflict came about, but it does this using a deeply ingrained sexist and racist gaze. It contains a clichéd depiction of a Black woman whose alleged loose morals caused the riot.

Miss Merrimac and the Monitor is a color light-and-shadow projection based on the simplest of technical means. Using a trans-

parent foil and an overhead projector, the silhouette of a crawling female figure wearing Southern states attire and holding a sword in her hand is projected onto the wall. Above her is a mix of cloud shapes and monsters, and overlapping or on top of her are balanced four miniature black paper cuts that represent further small figures. “Miss Mary Mack” is a well-known clapping game in the USA. The title of this work also refers to the famous sea battle of Hampton Roads during the American Civil War, which ignited over the issue of slavery. In this battle, the Southern and Northern states faced up to each other with the battleships *Virginia* (built from the rump of the sunk warship *Merrimack*) and *Monitor*. (JT)

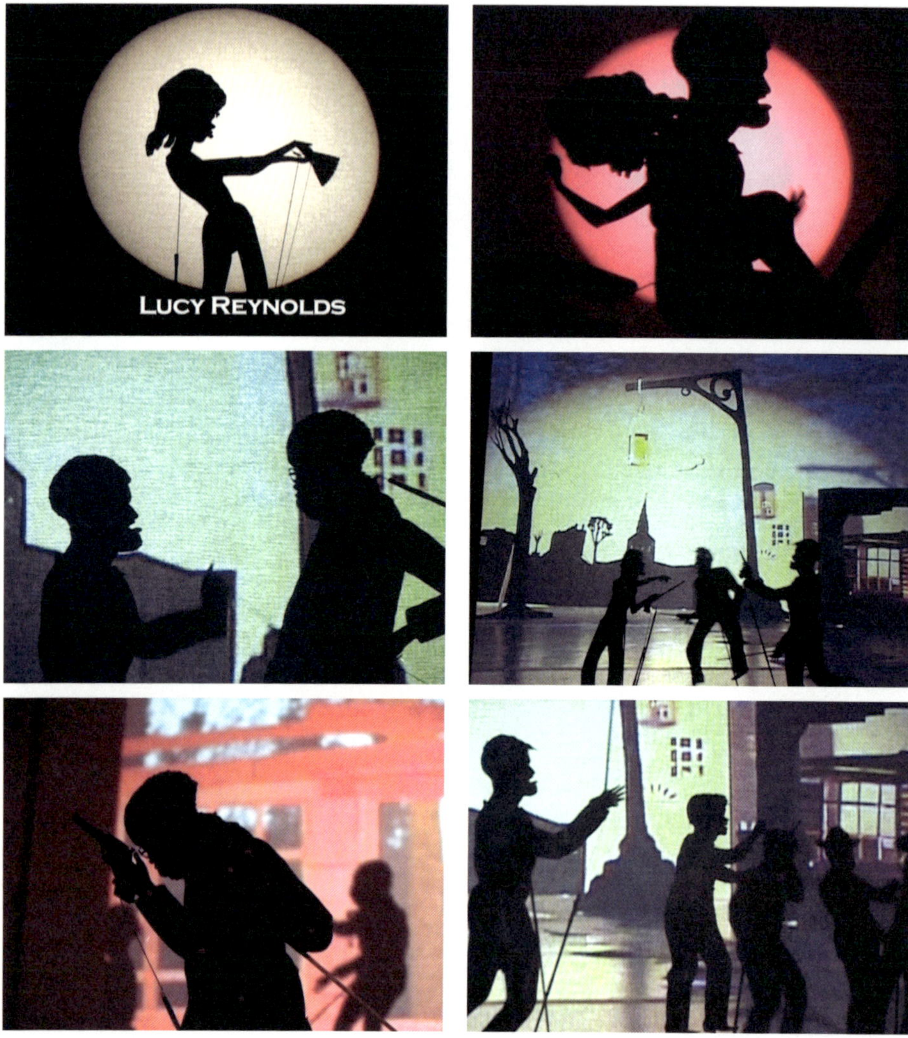

National Archives Microfilm M999 Roll 34: Bureau of Refugees, Freedmen and Abandoned Lands: Lucy of Pulaski, 2009

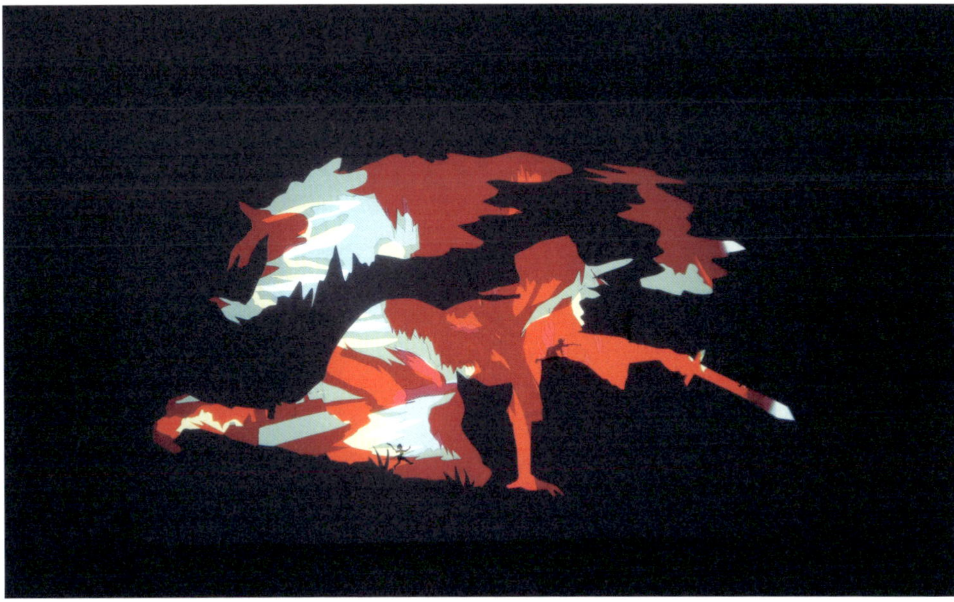

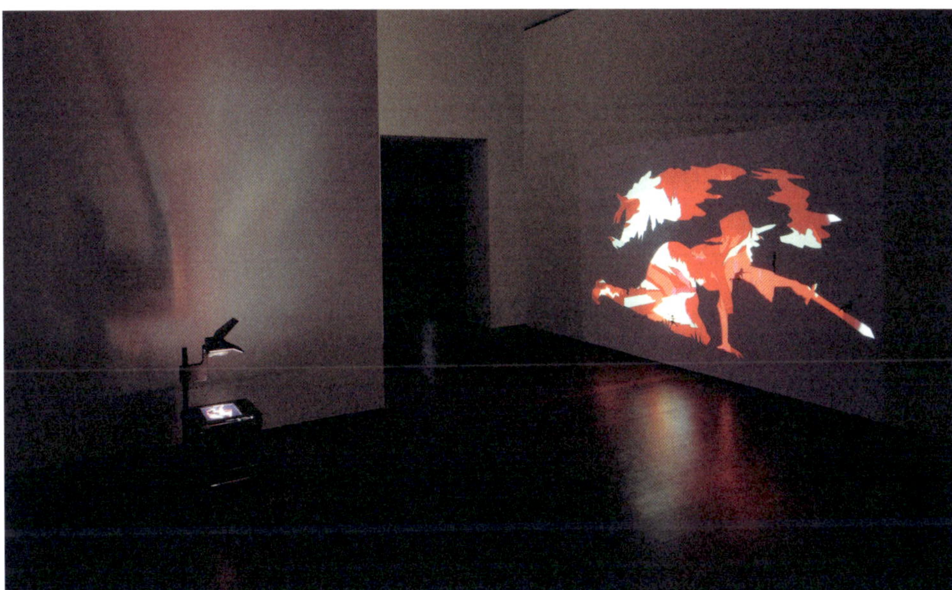

Miss Merrimac and the Monitor, 2001

DAS BEGEHREN NACH ANDEREN BILDERN IM GESPRÄCH MIT BELINDA KAZEEM-KAMIŃSKI

Stefanie Grünangerl und Jürgen Tabor

Jürgen Tabor: Eine Grundlage deiner künstlerischen Arbeit wie auch deiner wissenschaftlichen Forschung ist die Schwarze feministische Theorie und Praxis. Sprechen wir zuerst über die Methodik deiner Arbeit, über ihre Aufteilung in eine künstlerische und eine wissenschaftliche, kritisch-theoretische Seite. Deine Arbeit manifestiert sich in fast gleichem Maße in diesen beiden Formen der Auseinandersetzung. Welche Seite war zuerst da?

Belinda Kazeem-Kamiński: Ich würde es anders formulieren und sagen: Welche Seite zeigte sich zuerst? Da kann ich klar sagen, zuerst kam die wissenschaftliche Auseinandersetzung und damit ergaben sich auch Publikationsmöglichkeiten. Doch eigentlich war die Schwerpunktsetzung in meinem Studium der Internationalen Entwicklung an der Universität Wien bereits stark von der Arbeit mit und innerhalb der Schwarzen Frauen Community, einer Selbstorganisation von Schwarzen Frauen in Wien, geprägt. Meine Interessen haben sich zuerst in der wissenschaftlichen Arbeit gezeigt, weil ich dort die Möglichkeit hatte, relativ schnell zu publizieren. Das heißt aber nicht, dass die künstlerische Auseinandersetzung nicht auch schon da war. Seit meiner Jugend interessiere ich mich für Fotografie und Bilder im Allgemeinen – für Bilder, die die Realität widerspiegeln, aber auch für Bilder als Möglichkeit, andere Realitäten zu eröffnen.

Mein inhaltlicher Fokus spiegelte sich in den Theorien wider, die ich durch befreundete Aktivist:innen und Kulturwissenschaftler:innen kennengelernt habe. Und das waren vor allem Schwarze feministische Theorien und Praktiken. Was ich dort las und lernte, das machte Sinn in Übereinstimmung mit meiner Realität, mit meinen eigenen Erfahrungen. Dies war auch das erste Mal, dass ich in einem wissenschaftlichen Zusammenhang das Beharren auf genau diesen Erfahrungen erlebte, auf der Nutzung von Erfahrungswissen für die Bildung von Theorien. Das hat mich sehr angesprochen. Aus diesen Überlegungen heraus habe ich begonnen, mehr zu schreiben, aber auch recht schnell erkannt, dass mein Schreibstil oder das, was ich erreichen wollte, nicht einem geradlinigen „wissenschaftlichen" Stil entsprach. Das war und ist mir zu eng – diese

THE DESIRE FOR OTHER PICTURES IN CONVERSATION WITH BELINDA KAZEEM-KAMIŃSKI

Stefanie Grünangerl and Jürgen Tabor

Jürgen Tabor: A foundation of your artistic works and also your academic research is Black feminist theory and practice. We would like to begin by talking about the methodology of your work, its division into an artistic side and an academic and critical theoretical side. Your work is evident in almost equal measure in these two forms of investigation. Which side of your work came first?

Belinda Kazeem-Kamiński: I would put it differently and say, which side showed itself first. I can then clearly say that academic research and ensuing opportunities to publish came first. But in fact my focus during my studies in International Development at the University of Vienna was already strongly shaped by work with and within the self-organized Black women's community in Vienna. My interests were first evident in academic work, as I had the opportunity there to publish relatively quickly. But that does not mean that my artistic work was not yet present. Since my youth I have been interested in photography and pictures in general—pictures that reflect reality and also pictures that make it possible to open up different realities.

My thematic focus was reflected in matters that I got to know through friends who were activists and cultural studies scholars. These were above all Black feminist theories and practices. What I read and learned about there made sense in terms of my own reality and my own experiences. That was the first time in an academic context that I noted an insistence on precisely these experiences, on the use of experiential knowledge for the formation of theories. That greatly appealed to me. Based on these ideas I began to write more but then very quickly realized that my writing style, or what I wanted to achieve, did not correspond to any "straight" academic style. That was and still is too restricted for me, these academic paths saying "this is the way to write" and perhaps in the worst case this "not becoming subjective." Fortunately that is now becoming more and more fluid.

I do not have any artistic training in the classical sense. I studied International Development at the University of Vienna. Then in 2014 and 2015 I attended the

akademischen Bahnen im Sinne von „so wird es geschrieben" und vielleicht im schlimmsten Fall dieses „Nicht-subjektiv-Werden". Glücklicherweise weicht das mehr und mehr auf.

Eine künstlerische Ausbildung im klassischen Sinne habe ich nicht. Ich habe Internationale Entwicklung an der Universität Wien studiert. Danach habe ich von 2014 bis 2015 die Schule für künstlerische Photographie Friedl Kubelka besucht und die Aufnahmeprüfung für das PhD-Studium an der Akademie der bildenden Künste Wien abgelegt. Als ich meinen Abschluss an der Schule Friedl Kubelka machte, fiel es mir noch schwer, mich als Künstlerin zu bezeichnen. Ich meinte eher, dass ich eine Person bin, die schreibt und die sich für Kunst interessiert. Inzwischen würde ich sagen, dass ich theorieinformiert und theoriebasiert bin und diese Basis für die künstlerische Produktion nutze. Umgekehrt ist jedoch das Wissenschaftliche ohne das Künstlerische für mich nicht mehr denkbar. Die Basis ist für mich immer das Schreiben. Es spielt keine Rolle, ob es sich um einen Text handelt, der als „wissenschaftlich" bezeichnet wird, oder um eine künstlerische Arbeit. Ich finde es spannend, etwas zu schreiben, dann etwas Visuelles daraus zu machen und dann wieder darüber zu schreiben, wohin ich gekommen bin. Verschiedene Medien geben mir verschiedene Möglichkeiten.

Stefanie Grünangerl: Das wissenschaftliche Schreiben mit seinen Regeln setzt gewisse Grenzen, zum Beispiel ist ein persönlicher Bezug zum Untersuchungsgegenstand verpönt. Persönliche Erfahrungen werden als nicht-wissenschaftlich ausgeschlossen. Eröffnet die künstlerische Ebene hingegen die Möglichkeit, genau diese persönliche Involviertheit zu thematisieren?

BKK: In meinem Fall war es so. Was du beschreibst, war sicher einer der Gründe, warum mir die Konzentration auf das akademische Schreiben zu eng wurde. Die künstlerische Arbeit gibt mir Räume, die mir die akademische nicht geben kann. Bei der künstlerischen Arbeit hat mir noch nie jemand gesagt, sie sei zu persönlich. Dort kann ich persönliche Erfahrungen mit Theorie verbinden. Ich mache das zunehmend auch andersherum, also im wissenschaftlichen Bereich, aber hier muss ich verhandeln, wenn ich zum Beispiel für ein Journal schreibe. Da geht es oft darum, auszuhandeln, was für die Herausgeber:innen möglich ist.

School Friedl Kubelka for Artistic Photography and took admission examinations for Ph.D. studies at the Academy of Fine Arts Vienna. After I graduated from the School Friedl Kubelka I still found it difficult to say that I was an artist. I rather thought that I was a person who writes and is interested in art. Now I would say that I am informed about and grounded in theory and that I use this basis for my artistic production. Seen the other way, academic work is no longer conceivable for me without the artistic side. My basis is always writing, and it does not matter if I am writing a text that would be seen to be "academic" or an artistic work. I find it exciting to write something and then make something visual out of it, and then again to write about where I have got to. Different media give me different opportunities.

Stefanie Grünangerl: Academic writing and its rules set certain limits. Personal points of reference to the object of research, for example, are disapproved of. Personal experiences are excluded because they are not scholarly. Does the artistic level on the other hand open up the possibility of addressing precisely this personal involvement?

BKK: In my case, yes. What you have described was certainly one of the reasons why I found concentrating on only academic writing was becoming too restrictive. Artistic work gave me spaces that academic work cannot. No one has ever told me that my artistic work was too personal. There I can combine personal experiences with theory. Increasingly, I also do this the other way around, in research and academia, but here I need to negotiate this, when I am writing for a journal for example. Often this is about working out what the publishers and editors will accept.

JT: Let's turn to the thematic grounding of your artistic and academic work. Can you describe the roots of your investigations?

BKK: Before I met the people who were active in and around the Black women's community in Vienna, I often thought that I was facing racist and sexist experiences because there was something not right with myself. In conversation and exchange I then understood that many Black people had the same experiences. I realized then that there was something wrong with social structures, and that this had nothing directly to do with me. It may be played out on

JT: Kommen wir zu den inhaltlichen Grundlagen deiner künstlerischen und wissenschaftlichen Arbeit. Wo liegen die Wurzeln deiner Auseinandersetzung?

BKK: Bevor ich die Menschen traf, die in und um die Schwarze Frauen Community herum aktiv waren und sind, hatte ich oft den Gedanken, dass ich rassistisch-sexistische Erfahrungen machen musste, weil mit mir als Individuum etwas nicht stimmte. Im Gespräch und im Austausch habe ich dann jedoch verstanden, dass viele Schwarze Menschen die gleichen Erfahrungen machen. Da wurde mir klar, dass etwas mit der sozialen Struktur nicht stimmt, und das hat nicht direkt mit mir zu tun. Es wird vielleicht an mir ausgelassen, aber es geht um etwas Strukturelles. Das zu verstehen, hat mich geprägt. Zuvor war mir die Geschichte des Kolonialismus und der Versklavung nicht bewusst. Natürlich wusste ich davon, aber mir war nicht klar, welche massiven Auswirkungen das auf die Welt und die Möglichkeit, sich in dieser zu bewegen, hatte und hat. Und wie schwer das zu ändern ist, wie sich die Gewalt verhärtet hat, woher die Stereotype tatsächlich kommen und wie alt sie schon sind.

Eine weitere Wurzel meiner Arbeit war und ist das Lesen. Eine Freundin von mir, die Kulturwissenschaftlerin Araba Evelyn Johnston-Arthur drückte mir zum Beispiel das Buch *Black Looks* von bell hooks in die Hand und sagte: „Hier, lies das mal, vielleicht wäre das etwas für dich, da du dich doch so sehr für Fotografie und Bilder interessierst." Es war, als würden Glühbirnen in meinem Kopf angehen. Denn dort sind Dinge beschrieben, die ich aus meiner Erfahrung kannte, aber nie so in Worte hätte fassen können. Schwarze feministische Theorie und Praxis, Autorinnen wie bell hooks und Audre Lorde oder aus dem deutschsprachigen Raum Autorinnen wie May Ayim, Peggy Piesche, Fatima El-Tayeb waren und sind wichtige Bezugspunkte für mich. Natürlich gibt es noch viele andere, die inzwischen dazugekommen sind, wie Saidiya Hartman oder Christina Sharpe. Sie sind für mich auch deshalb wichtig, weil sie gegen die Trennung von Theorie und Praxis arbeiten. Sie argumentieren, dass das, was wir erleben, Wissen ist, Erfahrungswissen. Saidiya Hartman oder Christina Sharpe sind Denkerinnen, die für mich in der letzten Zeit auch wichtig geworden sind, weil sie mir geholfen haben, über den Begriff „Mensch" nachzudenken. Sie stellen fest, dass die Kategorie „Mensch" Schwarze Personen nicht einschloss, und sie erinnern in diesem Zusammenhang daran, wie wesentlich der Prozess der Versklavung war – ein Prozess, der Afrikaner:innen zu Objekten machte, zu

me, but it is nonetheless something structural. Understanding that shaped me. Previously I was not aware of the history of colonialism and slavery. Of course I knew about them, but I was not aware of the massive effects they had and have on the world and on people's opportunities in the world. And how hard it is to change this, how the violence has hardened, where the stereotypes really come from, and how old they already are.

Another root of my work is reading. For example, a friend of mine, cultural studies scholar Araba Evelyn Johnston-Arthur, gave me the book *Black Looks* by bell hooks and said: "Here you are, read this, perhaps this will be something for you, as you are so interested in photography and pictures." It was as if lamps were lit up in my mind. Things are described there that I knew from my own experience but could never have put into words in that way. Black fe-minist theory and practice, authors like bell hooks and Audre Lorde, or German-language authors like May Ayim, Peggy Piesche, and Fatima El-Tayeb, have been and still are important points of reference for me. Of course there are many more that I have discovered since, like Saidiya Hartman and Christina Sharpe. They are also important to me because they work against the separation of theory and practice. They argue that the things we experience are knowledge, the knowledge of experience. Saidiya Hartman and Christina Sharpe are thinkers who have become very important for me recently, because they have helped me to rethink the concept of the "human." They note that the category "human being" did not include Black people, and they recall in this context how important the process of enslavement was—a process that made Africans into objects, commodities that could be traded, and that all kinds of things were done to them that were not done to *white* people, or at least not to this extent. This is an important point for me, in order to understand this stickiness of racism in human relations. I often meet people who say: "You talk of liberation, of equality, but we already have all of that!" Then I laugh, because this is not the case. If we think of violence against Black people, then we can see that we have attained neither liberation nor equality. A closer look shows that these acts of violence, as Grada Kilomba argues in her book *Plantation Memories*, for example, are rearticulations and reenactments of a violent past in the here and now.

Waren, die gehandelt werden konnten, und mit denen alle möglichen Dinge getan wurden, die *weißen* Menschen nicht oder nicht in diesem Ausmaß zugefügt wurden. Dieser Punkt ist für mich wichtig, um diese Stickyness, diese Klebrigkeit des Rassistischen in den menschlichen Verhältnissen, zu verstehen. Ich treffe oft Leute, die sagen: „Du redest von Befreiung, von Gleichberechtigung, aber das haben wir doch alles schon!" Ich lache dann, weil dem nicht so ist. Wenn wir uns beispielsweise die Gewalt gegen Schwarze Menschen vergegenwärtigen, erkennen wir doch, dass wir weder Befreiung noch Gleichberechtigung schon erreicht haben. Bei näherer Betrachtung zeigt sich, dass diese Gewalt – wie Grada Kilomba beispielsweise in ihrem Buch *Plantation Memories* argumentiert – Reartikulationen und Reinszenierungen einer gewaltsamen Vergangenheit im Hier und Jetzt sind.

Wichtig sind mir Ansätze, die hinterfragen, was wir überhaupt als Vergangenheit, Gegenwart, Zukunft verstehen. Denn diese Vergangenheit, Gegenwart, Zukunft wird oft als eine Entwicklungsgeschichte, als eine Erfolgsgeschichte erzählt. Im Gegensatz dazu halte ich es für wichtig, zu benennen, was das eigentlich ist, dass sich in unser aller Gegenwart reartikuliert. Spannend finde ich Ansätze, die nicht davon sprechen, dass diese Vergangenheit überhaupt überwunden werden kann. Saidiya Hartman beschreibt in einem Essay, dass Schwarzen Menschen oft vorgeworfen wird, rückwärtsgewandt zu sein, sich ständig an die Vergangenheit zu erinnern. Sie argumentiert jedoch, dass wir das nicht tun, weil wir irgendwie nostalgisch sind oder weil es früher so viel besser war, sondern um aufzuzeigen, dass diese Vergangenheit nicht wirklich vergangen ist. Calvin Warren beispielsweise prägte den Begriff „Black Time". „Black Time" ist ein Verständnis von Zeit, in der die Vergangenheit gegenwärtig bleibt und nicht etwas zu Überwindendes ist. Für viele war etwa die Wahl von Barack Obama zum US-Präsidenten ein Zeichen dafür, dass Diskriminierung nun überwunden ist. Aber das Interessante ist doch, dass mit seiner Wahl gleichzeitig die Gewalt gegen Schwarze Personen, die es schon immer gab, wieder zugenommen hat. Das war nicht zu übersehen. Und auch darüber sollten wir nachdenken. Warum gerade dort und zu diesem Zeitpunkt?

JT: Eines der Ziele unserer Ausstellung *This World Is White No Longer* war es, künstlerische Arbeiten zu zeigen, die genau diese versteckten, unbewältigten rassistischen Strukturen bewusst machen und reflektieren.

I find approaches important that question what we understand as being past, present, and future. This past, present, and future is often narrated as a history of development and a success story. To counter this, I think it is important to say what it really is that is rearticulated in everyone's present. I find approaches interesting that do not talk of it being possible to overcome this past. Saidiya Hartman describes in her essay that Black people are often accused of being backward-looking and permanently recalling the past. But she argues that we do not do this because we are perhaps nostalgic or because things were much better in the past, but instead to show that this past is not really past. Calvin Warren, for example, coined the term "Black time." Black time is an understanding of time in which the past remains present and there is nothing to overcome. For many people, the election of Barack Obama as US president was a sign that discrimination was now overcome. But the interesting thing is that at the same time as his election violence against Black people, which has always existed, was again on the increase. That was impossible to ignore. And we should think about that too. Why just at this time?

JT: One of the aims of our exhibition *This World Is White No Longer* was to show artistic works that make us aware of and reflect on precisely these hidden racist structures, that have not been overcome.

StG: It was about a critique of approaches that ignore and blend out racist structures and that speak in connection with racism of isolated cases and individual fates that should be addressed on the individual level. But the challenge lies in the larger social structures that are behind this.

BKK: That is an important point. The problem with this kind of individualization, which is almost something like outsourcing, is that it works much more simply than addressing the structure. When racism is individualized then there is only this one person. If we then talk of a perpetrator then this one person has committed an error, and either it was bad and we have to punish them, if we can agree to that, or this person knew no better and these things just sometimes happen. But in reality it isn't so bad, it only affects a single person. There is no need at all to think about how we ourselves contribute every day to racist conditions, and also to sexist, ableist, and all kinds of discriminatory states. If we always outsource this and attribute it to the individual, then only

StG: Es geht auch um eine Kritik an Haltungen, die rassistische Strukturen ignorieren und ausblenden und die im Zusammenhang mit Rassismus von Einzelfällen und Einzelschicksalen sprechen, die auf individueller Ebene zu lösen seien. Die Herausforderung sind aber die gesamtgesellschaftlichen Strukturen, die dahinterstehen.

BKK: Das ist ein wichtiger Punkt. Das Problem mit dieser Form der Individualisierung, die fast so etwas wie Outsourcing ist, besteht darin, dass sie viel einfacher funktioniert als die Arbeit an der Struktur. Bei der Individualisierung von Rassismus gibt es nur diese eine Person. Wenn wir jetzt von einem Täter oder einer Täterin sprechen, dann hat sich diese eine Person einen Fehltritt erlaubt, und entweder war es schlimm und wir müssen sie bestrafen, wenn wir uns darauf einigen können. Oder sie hat es nicht besser gewusst und das passiert dann halt einmal. Aber eigentlich ist es gar nicht so schlimm, denn es betrifft ja nur eine Person. Wir müssen gar nicht darüber nachdenken, was wir selbst jeden Tag zu rassistischen Verhältnissen, aber auch zu sexistischen, ableistischen, zu allen diskriminierenden Verhältnissen beitragen. Wenn wir das immer wieder auslagern und dem Individuum zuschieben, dann ist nur dieses verantwortlich, nicht wir alle zusammen. Es handelt sich jedoch um eine gesellschaftspolitische, historische Struktur. Wir sind es, die diese Struktur bestimmen, indem wir tagtäglich unser Handeln wiederholen. Hier liegen die Eingriffsmöglichkeiten, die wir haben. Die Herausforderung besteht darin, dass das Engagement nicht auf einen einzigen Moment beschränkt bleibt, sondern ein ständiges Commitment darstellt. Dieses Commitment mag schwierig sein. Aber wenn wir das schaffen, können sehr ermutigende Prozesse entstehen.

JT: Deine Arbeit basiert oft auf Recherchen über unterdrückte Geschichten und Sichtweisen Schwarzer Menschen, die du in Archiven, Bibliotheken und anderen Sammlungen findest. Die Ordnungen und Perspektiven, die diesen Institutionen zugrunde liegen, sind ein wichtiger Ausgangspunkt deiner Arbeit. Oft ist es eine *weiße* Perspektive, die du herausschälst und der du oppositionelle Blicke gegenüberstellst. Können wir in diesem Zusammenhang über die *Library of Requests* sprechen? Deine Reihe *Library of Requests* ist ein fortlaufendes Projekt, das sich mit Bibliotheken und Archiven als Wissensspeicher und Faktor von Identitätspolitiken und damit verbundenen Ein- und Ausschlüssen beschäftigt.

this individual is responsible, and not all of us together. But this is a sociopolitical historical structure. We are the ones who determine this structure by repeating our behaviors and actions day by day. This is where our possibilities for intervention lie. The challenge is not to let commitment be restricted to a single moment, but to make it a permanent commitment. This commitment might be difficult. But if we manage it, then very encouraging processes can emerge.

JT: Your work is often based on research into repressed histories and the views of Black people that you find in archives, libraries, and other collections. The systems and perspectives that these institutions are based on are an important starting point for your work. Often it is a *white* perspective that you coax out, and which you counter with opposing views. Can we talk about the *Library of Requests* in this context? Your series *Library of Requests* is an ongoing project that addresses libraries and archives as stores of knowledge and a factor in identity politics and the appertaining inclusions and exclusions.

BKK: I really like bookstores and libraries. The idea was born in 2016 in the course of the exhibition project *Anti*Colonial Fantasies / Decolonial Strategies*. During my studies I often experienced wanting to read a book that was not in our library. That is ok, not every book that you want has to be there. But when that happens so much you have to buy every book for yourself. And then I asked myself: It is interesting that these books are important points of reference for me, but they are not in my university library—why is this the case? Years later I conducted a survey with students of color at the Academy of Fine Arts Vienna, wanting to find out which books were their important terms of reference, to which they repeatedly turn because they empower and encourage them. Many people took part, and the first edition of the project listed around seventy titles. I compared these with the catalogue of the library. Of these seventy titles there were just under sixty that the library did not have. I set the project up as an installation, and the library then bought all of these books and integrated them all at once. That was the first and second edition.

The project was invited to further exhibitions and I began to devote the different editions to specific themes. I asked myself where I actually wanted to bring all of these books, it did not have to always be a place where they were missing. It could also be a place where they are needed. This was my aim with

BKK: Büchereien und Bibliotheken liegen mir sehr am Herzen. Die Idee entstand 2016 im Rahmen des Ausstellungsprojekts *Anti*Colonial Fantasies / Decolonial Strategies*. Während meines Studiums ging es mir oft so, dass ich Bücher lesen wollte, die in unserer Bibliothek nicht vorhanden waren. Das ist okay, es muss ja nicht jedes Buch geben, das du willst. Aber wenn das zuhauf passiert, musst du dir jedes Buch kaufen. Und dann habe ich mich gefragt: Es ist spannend, dass diese Bücher für mich wichtige Bezugspunkte sind, aber dass sie in meiner Universitätsbibliothek nicht vorkommen – warum ist das so? Jahre später habe ich eine Umfrage unter den Students of Color an der Akademie der bildenden Künste Wien durchgeführt, um herauszufinden, welche Bücher für sie wichtige Bezugspunkte sind, zu denen sie immer wieder zurückkehren, weil sie sie empowern und bestärken. Viele haben sich beteiligt. In der ersten Auflage kamen so etwa siebzig Titel zusammen. Ich habe diese Titel mit dem Bestandskatalog der Bibliothek verglichen. Von diesen 70 Titeln waren knapp 60 nicht in der Bibliothek vorhanden. Ich baute das Projekt als eine Installation auf. Die Bibliothek kaufte schließlich alle diese Bücher und integrierte sie in einem Zug. Das war die erste und zweite Auflage.

Das Projekt wurde zu weiteren Ausstellungen eingeladen, und ich begann, die einzelnen Ausgaben bestimmten Themenkomplexen zu widmen. Ich fragte mich, wohin ich diese Bücher eigentlich bringen wollte. Es muss nicht immer ein Ort sein, an dem sie fehlen. Es kann auch ein Ort sein, an dem sie gebraucht werden. In diesem Sinne ging es bei der vierten Ausgabe, die ich zusammen mit der Schwarzen Frauen Community in Wien organisiert habe, um das Sammeln von Büchern für Schwarze Kinder und Jugendliche. Ziel war es, den Grundstock für eine Bibliothek anzulegen, in der Kinder empowernde Literatur finden können. Die *Library of Requests* hat immer damit gearbeitet, dass nicht ich die Expertin bin, die alles allein entscheidet, sondern dass es andere Expert:innen gibt, die das tun. Kinder, Sozialarbeiter:innen, Aktivist:innen, Theoretiker:innen, Radio-Moderator:innen haben Bücher vorgeschlagen. Die Ausgabe in der Ausstellung im Museum der Moderne Salzburg war die erste, bei der ich alleine eine Auswahl getroffen habe. Ich habe mir hier die Freiheit genommen, eine Sammlung von Büchern zusammenzustellen, die ich gerne schon früher gehabt hätte: eine Sammlung von Texten Schwarzer, feministischer Frauen aus dem deutschsprachigen Raum, die sich aus einer selbstbestimmten Perspektive mit Schwarzsein beschäftigen. Die Sammlung erhebt

the fourth edition which I organized together with the Black women's community in Vienna, collecting books for Black children and youth. The goal now was to establish the basis of a library where children could find empowering literature. The *Library of Requests* has always worked on the premise that I am not the expert who decides everything alone, but that there are other experts who do this. Children, social workers, activists, theorists, radio presenters all suggested books. The edition at the exhibition in the Museum der Moderne Salzburg was the first where I made the selection alone. I allowed myself the freedom to put together a collection of books that I would have liked to have when I was younger, a collection of texts by Black feminist women from the German-speaking world, addressing being Black from a self-determined perspective. The collection does not claim to be definitive, but it rather wishes to inspire people to collect more texts. Looking at the theory and practice of Black women in the German-speaking context intends to counter the often used strategy that locates the discrimination of Black people and also resistance against this discrimination not in your own country but in the USA, France, or the United Kingdom.

StG: The so-called institutions of memory—archives, museums, libraries—have very specific systems of knowledge, not seldom a colonial system. What challenges or difficulties arise for you in dealing with materials that represent such a colonial and racist system?

BKK: The challenge that I often see is that I have to think my way into this kind of institutional logic. This logic is evident for example in the use of racist concepts for indexing categories. This is not only about common racist terms, but also the underlying system of thought. At the same time this is not particularly difficult, as I grew up with this great corset of categories. This dichotomous thinking, thinking in opposites, is to this day a basis that our society is anchored in. It is shocking how much I can find there and what has become like a sediment within myself. This is why this work is a personal practice in which I have to negotiate a lot with myself.

StG: How can you work with this material without reproducing the underlying thought system? How are contrary reading, critique, and inquiry possible without repeating the inherent racist gaze?

keinen Anspruch auf Vollständigkeit, vielmehr soll sie dazu anregen, noch mehr Texte zu sammeln. Die Aufmerksamkeit auf die Theorie und Praxis Schwarzer Frauen im deutschsprachigen Raum will der gerne angewendeten Strategie Einhalt gebieten, die Diskriminierung Schwarzer Menschen, aber auch den Widerstand gegen Diskriminierung nicht im eigenen Land, sondern in den USA, Frankreich oder Großbritannien zu verorten.

StG: Die sogenannten Gedächtnisinstitutionen – Archive, Museen, Bibliotheken – haben sehr spezifische Wissensordnungen, nicht selten eine koloniale Wissensordnung. Welche Herausforderungen oder Schwierigkeiten ergeben sich für dich im Umgang mit Materialien, die eine solche koloniale, rassistische Ordnung repräsentieren?

BKK: Die Herausforderung, die ich oft sehe, ist, dass ich mich in eine solche institutionelle Logik hineindenken muss. Diese Logik zeigt sich zum Beispiel in der Verwendung rassistischer Begriffe für Verschlagwortungen. Dabei geht es nicht nur um gängige rassistische Begriffe, sondern auch um das Denksystem dahinter. Gleichzeitig ist das nicht besonders schwierig, weil ich mit diesem ganzen Korsett von Kategorien aufgewachsen bin. Dieses dichotome Denken, das Denken in Gegensätzen – das ist nach wie vor eine Grundlage, die in unserer Gesellschaft verankert ist. Es ist erschreckend, wie viel ich dort finden kann und was sich auch in mir ablagert. Deshalb ist diese Arbeit auch eine persönliche Praxis, bei der ich viel mit mir selbst ausverhandeln muss.

StG: Wie kannst du mit diesem Material arbeiten, ohne das dahinterstehende Denksystem zu reproduzieren? Wie ist ein Querlesen, eine Kritik und eine Hinterfragung möglich, ohne den darin verborgenen rassistischen Blick zu wiederholen?

BKK: Dies ist zum Beispiel eine zentrale Frage in meinem Film *Unearthing. In Conversation* (2017), der sich mit historischen Fotografien beschäftigt, die der österreichisch-tschechische Ethnograf Paul Schebesta in den 1930er-Jahren in der belgischen Kolonie Kongo aufgenommen hat. Ich löse diese Frage nicht, oder besser gesagt, die Unmöglichkeit, sie zu beantworten, wird am Ende des Films deutlich. Für mich stellte sich immer die Frage, was es bewirkt, wenn ich rassistisches oder gewaltvolles Material nehme, weil ich darüber sprechen will.

BKK: This is a key question in my film *Unearthing. In Conversation* (2017), for example, which looks at historical photographs taken by Austrian-Czech ethnographer Paul Schebesta in the 1930s in the Belgian colony of Congo. I do not resolve this question, or put better, the impossibility of answering it becomes clear at the end of the film. I always face the question as to what the effect is when I take racist or violent material, because I wish to speak about it. With the good intention of speaking about it, because it has something to tell us about our present day. What is the effect when I use it as it is? Is that not repeating violence, when I think that the audience consists of people like myself who have various minoritized and perhaps marginalized positions? What does this have to say to these people, who know this material anyway in a different form? For me there is always the question: How can I speak about this violence without reproducing this material? That is why I see visual interventions, such as overlapping or cutting out, as a way of indicating something and guiding the gaze of the beholder in a certain way. In order to draw attention to the thought systems that are deposited in us all. And to ask the question whether we really want to have these. More and more this is connected to the need to create very different images.

JT: In the exhibition *This World Is White No Longer* it was important for us, in addition to showing works that (self-)critically challenge racist structures, to also present works and projects that practice specific perspective shifts and also reflect on these as methods. Adrian Piper makes such a perspective shift, between a Black and a *white* perspective, really tangible in her multimedia installation *Black Box/White Box* (1992). Works in which a real perspective shift is clearly shown can be productive for a different view of the world.

BKK: Seen from my artistic viewpoint, a critique of images is not the most satisfying approach. That is part of my work, but not the aim. The aim is to learn through this critique of existing images about the different images that can be desired. That is a reinforcing moment for me. I think that many of us can agree that there are highly dubious colonially influenced fields in science, and that these are racist, sexist, and the like. But the question is how we go on, what we do in spite of all of this. This question is relevant for everyone, independent of their positions. We must find a way of dealing with this past. In art production I can test out different ways.

Mit der guten Absicht, darüber zu sprechen, weil es uns etwas über unsere Gegenwart zu sagen hat. Was bringt es, wenn ich es so verwende, wie es ist? Ist es nicht eine Wiederholung von Gewalt, wenn ich bedenke, dass das Publikum auch Menschen wie ich sind, die verschiedene minorisierte und vielleicht marginalisierte Positionen einnehmen? Wie kann ich über diese Gewalt sprechen, ohne dieses Material zu reproduzieren? Deshalb sind für mich visuelle Interventionen, wie etwas zu überlagern oder auszuschneiden, eine Möglichkeit, auf etwas hinzuweisen und den Blick der Betrachter:innen auf eine bestimmte Weise zu lenken. Um die Aufmerksamkeit auf die Denksysteme zu lenken, die in uns allen abgelagert sind. Und die Frage zu stellen, ob wir diese so tatsächlich haben wollen. Mehr und mehr verbindet sich dies mit dem Bedürfnis, überhaupt andere Bilder zu schaffen.

JT: In der Ausstellung *This World Is White No Longer* war es uns wichtig, parallel zu Arbeiten, die rassistische Strukturen (selbst)kritisch befragen, Werke und Projekte zu zeigen, die Perspektivenwechsel konkret praktizieren und diese auch als Methode reflektieren. Adrian Piper macht einen solchen Perspektivenwechsel – den Wechsel zwischen einer Schwarzen und einer *weißen* Perspektive – in ihrer Multimedia-Installation *Black Box / White Box* (1992) anschaulich erfahrbar. Werke, in denen ein tatsächlich vollzogener Perspektivenwechsel nachvollziehbar wird, können produktiv für eine andere Sicht auf die Welt sein.

BKK: Von meinem künstlerischen Standpunkt aus gesehen, ist die Kritik an Bildern nicht die befriedigendste Sache. Das ist ein Teil meiner Arbeit, aber nicht das Ziel. Das Ziel ist, dass ich durch diese Kritik an bestehenden Bildern lernen kann, nach welchen anderen Bildern es ein Begehren gibt. Das ist ein bestärkendes Moment für mich. Ich denke, viele von uns können sich darauf einigen, dass es höchst fragwürdige, kolonial geprägte Wissenschaftsfelder gibt und dass diese rassistisch, sexistisch und dergleichen mehr sind. Aber die Frage ist ja, wie wir weitermachen, wie wir trotz allem weitermachen. Diese Frage stellt sich für alle Menschen, unabhängig von ihrer Positionierung. Wir müssen einen Weg finden, mit dieser Vergangenheit umzugehen. In der Kunstproduktion kann ich diesen Umgang erproben.

THIS WORLD IS WHITE NO LONGER
Ansichten einer dezentrierten Welt
Museum der Moderne Salzburg, Rupertinum
24. April – 10. Oktober 2021

THIS WORLD IS WHITE NO LONGER
Views of a Decentered World
Museum der Moderne Salzburg, Rupertinum
April 24—October 10, 2021

Presented by GENERALI

Werkliste | List of Works

Die Werke sind nach Künstler:innen alphabetisch gereiht.

Works are listed by artist in alphabetical order.

KARO AKPOKIERE
1981 Lagos, NG – Lagos, NG und Hamburg, DE
1981 Lagos, NG—Lagos, NG and Hamburg, DE

Zwischen Lagos und Berlin, 2015
50 Zeichnungen
Bleistift, Kugelschreiber, Marker, Gouache auf Papier
Je 42 × 29,7 cm
Courtesy of the artist

Zwischen Lagos und Berlin, 2015
50 drawings
Pencil, ballpoint pen, marker, gouache on paper
42 × 29.7 cm each
Courtesy of the artist

LOTHAR BAUMGARTEN
1944 Rheinsberg, DE – 2018 Berlin, DE
1944 Rheinsberg, DE—2018 Berlin, DE

Unsettled Objects, Pitt Rivers Museum, Oxford, 1968/69
Lichtbildprojektion
81 Diapositive (35 mm, Farbe, nummeriert, inkl. 1 Schwarzdiapositiv), Diaprojektor
13:30 Min.
Sammlung Generali Foundation – Dauerleihgabe am Museum der Moderne Salzburg

Unsettled Objects, Pitt Rivers Museum, Oxford, 1968/69
Slide projection
81 slides (35 mm, color, numbered, 1 black slide), slide projector
13:30 min
Generali Foundation Collection—Permanent Loan to the Museum der Moderne Salzburg

IICA DAKIĆ
2 Sarajevo, BA – Düsseldorf, DE
2 Sarajevo, BA—Dusseldorf, DE

ƆORADO. Gießbergstraße, 2006/07
‹anal-Videoprojektion (HDV, Farbe, Ton)
9 Min.
positiv im Leuchtkasten
× 47 × 10 cm
ırtesy of the artist

DORADO. Gießbergstraße, 2006/07
gle-channel video projection (HDV, color,
nd)
39 min
positive in light box
× 47 × 10 cm
ırtesy of the artist

RENSIC ARCHITECTURE
1 gegründet am Centre for Research
hitecture, Goldsmiths, University of
ıdon
ınded in 2011 at the Centre for Research
hitecture, Goldsmiths, University of
ıdon

**rder Violence Across the Evros/Meriç
er: Six Investigations**, 2019–21
ideos (Farbe, Ton), 10:49 Min., 10:08 Min.,
18 Min., 17:03 Min., 21:26 Min., 32:15 Min.
rafiken, Maße variabel
urtesy of the artist

**shbacks Across the Evros/Meriç River:
leo Evidence**, 2019
leo (Farbe, Ton), 10:49 Min.

rensic Architecture Team
rantwortliche Forscherin: Christina Varvia
ojektkoordinator: Stefanos Levidis
rschung & Videountersuchung: Dimitra
Andritsou, Kishan San
Forschungsassistenz: Martyna Marciniak,
Phevos Kororos-Simeonidis
Forschungsaufsicht: Eyal Weizman
Projektunterstützung: Sarah Nankivell,
Robert Trafford

In Zusammenarbeit mit Der Spiegel und
HumanRights360

**Pushbacks Across the Evros/Meriç River:
The Case of Ayse Erdogan**, 2020
Video (Farbe, Ton), 10:08 Min.

Forensic Architecture Team
Verantwortliche Forscherin: Christina Varvia
Projektkoordinator: Stefanos Levidis
Forschung & Videountersuchung: Dimitra
Andritsou, Kishan San
Forschungsassistenz: Ifor Duncan, Sofia
Georgovassili, Phevos Kororos-Simeonidis
Forschungsaufsicht: Eyal Weizman
Projektunterstützung: Sarah Nankivell,
Robert Trafford

In Zusammenarbeit mit HumanRights360
und Greek Council for Refugees

The Killing of Muhammad Gulzar, 2020
Video (Farbe, Ton), 16:18 Min.

Forensic Architecture Team
Verantwortliche Forscherin: Christina Varvia
Projektkoordinator: Stefanos Levidis
Forschung & Videountersuchung: Dimitra
Andritsou, Kishan San, Nour Abuzaid
Forschungsassistenz: Lola Conte
Projektunterstützung: Sarah Nankivell,
Robert Trafford
Forschungsaufsicht: Eyal Weizman

Produziert in Partnerschaft mit Bellingcat
und Lighthouse Reports

Erweitertes Team
Akustische Analyse: Beck Audio Forensics
Besonderer Dank an: Stephanie Walcott (Department of Forensic Science, Virginia Commonwealth University)
Satellitenbilder courtesy of Planet Labs

In Zusammenarbeit mit Der Spiegel und HumanRights360

The Killing of Muhammad Al-Arab, 2020
Video (Farbe, Ton), 17:03 Min.

Forensic Architecture Team
Verantwortliche Forscherin: Christina Varvia
Projektkoordinator: Stefanos Levidis
Forschung & Videountersuchung: Kishan San, Dimitra Andritsou, Nour Abuzaid
Forschungsaufsicht: Eyal Weizman
Forschungsassistenz: Lola Conte, Bashar Deeb
Projektunterstützung: Sarah Nankivell, Robert Trafford

Erweitertes Team
Beck Audio Forensics (Akustische Analyse)

In Zusammenarbeit mit HumanRights360

Situated Testimony: The Case of Fady, 2020
Situated Testimony: The Case of Kuzey, 2020
Video (Farbe, Ton), 21:26 Min., 32:15 Min.

Forensic Architecture Team
Hauptermittler: Eyal Weizman
Verantwortliche Forscherin: Christina Varvia
Projektkoordinator: Stefanos Levidis
Forschung: Dimitra Andritsou, Kishan San
Interviewführung: Dimitra Andritsou
Softwareentwicklung: Alican Aktürk, Nour Abuzaid, Zac Ioannidis
Forschungsentwicklung: Phevos Kororos-Simeonidis, Lachlan Kermode, Hanieh Fatouraee, Mhamad Safa, Ifor Duncan, Samaneh Moafi
Projektunterstützung: Sarah Nankivell, Robert Trafford

Erweitertes Team
Dreharbeit: Iason Arvanitakis, Giorgos Valsamis, Sofia Georgovassili
Übersetzung: Baris Karadeniz, Katerina Polychroni, Fares Nidal, Jalal Barekzai
Sounddesign: Odinn Ingibergsson
Besonderen Dank an: Lena Karamanidou, Sam Blair, Natalie Fiennes

In Zusammenarbeit mit HumanRights360, HIAS Greece, Global Legal Action Network (GLAN), Greek Council for Refugees

Border Violence Across the Evros/Meriç River: Six Investigations, 2019–21
6 videos (color, sound), 10:49 min, 10:08 min, 16:18 min, 17:03 min, 21:26 min, 32:15 min
2 printed graphics, dimensions variable
Courtesy of the artist

Pushbacks Across the Evros/Meriç River: Video Evidence, 2019
Video (color, sound), 10:49 min

Forensic Architecture Team
Researcher in Charge: Christina Varvia
Project Coordinator: Stefanos Levidis
Research & Video Investigation: Dimitra Andritsou, Kishan San
Research Assistance: Martyna Marciniak, Phevos Kororos-Simeonidis
Research Supervision: Eyal Weizman
Project Support: Sarah Nankivell, Robert Trafford

In collaboration with Der Spiegel and Human Rights360

**shbacks Across the Evros/Meriç River:
e Case of Ayşe Erdoğan**, 2020
eo (color, sound), 10:08 min

ensic Architecture Team
searcher in Charge: Christina Varvia
oject Coordinator: Stefanos Levidis
search & Video Investigation: Dimitra
dritsou, Kishan San
search Assistance: Ifor Duncan, Sofia
orgovassili, Phevos Kororos-Simeonidis
search Supervision: Eyal Weizman
oject Support: Sarah Nankivell, Robert
afford

collaboration with HumanRights360 and
e Greek Council for Refugees

e Killing of Muhammad Gulzar, 2020
eo (color, sound), 16:18 min

ensic Architecture Team
searcher in Charge: Christina Varvia
oject Coordinator: Stefanos Levidis
search & Video Investigation: Dimitra
dritsou, Kishan San, Nour Abuzaid
search Assistance: Lola Conte
oject Support: Sarah Nankivell, Robert
afford
search Supervision: Eyal Weizman

oduced in partnership with Bellingcat and
ghthouse Reports

tended Team
oustic Analysis: Beck Audio Forensics
ecial thanks to: Stephanie Walcott (Depart-
ent of Forensic Science, Virginia Common-
alth University)
tellite imagery courtesy of Planet Labs

collaboration with Der Spiegel and Human-
ghts360

The Killing of Muhammad Al-Arab, 2020
Video (color, sound), 17:03 min

Forensic Architecture Team
Researcher in Charge: Christina Varvia
Project Coordinator: Stefanos Levidis
Research & Video Investigation: Kishan San, Dimitra Andritsou, Nour Abuzaid
Research Supervision: Eyal Weizman
Research Assistance: Lola Conte, Bashar Deeb
Project Support: Sarah Nankivell, Robert Trafford

Extended Team
Beck Audio Forensics (Acoustic Analysis)

In collaboration with HumanRights360

Situated Testimony: The Case of Fady, 2020
Situated Testimony: The Case of Kuzey, 2020
Video (color, sound), 21:26 min, 32:15 min

Forensic Architecture Team
Principal Investigator: Eyal Weizman
Researcher in Charge: Christina Varvia
Project Coordinator: Stefanos Levidis
Research: Dimitra Andritsou, Kishan San
Interviewing: Dimitra Andritsou
Software Development: Alican Aktürk, Nour Abuzaid, Zac Ioannidis
Research Assistance: Phevos Kororos-Simeonidis, Lachlan Kermode, Hanieh Fatouraee, Mhamad Safa, Ifor Duncan, Samaneh Moafi
Project Support: Sarah Nankivell, Robert Trafford

Extended Team
Filming: Iason Arvanitakis, Giorgos Valsamis, Sofia Georgovassili
Translation: Baris Karadeniz, Katerina Polychroni, Fares Nidal, Jalal Barekzai

Sound Design: Odinn Ingibergsson
Special Thanks To: Lena Karamanidou, Sam Blair, Natalie Fiennes

In collaboration with HumanRights360, HIAS Greece, Global Legal Action Network (GLAN), Greek Council for Refugees

SAMUEL FOSSO
1962 Kumba, CM – Bangui, CF und Paris, FR
1962 Kumba, CM—Bangui, CF and Paris, FR

70's Lifestyle, 1974–78
Silbergelatineabzug
100 × 100 cm
Courtesy of the artist und JM Patras, Paris

Self-Portrait (Angela Davis),
aus der Serie: **African Spirits**, 2008
Silbergelatineabzug
101,75 × 76 cm
Courtesy of the artist und JM Patras, Paris

Self-Portrait (Malcolm X),
aus der Serie: **African Spirits**, 2008
Silbergelatineabzug
101,75 × 76 cm
Courtesy of the artist und JM Patras, Paris

Self-Portrait (Martin Luther King Jr.),
aus der Serie: **African Spirits**, 2008
Silbergelatineabzug
101,75 × 76 cm
Courtesy of the artist und JM Patras, Paris

Self-Portrait (Tommie Smith),
aus der Serie: **African Spirits**, 2008
Silbergelatineabzug
101,75 × 76 cm
Courtesy of the artist und JM Patras, Paris

Emperor of Africa, 2013
Chromogener Farbabzug
166,5 × 124,5 cm
Courtesy of the artist und JM Patras, Paris

Black Pope, 2017
Chromogener Farbabzug
240 × 180 cm
Courtesy of the artist und JM Patras, Paris

70's Lifestyle, 1974–78
Gelatin-silver print
100 × 100 cm
Courtesy of the artist and JM Patras, Paris

Self-Portrait (Angela Davis),
from the series **African Spirits**, 2008
Gelatin-silver print
101.75 × 76 cm
Courtesy of the artist and JM Patras, Paris

Self-Portrait (Malcolm X),
from the series **African Spirits**, 2008
Gelatin-silver print
101.75 × 76 cm
Courtesy of the artist and JM Patras, Paris

Self-Portrait (Martin Luther King Jr.),
from the series **African Spirits**, 2008
Gelatin-silver print
101.75 × 76 cm
Courtesy of the artist and JM Patras, Paris

Self-Portrait (Tommie Smith),
from the series **African Spirits**, 2008
Gelatin-silver print
101.75 × 76 cm
Courtesy of the artist and JM Patras, Paris

Emperor of Africa, 2013
Chromogenic print
161.5 × 124.5 cm
Courtesy of the artist and JM Patras, Paris

ıck Pope, 2017
romogenic print
) × 180 cm
urtesy of the artist and JM Patras, Paris

ARLOTTE HASLUND-CHRISTENSEN
53 Kopenhagen, DK – Kopenhagen, DK
53 Copenhagen, DK—Copenhagen, DK

PE & FEAR, 2016
eikanal-Videoinstallation (Farbe, Ton)
:40 Min.
urtesy of the artist

PE & FEAR, 2016
ree-channel video installation (color, sound)
:40 min
urtesy of the artist

FREDO JAAR
56 Santiago de Chile, CL – New York, NY, US
56 Santiago de Chile, CL—New York, NY, US

titled (Newsweek), 1994
leo (HD, ohne Ton)
:0 Min.
urtesy of the artist und Galerie Hubert
nter, Wien

FE Magazine, April 19, 1968, 1995
Leuchtboxen, C-Print auf Duratrans
183 × 120 cm
urtesy of the artist und Galerie Hubert
nter, Wien

arching for Africa in LIFE, 1996
Leuchtboxen, analoger C-Print auf Dura-
ans
152,4 × 101,6 cm
urtesy of the artist und Galerie Hubert
nter, Wien

Untitled (Newsweek), 1994
Video (HD, without sound), 7:20 min
Courtesy of the artist and Galerie Hubert
Winter, Vienna

LIFE Magazine, April 19, 1968, 1995
3 light boxes, analog C-print on Duratrans
183 × 120 cm each
Courtesy of the artist and Galerie Hubert
Winter, Vienna

Searching for Africa in LIFE, 1996
5 light boxes, analog C-print on Duratrans
152.4 × 101.6 cm each
Courtesy of the artist and Galerie Hubert
Winter, Vienna

VOLUSPA JARPA
1971 Rancagua, CL – Santiago de Chile, CL
1971 Rancagua, CL—Santiago de Chile, CL

The Emancipating Opera, 2019
Video (HD, Farbe, Ton)
11:49 Min.
Courtesy of the artist und mor charpentier,
Paris

The Emancipating Opera, 2019
Video (HD, color, sound)
11:49 min
Courtesy of the artist and mor charpentier,
Paris

BELINDA KAZEEM-KAMIŃSKI
1980 Wien, AT – Wien, AT
1980 Vienna, AT—Vienna, AT

In Search of Red, Black, and Green, 2021
3 chromogene Farbabzüge
je 81 × 54,3 cm
Courtesy of the artist

Library of Requests #7 (solo edition), 2021
Sammlung von Büchern und Texten Schwarzer, feministischer Frauen aus dem deutschsprachigen Raum (31 Bücher, 3 Artikel)
Display: Holz, 134,2 × 84 × 42 cm, Entwurf: Carolina Frank, Ausführung: Arnold Löschnauer
Courtesy of the artist

In Search of Red, Black, and Green, 2021
3 chromogenic prints
81 × 54.3 cm each
Courtesy of the artist

Library of Requests #7 (solo edition), 2021
Collection of books and texts by Black, feminist women from German-speaking countries (31 books, 3 articles)
Display: wood, 134.2 × 84 × 42 cm, design: Carolina Frank, construction: A. Löschnauer
Courtesy of the artist

ADRIAN PIPER

1948 New York, NY, US – Berlin, DE
1948 New York, NY, US—Berlin, DE

Black Box / White Box, 1992
Multimedia-Installation, schwarzer Raum und weißer Raum, je 244 × 244 × 244 cm
Sammlung Generali Foundation – Dauerleihgabe am Museum der Moderne Salzburg

Im schwarzen Raum: Schwarz-Weiß-Fotografie (Rodney King), digitaler Fotodruck zwischen halbtransparentem Spiegel und Plexiglas, 81 × 56 cm; Halogen-Lichtspot mit Timer; Audio-Monolog (Rodney King), 5:46 Min.
Im weißen Raum: Video (Polizeigewalt gegen Rodney King, Amateuraufnahme), Ton (Musikkompilation von Adrian Piper), Audio-Monolog (Ausschnitt aus einer Ansprache von George Bush senior), 30 Min.
In beiden Räumen: Schwarz-Weiß-Fotografi (jeweils Bild von George Bush senior), 73,5 × 101,5 cm; Lederstuhl, Tisch, Taschentuchbo Papierkorb; Wandtext, dt. Übersetzung: „De ein Mensch, dem sie alles weggenommen haben, ist außerhalb ihres Machtbereiches, ist wieder frei.“ Alexander I. Solschenizyn (D erste Kreis der Hölle)

Black Box / White Box, 1992
Multimedia installation, black room and whi room, 244 × 244 × 244 cm each
Generali Foundation Collection—Permanent Loan to the Museum der Moderne Salzburg

In the black box: black-and-white photography (Rodney King), digital photo print betwe semi-transparent mirror and perspex, 81 × 56 cm; halogen light spot with timer; audio monologue (Rodney King), 5:46 min
In the white box: video (police violence agai Rodney King, amateur recording), sound (music compilation by Adrian Piper), audio monologue (excerpt from a speech by Georg Bush senior), 30 min
In both boxes: black-and-white photography (both pictures George Bush senior), 73.5 × 101.5 cm; leather chair, table, handkerchief box, waste basket; wall text: “Once you have taken everything away from a man, he is no longer in your power. He is free.” Alexander Solzhenitsyn (The First Circle)

LISL PONGER

1947 Nürnberg, DE – Wien, AT
1947 Nuremberg, DE—Vienna, AT

Teilnehmende Beobachterin / Participant Observer, 2016
Leuchtbox, analoger C-Print auf Duratrans
140 × 120 cm
Museum der Moderne Salzburg

lnehmende Beobachterin / Participant
server, 2016
ht box, analog C-print on Duratrans
) × 120 cm
useum der Moderne Salzburg

RA WALKER
69 Stockton, CA, US – New York, NY, US
69 Stockton, CA, US—New York, NY, US

tional Archives Microfilm M999 Roll 34:
reau of Refugees, Freedmen and Aban-
ned Lands: Lucy of Pulaski, 2009
deo (Farbe, Ton)
08 Min.
urtesy of the artist, Sprüth Magers und
kema Jenkins & Co.

ss Merrimac and the Monitor, 2001
er Scherenschnitte, vier Folien, Licht-
ojektor
mmlung Deutsche Bank

tional Archives Microfilm M999 Roll 34:
reau of Refugees, Freedmen and Aban-
ned Lands: Lucy of Pulaski, 2009
deo (color, sound)
:08 min
ourtesy of the artist, Sprüth Magers and
kema Jenkins & Co.

iss Merrimac and the Monitor, 2001
ur paper cuts, four foils, light projector
mmlung Deutsche Bank

THIS WORLD IS WHITE NO LONGER
Ein Projekt mit der Klasse für Fotografie und Neue Medien, Universität Mozarteum Salzburg

THIS WORLD IS WHITE NO LONGER
A Project with the Class for Photography and New Media, Mozarteum University Salzburg

PART II

INHALT
CONTENTS

VORWORT

Gregor Neuerer

In der Beschäftigung mit Rassismus gibt es keine unpolitische Haltung: Sich *nicht* mit rassistischen Strukturen in unserer Gesellschaft und Kultur zu konfrontieren oder sich selbst glücklich zu schätzen, dass der eigene Alltag kaum von den Folgen von Rassismus betroffen zu sein scheint, ist ebenso politisch wie das Gegenteil, nämlich sich *aktiv* mit Rassismus auseinanderzusetzen und für sich selbst eine mögliche Verstricktheit mit einer rassistischen Kultur anzunehmen. Genau deshalb bin ich beeindruckt, mit welch unmittelbarer Notwendigkeit und persönlichem Engagement sich die Studierenden seit dem Sommer 2020 dazu äußern. Mir ist bewusst, dass es mitunter leichter – und auch weniger schmerzhaft – ist, das Thema auszublenden und das eigene Umfeld auf einen Radius zu reduzieren, in dem Rassismus zu verschwinden scheint. Wir haben gelernt, dass es in Österreich rassistische Übergriffe gibt. Und wir sehen laufend, dass die meisten dieser Übergriffe nie als solche benannt werden, kaum zur Sprache kommen oder zu oft als ungeschickte Geste entschuldigt werden. Wir wissen, dass Rassismus nicht als Einzelfall existiert, sondern als Kultur.

Die institutionelle Unterstützung und die Initiative, die wir über die letzten Monate von Direktor Thorsten Sadowsky, von den beiden Kurator:innen Stefanie Grünangerl und Jürgen Tabor seitens des Generali Foundation Studienzentrums sowie den Mitarbeiter:innen des Museum der Moderne Salzburg angeboten bekamen, waren nicht nur eine Möglichkeit, mit den Mitteln der Kunst zu sprechen, sondern sie verdeutlichten ebenso die Bereitschaft aller Beteiligten, die Rolle von Institutionen wie Museen und Universitäten innerhalb dieses Problems anzusprechen.

Ich selbst bin weiß und lehre eine Gruppe vor allem weißer Studierender – dies ist die Perspektive, aus der wir auf ein Ausstellungsangebot, das die Frage nach Rassismus in meiner und unserer Welt stellt, reagieren. Die Arbeiten von 16 Studierenden und der Sculpting Feminism Reading Group, die in einem Teil der Ausstellung gezeigt werden, sind das Ergebnis komplexer und komplizierter Diskussionen, die in unseren Ateliers und in zahlreichen Zoom-Meetings entstanden sind. Sie sind ebenso der Versuch, offen und persönlich über Rassismus

FOREWORD

Gregor Neuerer

There can be no apolitical attitude in terms of racism. Not confronting our society and culture's racist structures or thinking yourself fortunate that your own everyday life is hardly affected by the consequences of racism is just as political as the opposite, namely the active addressing of racism and the acceptance of your own possible complicity in a racist culture. That is precisely why I have been so impressed by the urgency and personal commitment that the contributing students have displayed in expressing themselves on the issue of racial injustice since the summer of 2020. I am aware that it can sometimes be more convenient—and less painful—to ignore the subject and reduce your own environment to parameters within which racism would seem to be non-existent. We must acknowledge that there are racist attacks in Austria. And we have repeatedly observed that most of these abuses are never named as such, are rarely spoken about with seriousness, or are too frequently excused as social faux pas. We know that racism exists not in isolated cases but as a culture.

The institutional support and determination that we have been offered over the last few months by the Museum der Moderne Salzburg and Generali Foundation, by director Thorsten Sadowsky, by the two curators Stefanie Grünangerl and Jürgen Tabor, as well as by the staff, provided not just an opportunity for us to speak out using the vehicle of art, but it also revealed the willingness, of all those involved, to address the complicity of public institutions, such as museums and universities, in systemic racism.

I am white myself and teach a group of predominantly white students—it can therefore only be this perspective from which we could respond to the offer of an exhibition that examines racism in my and our world. Works by 16 students and the Sculpting Feminism Reading Group, featured in our section of the exhibition, are the result of complex and complicated discussions that emerged in both our studios and during numerous online meetings. They speak openly and personally about racism here and now in Salzburg. To this end, each student examined the cultural, social, and political circumstances of their own biography, thoroughly exploring their environment and involvement,

jetzt und hier in Salzburg zu sprechen. Jede:r Studierende hat sich dafür in die kulturellen, sozialen und politischen Bedingungen der eigenen Biografie begeben, das eigene Umfeld und die eigene Involviertheit präzise betrachtet sowie die oft selbstverständlich erscheinenden Pfeiler der eigenen sozialen und kulturellen Zugehörigkeit befragt. Das alles war gut ein halbes Jahr lang eine signifikante Herausforderung für uns alle. Als wir begannen, gemeinsam nachzudenken und zu arbeiten, realisierten wir bald, dass unsere Position unter dem Gesichtspunkt sozialer Gerechtigkeit voller Ambivalenz ist. Wir entdeckten uns selbst innerhalb von Lebensbedingungen und -voraussetzungen, die wir nicht aufrechterhalten wollen und noch weniger verteidigen können. Wir realisierten auch, dass Salzburg, Österreich und die westliche Welt eine fundamentale Umstrukturierung zu durchlaufen haben. Wie können wir als diejenigen, die wir sind, einen Beitrag zu einer Ausstellung über Rassismus leisten oder einen relevanten Diskurs herstellen, der das thematisiert, was hier und jetzt tatsächlich passiert?

Bereits der Titel der Ausstellung *This World Is White No Longer* hat uns mit einer Schwierigkeit konfrontiert: Sowohl die Verantwortlichen im Museum als auch wir Lehrende und Studierende repräsentieren Gruppen, die vielfach von Marginalisierung und Rassismus abgeschirmt sind. Die meisten der Stimmen, die hier zu hören sein werden, bleiben also die „weißen". Eingeschlossen sind die Organisator:innen, die begehrte Jobs in den involvierten Institutionen, der Universität Mozarteum, der Sammlung Generali Foundation und dem Museum der Moderne Salzburg, innehaben – Menschen, die sich dafür aufgrund ihrer kulturellen und wirtschaftlichen Sozialisierung qualifizierten, sowie jene, die die Möglichkeit haben, an einer Kunstuniversität zu studieren, die wiederum von einer weißen Administration geleitet wird, in einem Land mit einer Regierung, die homogen eine westlich-weiße Kultur repräsentiert. Kurzum: Wir können nicht anders, als aus einer weißen Perspektive zu agieren, und die Stimmen, die hier gehört werden, sind demnach weiße. Wie können wir also von diesem Platz aus zu Rassismus Stellung beziehen? Wie kann das Set-up unserer Machtstruktur mit dem aufrichtigen Anliegen einhergehen, unsere Gesellschaft als Ganzes zu adressieren und dieses wichtige Sprechen gleichwertig mit Minderheiten zu teilen? Wie kann sich eine Stadt wie Salzburg, in der diese Ausstellung stattfindet, als eine Gesellschaft und Kultur darstellen, die Diversität auf allen Ebenen lebt?

and questioning the pillars of their own social and cultural affiliations. This process presented a significant challenge to everyone involved throughout six months of collaborative and mutual engagement. As we began to think and work together as a group, we soon realized that our position in terms of social justice is itself in question. The group urgently felt that we were living under conditions and premises that we have no desire to maintain, much less defend. We also came to realize that Salzburg, Austria, and the Western world need to undergo a fundamental restructuring. How are we, in terms of who we are, able to contribute to an exhibition about racism or create a relevant discourse addressing what is actually happening here and now?

The title of the exhibition *This World Is White No Longer* already confronted us with a challenge. Not only the museum staff but also we as tutors and students represent groups that are shielded from marginalization and racism. The majority of the voices being provided with a platform here remain "white ones." This includes the organizers who work in central positions in the institutions involved, the Mozarteum University, the Generali Foundation Collection, and the Museum der Moderne Salzburg—people who are professionally qualified for what they do as a result of their cultural and economic socialization, as well as those who have been given the opportunity of studying at an art college run by a white administration, in a country with a government that homogeneously insists to represent Western, white culture. In short, we cannot help but operate from a white perspective, and the voices heard here will therefore be white-biased. So how can we take a stand on racism from such a position? How can the composition of our power structures go hand in hand with sincere concerns in addressing our society as a multifaceted whole and in sharing the crucial opportunity of having a voice equally with those who are not white, German-speaking, heteronormative, and Catholic? How can a city like Salzburg, where this exhibition is taking place, present itself as a society and culture that lives diversity at every conceivable level?

On the one hand, we are aware that this world will remain white somewhat longer. On the other, we are making individual choices as a privileged group, in that we are consciously learning about injustice across all levels of our daily lives. How can we step out of this privileged space, abandon a culture that we no longer want to represent, and reach out to new generations and

Auf der einen Seite sind wir uns im Klaren darüber, dass diese Welt noch länger weiß bleiben wird – *that this world will stay white much longer.* Auf der anderen Seite treffen wir für uns als Gruppe privilegierter Menschen Entscheidungen, um über die Ungerechtigkeit auf allen Ebenen des eigenen täglichen Lebens zu lernen. Wie können wir versuchen, aus diesem Raum des Privilegiertseins herauszutreten, eine Kultur aufzugeben, die wir nicht mehr vertreten wollen, und auf neue Generationen von Menschen zuzugehen, die sich mit uns solidarisieren, um diese schwierigen Fragen an uns selbst offenzulegen?

Die künstlerischen Arbeiten und Überlegungen, die in dieser Ausstellung formuliert sind, kommen aus genau dieser Haltung. Die vorgestellten Schritte sind aufrichtig, offen, mutig und willens, einen neuen gesellschaftlichen und kulturellen Raum zu definieren – bereit, dafür den eigenen Komfortbereich zu verlassen. Die Beiträge sprechen von den eigenen Vorurteilen, von der Unsicherheit zu erkennen, wie eine gerechtere Gesellschaft aussehen kann, wie sich die eigene Bildung dahingehend adaptiert und wie wir Platz machen können, um eine Kultur, die anders ist als die, in der wir heute leben, entstehen zu lassen. Dieses Projekt setzt viel Vertrauen in die Möglichkeiten künstlerischer Methoden und Sprachen, in die Werkzeuge der Kunst und in die Möglichkeit, aus der eigenen Erfahrung zu sprechen und Realität zu transformieren. Es zeigt das eigene künstlerische Handeln als Grundlage, über sich selbst zu sprechen und sich selbst in eine kollektive Veränderung einzubinden. Dieses Projekt, das zugleich Ausstellung und Lernprozess ist, hat das Ziel, einen Weg aus einer Welt zu zeichnen, mit der wir uns nicht mehr zur Gänze identifizieren möchten, und lädt ein, einer Veränderung entgegenzusteuern, deren Teil wir sein wollen. Die Studierenden und wir Lehrende – Sigrid Langrehr, Peter Schreiner, Michael Mauracher und ich – haben diese Herausforderung angenommen und werden dem Rassismus unserer Gegenwart nicht mit Schweigen begegnen.

Meiner eigenen Erfahrung Sprache zu verleihen, wäre ohne meine Familie, ohne Freunde und Freundinnen, Aktivist:innen und Künstler:innen während der letzten Jahre unmöglich gewesen. Deshalb möchte ich mich insbesondere bei Elka Krajewska, Andrea Lumplecker, Dženeta Karabegović, Farid Hafez, Ana Hoffner, der Aktivist:innengruppe Rise and Resist und den Kolleg:innen und Studierenden am Department für bildende Kunst und Gestaltung der Universität Mozarteum aufrichtig bedanken.

perspectives, willing to join us in approaching the challenging questions around racism that we need to think about?

The works and thinking being formulated in this exhibition have been inspired by precisely such an attitude and accept the challenge, employing all the resources available to the students. The steps the students are presenting are sincere, open, and willing to redefine their social and cultural space, while also abandoning established comfort zones. The contributions speak of the individual's own prejudices, of the insecurities involved in recognizing what a fairer society could actually demand, how an individual's own education may be adapted, and in what way they can create space for a culture to emerge that is different from the one they live in today.
This project places a lot of faith in the potential of approaches and languages based in visual art, in art's tools, and the possibility of speaking from individual experience to transform social reality. It presents individual artistic practices as a basis for speaking about the individual and involving them in collective transformation. This project, which is both an exhibition and a mutual learning process, aims to delineate ways out of the racist world which we no longer wish to identify with, and presents an invitation to take a different path to social equity, one that we can follow in good conscience. The students and we tutors—Sigrid Langrehr, Peter Schreiner, Michael Mauracher, and myself—have accepted this challenge to confront the racism of our time out loud.

Giving voice to my own experience would have been impossible without the support of my family, as well as the friends, activists, and artists I've been in contact with over the past few years. I would therefore like to sincerely thank Elka Krajewska, Fatena Al Ghorra, Dženeta Karabegović, Farid Hafez, Andrea Lumplecker, together with the group of activists Rise and Resist, as well as colleagues and students at the Department of Fine Arts, Art and Craft Education at the University Mozarteum Salzburg.

DEM EIGENEN *WEISS*-SEIN BEGEGNEN. ZUR AUSSTELLUNG DER KLASSE FÜR FOTOGRAFIE UND NEUE MEDIEN DER UNIVERSITÄT MOZARTEUM SALZBURG

Stefanie Grünangerl

Die mit der Klasse für Fotografie und Neue Medien der Universität Mozarteum Salzburg entwickelte Ausstellung präsentierte in drei aufeinanderfolgenden Akten 18 neue Arbeiten und Projekte, die aus einer fast über ein Jahr andauernden Beschäftigung mit aktuellen Fragen von Rassismus und Xenophobie entstanden sind. Die Intention hinter der Zusammenarbeit zwischen der Sammlung Generali Foundation, dem Museum der Moderne Salzburg und der Klasse war es, die Sichtweise einer jungen Generation zu zeigen, die vor Ort in Salzburg lebt, studiert und arbeitet. Darüber hinaus sollte in den Herangehensweisen der jungen Künstler:innen jener Perspektivenwechsel erprobt werden, der in der parallel laufenden Ausstellung *This World Is White No Longer. Ansichten einer dezentrierten Welt* im Fokus stand. Die Zusammenarbeit verstand sich als ein Prozess, der sich nicht nur in abgeschlossenen Werken manifestieren sollte, sondern auch Diskussionen Raum gab, die sich teils wiederkehrenden, teils neu auftauchenden Fragestellungen, fragmentarischen Überlegungen und notwendig gewordenen Richtungswechseln widmeten. Das Prozesshafte war auch in der Ausstellung selbst präsent. Dokumentationstische gaben den Besucher:innen die Möglichkeit, auf die Ausstellung zu reagieren und sich in Form von Kommentaren mit ihren Ansichten und Haltungen in das Projekt einzuschreiben.

Wie kann in einer Ausstellung, einem Museum, einer universitären Lehrveranstaltung, deren Akteure und Akteurinnen in einer als *weiß* definierten Dominanzgesellschaft[1] fast ausschließlich der Gruppe der Privilegierten angehören, über Rassismus gesprochen werden? Diese Frage ist der rote Faden, der sich seit Projektbeginn durch nahezu alle Diskussionen ebenso wie durch die individuellen Arbeiten der Studierenden zog und schlussendlich zur Reflexion ihrer eigenen Position innerhalb von Kulturen und Ökonomien in Österreich und des damit einhergehenden Verhältnisses zu Rassismus führte. Rassismus wurde dabei nicht allein als das Handeln einzelner Personen, das sich in gewaltsamen Übergriffen oder verbalen Attacken manifestiert, verstanden, sondern vor allem als ein Machtverhältnis, das unsere Vorstellungen von gesellschaftlichem

MEET YOUR OWN WHITENESS. ON THE EXHIBITION BY THE CLASS FOR PHOTOGRAPHY AND NEW MEDIA AT THE MOZARTEUM UNIVERSITY SALZBURG

Stefanie Grünangerl

The exhibition, developed together with the class for photography and new media at the Mozarteum University in Salzburg, presented 18 new works and projects in a sequence of three sections, emerging from almost a year's work on issues involving racism and xenophobia. The intention behind the collaboration between the Generali Foundation Collection, the Museum der Moderne Salzburg, and the class was to make visible the perspective of a younger generation that lives, studies, and works locally in Salzburg. The young artists' approach was, in addition, to test the very change of perspective that was the focus of the concurrent exhibition *This World Is White No Longer. Views of a Decentered World*. The collaboration saw itself as a process not only manifesting itself in finished works, but also as one that was providing space for discussions that were dedicated partly to recurring and partly to newly emerging questions, fragmentary thoughts, and the changes of direction they entail. Such a process-based approach was likewise present in the exhibition itself. Tables of documentation materials provided visitors with an opportunity to react to the exhibition and to participate in the project with their own views and attitudes, in the form of comments.

How can racism be discussed in an exhibition, a museum, and university course whose protagonists, even in a *Dominanzgesellschaft* (predominating society)[1] defined as white, belong almost exclusively to the most privileged? The question is the common thread that has run through almost all of the discussions since the beginning of the project, as well as through the individual work of the students, ultimately encouraging them to consider their own position in the cultures and economies existent in Austria, and such systems' relationships to racism. Racism should not only be understood as the actions of individual people, manifesting itself in physical or verbal attacks but, above all, as a power relation shaping our notions of social coexistence and social hierarchies, and consequently our view of the world.[2] Kevin Klinger outlined such a distribution of power, in his video work *Exit the Box*, as an all-encompassing system of thought that—like a film continually being replayed—

Zusammenleben und sozialen Hierarchien – mithin unsere Sicht auf die Welt – prägt.[2] Kevin Klinger skizziert dieses Machtverhältnis in seiner Videoarbeit *Exit the Box* als ein alles umschließendes Denksystem, das sich – ähnlich wie ein stets aufs Neue abgespielter Film – unablässig reproduziert, solange nicht eine schonungslose und vermutlich schmerzhafte Konfrontation mit den eigenen Verstrickungen vonstattengeht. Zu diesem Sich-gewahr-Werden der eigenen Position in einer rassistischen Gesellschaft und zum Erkennen der eigenen Handlungsmacht fordert auch Hannah Imhoff mit ihrer Skulptur *Rassistische Gesellschaft (Eine Problemdarstellung mit offenem Ende)* auf. Das eigene *Weiß*-Sein in den Blick zu nehmen und es zugleich „zu befreien aus seiner ‚unmarkierten Normalität'"[3] steht im Mittelpunkt ihrer *Visitenkarte (Erinnerung an mich selbst).* Der eigenen Sichtweise auf die Welt und auf das Themenfeld Rassismus andere Stimmen gegenüberzustellen, wie es Leonie Lindinger in ihrem Videoessay *How Soon Is Soon?* vorschlägt, hilft nicht nur, Gemeinsamkeiten und Unterschiede offensichtlich werden zu lassen, sondern ermöglicht es, die eigene Perspektive als eine unter vielen anzuerkennen.

Das Nachdenken darüber, wie sehr rassistische Einstellungen Hintergrund ihrer eigenen Lebenswirklichkeiten sind und wie sehr sie ihr eigenes Denken und Handeln prägen, war für viele der Künstler:innen ein zentraler Ansatzpunkt. So legt Melanie Forsthuber durch die Art ihrer Verwendung exotistischer Bildwelten der Tourismusindustrie deren neokolonialen und eurozentristischen Blick auf die Welt offen und zeigt, wie dieser Blick unser eigenes Begehren nach dem Fernen und unsere „Weltaneignung" formt. Pia Geisreiter stellt rassistische Darstellungen im Comic in den Fokus eines mehrwöchigen Arbeitsprozesses, in dem sie ein bestimmtes Bild immer wieder übermalt, zerschneidet und zerstört, während dieses eine gewisse Wirkmächtigkeit zu behalten scheint. Die Auseinandersetzung mit den eigenen xenophoben Vorurteilen, die man sich selbst nicht eingestehen will und die dennoch den Umgang mit dem gerade dadurch konstruierten „Fremden" bestimmen, setzt Eva-Maria Schitter ins Zentrum ihrer Arbeit *Ich über mich über ihr über sie*, in der sie ihr Verhältnis zu einer Notreisenden in Salzburg reflektiert.

Marija Živojinović' Arbeit *I See Color* zeigt anhand der Kosmetikindustrie, wie sehr unser Alltag von rassistischen Momenten durchdrungen ist. Die für unterschiedliche Make-up-Produkte angebotene Palette an Hauttönen macht

constantly reproduces itself, as long as there is no rigorous, and perhaps painful, confrontation with individual complicity. In her sculpture *Rassistische Gesellschaft (Eine Problemdarstellung mit offenem Ende)* [Racist Society (Presenting an Open-Ended Issue)], Hannah Imhoff likewise encouraged people to become aware of their own position in a racist society and to recognize their own agency. Observing your own whiteness while at the same time "liberating it from its 'unmarked normality'"[3] was the focus of her *Visitenkarten (Erinnerung an mich selbst)* [Calling Cards (Reminder to Myself)]. Contrasting individual views of the world and the subject of racism with other voices, as Leonie Lindinger suggested in her video essay *How Soon Is Soon?*, not only assists in making similarities and differences evident, but also enables a recognition of your own perspective as just one among many.

Thinking about the extent to which racist stereotypes describe the backdrop of their own lived realities and shape their own thoughts and actions was a central point of departure for many of the artists. In employing the tourism industry's exotic imagery, Melanie Forsthuber exposed its neocolonial and Eurocentric view of the world, demonstrating how such a perspective forges our own desires for far-flung places as well as our "appropriation of the world." Pia Geisreiter focused on racist representations in comics in a working process lasting several weeks that involved her repeatedly painting over, cutting up, and destroying one particular image that nevertheless retained a certain power. The confrontation with individual xenophobic prejudices, ones which are difficult to admit to but which nevertheless determine how the resultingly constructed "alien" is encountered, was located at the center of Eva-Maria Schitter's work, *Ich über mich über ihr über sie* (Me about Me above Her about Her), in which she reflected on her relationship with a foreign homeless woman in Salzburg.

Marija Živojinović's work *I See Color* used the cosmetics industry to demonstrate how much our everyday life is permeated by instances of racism. The range of skin-tones offered by various make-up products makes evident the extent to which the term "skin color"[4] is defined as *white*—and *non-white* as a (negligible) deviation. Živojinović was likewise concerned with "color blindness,"[5] which negates the relevance of skin color, but in doing so denies the existence of racist structures and therefore the significance of people of color's experiences. Alba Malika Belhadj Merzoug addressed questions of identity

offensichtlich, wie sehr der Begriff „hautfarben“[4] als *weiß* definiert wird – und nicht-*weiß* als (vernachlässigbare) Abweichung. Živojinović geht es ebenso um „color blindness“[5], die die Relevanz von Hautfarbe negiert, dabei jedoch vor allem die Existenz rassistischer Strukturen leugnet und damit die Bedeutsamkeit der Lebenserfahrungen von People of Color in Abrede stellt. Der Auseinandersetzung mit Identitätsfragen und dem, was bleibt, wenn einem Menschen jene Angriffspunkte – wie eben die „Hautfarbe“ – genommen werden, an denen in unserer Gesellschaft Ungleichheitsregime festgemacht werden, stellt sich Alba Malika Belhadj Merzoug. Sie schafft dabei eine Figur, die dem Menschsein entrückt ist. Die Projektion wird selbst zur Projektionsfläche unserer Erwartungen, da es uns offensichtlich nur über die Zuordnung zu Identitätskategorien möglich erscheint, ein Individuum als solches zu erkennen.

Rassistisch motivierte Gewalt, insbesondere jene von staatlichen Organen, war in den vergangenen Jahren oft der Ausgangspunkt für die medial geführte gesellschaftspolitische Thematisierung von Rassismus. Charlotte Pann greift diese mediale Repräsentation auf und stellt in ihrer Installation die Frage nach ihrer eigenen Position und Involviertheit in einer Gesellschaft, die rassistische Übergriffe ermöglicht und hervorbringt. Judith Zaunschirm wirft einen anderen Blick auf das Thema Polizeigewalt und nutzt hierfür das Setting einer Fallbeschreibung. Beide Positionen verorten die Thematik in ihrem unmittelbaren Lebensumfeld in Österreich und wirken damit der verzerrten Wahrnehmung entgegen, systematische rassistische Gewalt sei ein primär US-amerikanisches Problem.

Die Proteste der letzten Jahre, die nicht allein durch Gewalttaten ausgelöst, sondern vor allem durch ein generelles Aufbegehren und den jahrelangen Kampf gegen rassistische Strukturen getragen werden, spielen sich neben dem öffentlichen Raum verstärkt auch auf Social-Media-Plattformen ab. Diese virtuellen Protestformen und den schmalen Grat zwischen Aktivismus und antirassistischem Engagement einerseits sowie Aktionismus und Selbstinszenierung andererseits nehmen Magdalena Heller und Vera Kern in den Blick. Heller tut dies, indem sie die Bilderwelt der Black-Lives-Matter-Proteste auf Instagram in das grundlegende Instrument jedes Straßenprotestes – nämlich das Protestschild – rückübersetzt und so an die Forderung nach realen Handlungen statt virtueller Solidaritätsbekundungen erinnert. Vera Kern nimmt ihren

and what remains when a person is detached from any markers of selfhood—such as “skin color”—which regimes of inequality in our society tend to adhere to. She was consequently able to create a figure whose status as human has dissipated. The projection itself becomes the surface on which our expectations are projected, since it seems only possible to recognize an individual as such by assigning it an identity from predetermined categories.

Racially motivated violence, especially that by organs of the state, has often been the point of departure for media-led, sociopolitical attempts to address racism in recent years. Charlotte Pann seized upon such media representations in her installation, questioning both her own point of view and involvement in a society that facilitates and spawns racist attacks. Employing a case study, Judith Zaunschirm took an alternative look at the subject of police violence. Both positions locate the issue within the immediate environment in which the two artists live in Austria, counteracting the distorted perception that systemic racial violence is primarily a US-American problem.

The protests of the last few years, which were not only precipitated by acts of violence, but have been conveyed, above all, by a general rallying and years of struggle against racist structures, are taking place not only in public space but also increasingly on social media platforms. Magdalena Heller and Vera Kern examined such virtual forms of protest and the fine line between activism and a commitment to anti-racism on the one hand, and the performative and staging the self on the other. Heller’s approach was to translate the imagery of the Black Lives Matter protests on Instagram back into the essential tool of every street protest, namely the protest sign, a reminder of the call for real actions rather than virtual expressions of solidarity. Vera Kern took her own social media consumption, in highly abstracted form, as a point of departure for questioning life within her own filtered bubble, but particularly the individual’s own responsibilities, that is, the potential of progressing from passive media use to committed engagement.

In a hierarchically constructed society, racism and xenophobia never act alone, but always in conjunction with other types of inequality, be it gender, religion, age, social and economic position, ill-health, and so on. Two projects in the exhibition pursued such an intersectional approach. Agnes Elena Kern

eigenen Social-Media-Konsum in stark abstrahierter Form zum Ausgangspunkt, um Fragen nach dem Leben in der eigenen Filterblase, insbesondere aber nach der eigenen Verantwortung zu stellen, d. h. nach den Möglichkeiten, von einer passiven Mediennutzung zu einer engagierten Position zu gelangen.

Rassismus und Xenophobie wirken in einer hierarchisch geprägten Gesellschaftsordnung niemals allein, sondern immer im Verbund mit anderen Ungleichheitskategorien, sei es Geschlecht, Religion, Alter, die soziale und ökonomische Stellung, Krankheit und dergleichen mehr. In der Ausstellung verfolgen zwei Projekte einen solchen intersektionalen Ansatz. Agnes Elena Kern setzt den über Tags und Graffiti im öffentlichen Raum geführten Debatten im Kampf gegen Diskriminierung Aufnahmen der privaten Lebenswelt der LGBTQIA+-Community gegenüber, ermöglicht uns einen Einblick „hinein in die Wohnzimmer derer, über deren Existenz draußen diskutiert wird"[6], und fordert zugleich Empathie ein. Eine zwar allgegenwärtige, aber ignorierte Diskriminierungsform nimmt die unter dem Pseudonym this world is Ego No longer auftretende Position zum Ausgangspunkt für eine interaktive Installation, die eine Vielzahl an teils sehr persönlichen Zeichnungen, Texten und Malereien umfasst. Hier geht es um (vermeintliche) Abweichungen von einer Vorstellung von „Gesund"- oder „Normal"-Sein, die immer noch als eines der wirksamsten und kaum hinterfragten Paradigmen unserer Gesellschaft gesehen werden kann. Mittlerweile fasst man dies unter dem Begriff Ableismus[7].

Auch Gegenentwürfe unter dem Leitmotiv eines „Was wäre, wenn die Verhältnisse andere wären?" schaffen Raum, um über unsere derzeitigen Lebensrealitäten zu reflektieren. Angelika Wienerroither beschäftigt sich in *Utopia (Why can't we all just get along with it?)* mit der Vorstellung einer Welt, in der eine Woman of Color an der Macht ist, und formuliert dabei nicht nur eine Repräsentationskritik westlich geprägter Darstellungen von Macht, sondern wirft in enger Zusammenarbeit mit ihren beiden Protagonistinnen die Frage auf, was Macht bedeutet, wozu sie dienen kann und warum sie uns wichtig erscheint. Einen poetischen Gegenentwurf, ebenso in Form einer vertieften Auseinandersetzung mit dem Werk zweier BIPoC-Künstlerinnen (bell hooks auf der Textebene und Tanya Tagaq auf der Tonebene), liefert Sabine Reisenbüchler. Sie erzählt von einer (vergangenen wie zukünftigen) Zeit „ohne den patriarchalen Anspruch auf Besitznahme von Natur, Tieren und Menschen"[8].

contrasted debates instigated by tags and graffiti in public space in the fight against discrimination with documentation of the private lives of the LGBTIQ+ community, providing a glimpse "into the living rooms of those whose existence is being discussed in the outside world,"[6] while at the same time making a call for empathy. The pseudonym "this world is Ego No longer" took an omnipresent yet ignored form of discrimination as the point of departure for an interactive installation encompassing a large number of drawings, texts, and paintings, some of which were very personal. The work addressed (alleged) deviations from received notions of being "healthy" or "normal," which remain one of the most effective but rarely questioned paradigms in our society, which is meanwhile being termed ableism.[7]

Under the leitmotif of "What would happen if the circumstances were different?" counter-concepts created space to reflect on our currently lived realities. In *Utopia (Why can't we all just get along with it?)*, Angelika Wienerroither addressed an image of a world in which a woman of color is in power, not only formulating a representational critique of Western-style depictions of power, but in close collaboration with her two protagonists approached questions of what power means, what purpose it serves, and why it seems so important to us. Sabine Reisenbüchler provided a poetic counter-concept, in the form of an in-depth examination of the work of two BIPOC artists (bell hooks in terms of text and Tanya Tagaq in terms of audio). The piece told of a (past and future) time without "any patriarchal right to take possession of nature, animals, and people."[8]

In order to provide such utopias any chance of becoming reality, it is primarily our responsibility as white people to not only recognize our own white privileges, but to also demonstrate active solidarity.[8] The Sculpting Feminism Reading Group sought to continue such a discussion by confronting all the above-mentioned issues as an ongoing process. It provided a pool of books and activated its call for "self-education" through weekly readings. We come full circle with Belinda Kazeem-Kamiński's *Library of Requests*, which acted as a prelude to the wider project in the Rupertinum's atrium. The two collections of books, as well as the two exhibitions, were not only an invitation but, above all, tasked everyone in carrying out a transformation of perspective that is situated at the beginning of any action whose objective is social change.

Um derartigen Utopien eine Chance auf Verwirklichung zu geben, liegt es vor allem an uns als *weiße* Personen, die eigenen *weißen* Privilegien nicht nur zu erkennen, sondern daraus ein solidarisches Handeln abzuleiten.[9] Diese Diskussion weitertragen sowie die Auseinandersetzung mit all den oben genannten Themensträngen als fortlaufenden Prozess verstehen, das will die Sculpting Feminism Reading Group. Sie stellt einen Bücher-Pool zur Verfügung und aktiviert ihre Aufforderung zur „self education" durch wöchentliche Lesungen. Hier schließt sich einerseits der Kreis zu Belinda Kazeem-Kamińskis *Library of Requests*, die im Atrium des Rupertinum den Auftakt zum Gesamtprojekt bildet. Andererseits sind diese beiden Büchersammlungen wie auch die beiden Ausstellungen nicht nur ein Angebot, sondern vor allem ein Auftrag an uns alle, einen Perspektivenwechsel zu vollziehen und ihn an den Beginn eines auf gesellschaftliche Veränderung abzielenden Handelns zu stellen.

1 Birgit Rommelspacher, *Dominanzkultur. Texte zur Fremdheit und Macht*, Berlin: Orlanda Frauenverlag, 1995.

2 Vgl. ebd., S. 39–54; Grada Kilomba, *Plantation memories. Episodes of everyday racism*, 6. Aufl., Münster: Unrast, 2020, S. 40–43.

3 Susan Arndt, „Weißsein. Die verkannte Strukturkategorie Europas und Deutschlands", in: Maureen Maisha Eggers et al., Hg., *Mythen, Masken und Subjekte. Kritische Weißseinsforschung in Deutschland*, 4. Aufl., Münster: Unrast, 2020, S. 24–28, hier: S. 28.

4 Susan Arndt, „Hautfarbe", in: Susan Arndt, Nadja Ofuatey-Alazard, Hg., *Wie Rassismus aus Wörtern spricht. (K)Erben des Kolonialismus im Wissensarchiv deutsche Sprache. Ein kritisches Nachschlagewerk*, 3. Aufl., Münster: Unrast, 2019, S. 332–342, hier: S. 340–341.

5 Robin DiAngelo, *What does it mean to be white? Developing white racial literacy*, überarb. Aufl., New York u. a.: Peter Lang, 2016, S. 129–132.

6 Agnes Elena Kern, Artist Statement in diesem Buch, S. 160.

7 Swantje Köbsell, „Ableism. Neue Qualität oder ‚alter Wein' in neuen Schläuchen?", in: Iman Attia, Swantje Köbsell, Nivedita Prasad, Hg., *Dominanzkultur reloaded. Neue Texte zu gesellschaftlichen Machtverhältnissen und ihren Wechselwirkungen*, Bielefeld: transcript, 2015, S. 21–34.

8 Sabine Reisenbüchler, Artist Statement in diesem Buch, S. 180.

9 Peggy McIntosh, *White privilege and male privilege. A personal account of coming to see correspondences through work in Women's Studies*, Working Paper 189, Wellesley, MA: Wellesley Centers for Women, 1988, https://nationalseedproject.org/Key-SEED-Texts/white-privilege-and-male-privilege (14.07.2021).

1 Birgit Rommelspacher, *Dominanzkultur. Texte zur Fremdheit und Macht*, Berlin: Orlanda Frauenverlag, 1995.

2 Cf. ibid., pp. 39–54; Grada Kilomba, *Plantation memories. Episodes of everyday racism*, 6th ed., Münster: Unrast, 2020, pp. 40–43.

3 Susan Arndt, "Weißsein. Die verkannte Strukturkategorie Europas und Deutschlands," in: Maureen Maisha Eggers et al., eds., *Mythen, Masken und Subjekte. Kritische Weißseinsforschung in Deutschland*, 4th ed., Münster: Unrast, 2020, pp. 24–28, here: p. 28.

4 Susan Arndt, "Hautfarbe," in: Susan Arndt, Nadja Ofuatey-Alazard, eds., *Wie Rassismus aus Wörtern spricht. (K)Erben des Kolonialismus im Wissensarchiv deutsche Sprache. Ein kritisches Nachschlagewerk*, 3rd ed., Münster: Unrast, 2019, pp. 332–342, here: pp. 340–341.

5 Robin DiAngelo, *What Does it Mean to Be White? Developing White Racial Literacy*, rev. ed., New York e.g.: Peter Lang, 2016, pp. 129–132.

6 Agnes Elena Kern, artist's statement in the present publication, p. 162.

7 Swantje Köbsell, "Ableism. Neue Qualität oder 'alter Wein' in neuen Schläuchen?," in: Iman Attia, Swantje Köbsell, Nivedita Prasad, eds., *Dominanzkultur reloaded. Neue Texte zu gesellschaftlichen Machtverhältnissen und ihren Wechselwirkungen*, Bielefeld: transcript, 2015, pp. 21–34.

8 Sabine Reisenbüchler, artist's statement in the present publication, p. 182.

9 Peggy McIntosh, *White Privilege and Male Privilege. A Personal Account of Coming to See Correspondences Through Work in Women's Studies*, Working Paper 189, Wellesley, MA: Wellesley Centers for Women, 1988, https://nationalseedproject.org/Key-SEED-Texts/white-privilege-and-male-privilege (July 14, 2021).

KÜNSTLER:INNEN / ARTISTS

Texte / Texts: Künstler:innen / Artists

ALBA MALIKA BELHADJ MERZOUG

2000 Salzburg, AT – Salzburg, AT

Was bleibt einem Menschen, wenn man ihm alles nimmt, was ihn auszumachen scheint? Dieser Frage nachgehend, vollzieht sich mein persönlicher Perspektivenwechsel; die Fotografie wird zum Machtapparat und Bildmanipulation zum Sinnbild für manipulative Konstrukte in unserer Gesellschaft.

Mich selbstsicher vom eigenen Selbst entfernend, mache ich mich verwundbar, bis jegliche Angriffsfläche verschwunden zu sein scheint. Was bleibt, ist ein Individuum jenseits von Individualität, eine entmenschlichte Figur, die trotz allem Mensch bleibt. Fernab von biografischen Hintergründen wird sie zur Projektionsfläche fremder Erwartungshaltungen und es bleibt die Frage, ob in all diesem Nichts noch ich bin.
(AMBM)

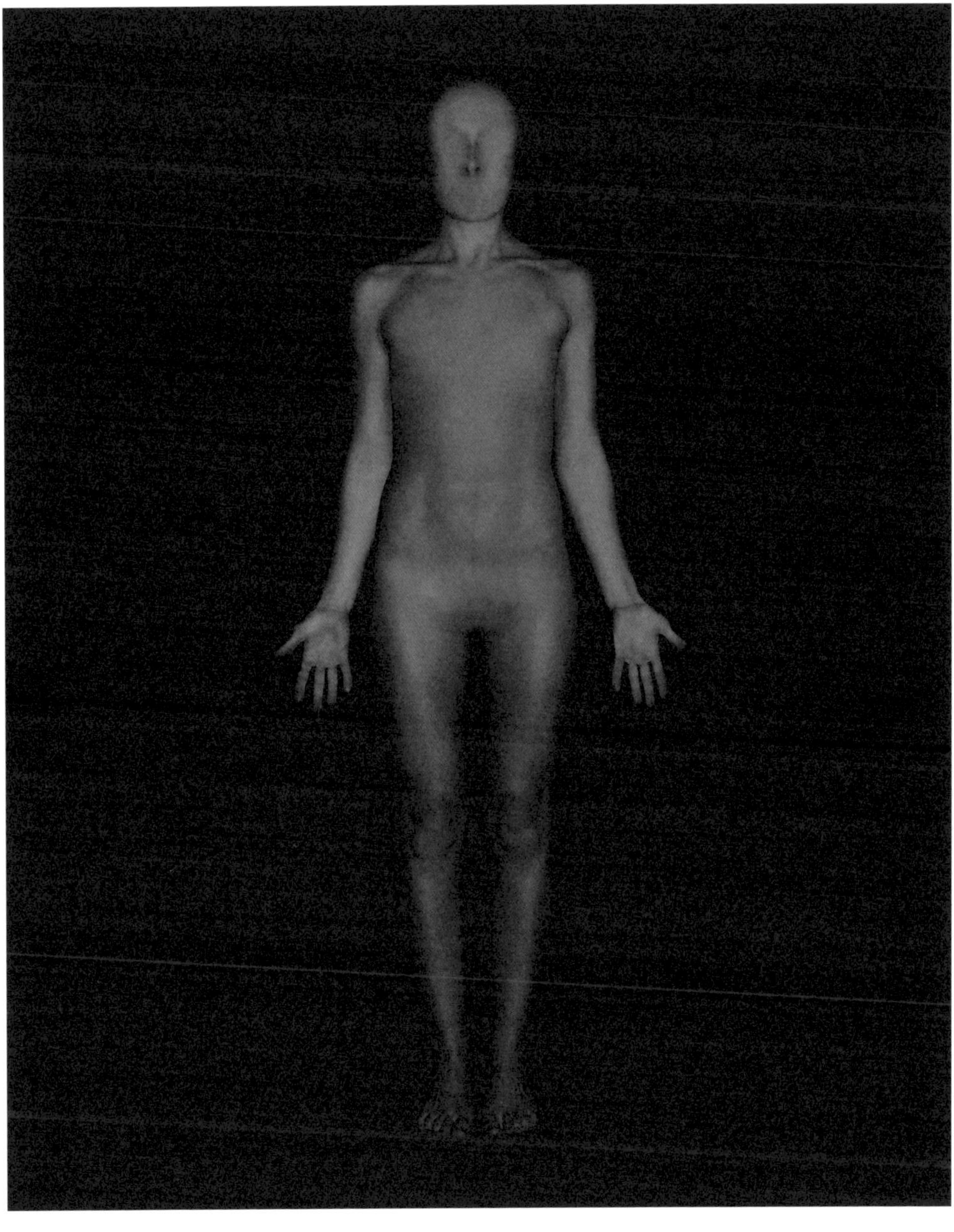

NichTS, 2020/21

ALBA MALIKA BELHADJ MERZOUG

2000 Salzburg, AT—Salzburg, AT

If you take away everything that seemingly makes up a person, what is left? In pursuing this question, I have experienced a shift in my own perspective, photography has become an instrument of power, and image manipulation a symbol for our society's manipulative constructs.

By confidently detaching from the self, I make myself vulnerable, until all of my edges seem to disappear. What is left is an individual beyond individuality—a dehumanized figure that, despite everything, remains human. Far removed from any kind of identity, the figure becomes a projecting surface for alien expectations. But the question remains: Do I still exist in all this nothingness? (AMBM)

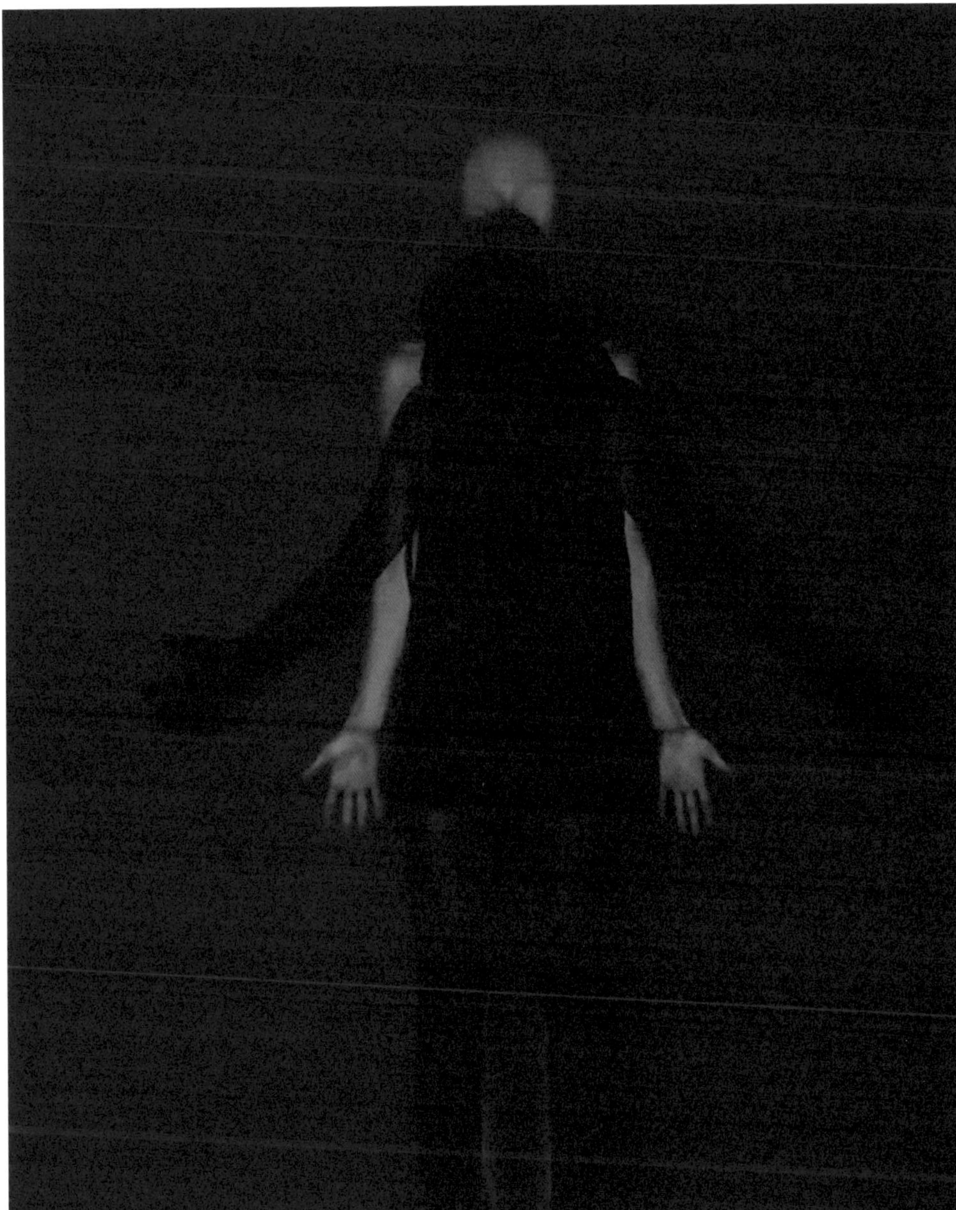

NichTS, 2020/21

MELANIE FORSTHUBER

2000 Grieskirchen, AT – Salzburg, AT

Auf den ersten flüchtigen Blick: farbenfroh, überwältigend, vielleicht sogar an ein Paradies erinnernd. Doch das Gesamtbild zerfällt, in verschiedene Perspektiven und Bildelemente. Merkwürdige und skurrile Szenen kommen zutage. Ein Paradies kann das nicht sein. Wie konstruieren wir uns Bilder über andere Länder, Kulturen oder Gesellschaften? Welche Rolle spielen dabei etwa Reisekataloge, Nachrichten, Filme oder Social Media? Sind diese konstruierten und zusammengestückelten Bilder in unseren Köpfen noch von kolonialem Denken verzerrt?

Ein Schwerpunkt meiner Arbeit ist das Thema Sextourismus. Aus unterschiedlichen Bildmaterialien, die zum Teil aus Reisekatalogen, zum Teil aus dem Internet stammen, „klebe" ich eine Welt zusammen, die zwar prachtvoll und schön wirken mag, jedoch von rassistischen und egoistischen Szenen geprägt ist. Die abgebildeten Handlungen zeigen unser eigenes (oftmals unbewusstes) Involviertsein in rassistischen Mustern und unsere Teilnahme am Kreieren postkolonialer Klischees und Vorurteile. Nicht zuletzt werden kritikwürdige Strukturen unserer Gesellschaft beleuchtet, in denen diese rassistischen Muster in verschiedensten, meist alltäglichen Situationen fortgesetzt werden.

Abseits der Fotocollage stehen persönliche Erinnerungsstücke aus Urlauben. Zwar besteht ein großer Kontrast zwischen diesen kleinformatigen, persönlichen Abbildungen und der bunten, großformatigen und zugleich bizarren Collage, doch in ihrer Beziehung zueinander sind sie Zeugen meines eigenen Eingebundenseins. Ich werde mir bewusst, dass auch ich als Mitglied unserer Gesellschaft Teil dieses von Rassismus geprägten Systems bin – auch wenn ich das nicht will. Aus der Distanz betrachtet, mag das Gesamtbild schön und gut wirken, begeben wir uns aber auf eine Mikroebene, zerfällt dieser Eindruck. (MF)

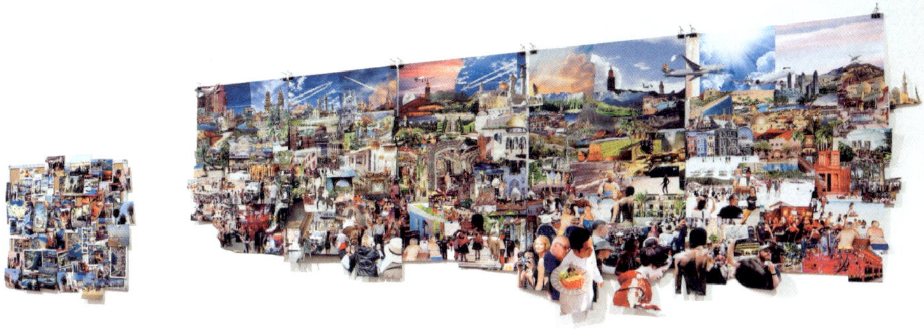

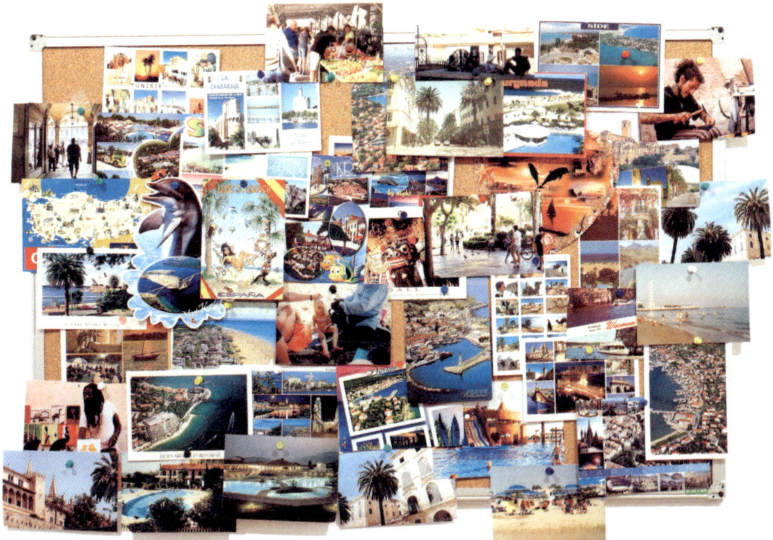

Paradies?, 2021

MELANIE FORSTHUBER

2000 Grieskirchen, AT—Salzburg, AT

At first glance: colorful, overwhelming, maybe even reminiscent of paradise. But the overall image fractures into differing perspectives and pictorial elements. Weird and bizarre scenes become apparent. It can't possibly be a paradise. How do we construct images of other countries, cultures, and societies? What role do travel catalogues, news, films, and social media play? Is such imagery, constructed and pieced together, in our minds still distorted by colonial thinking?

One focus of my work is the subject of sex tourism. Using differing sources of imagery, some of which originate from travel catalogues and some from the Internet, I "paste" together a world that may appear magnificent and beautiful, but is characterized by racist and self-serving scenarios. The activities being depicted display our own (frequently unconscious) involvement in both racist patterns and the creation of post-colonial clichés and prejudices. Not least, structures within our society are examined that are worthy of criticism, in which such racist patterns are prolonged in wide-ranging, mostly everyday circumstances.

Beyond the photographic collages, there are also personal mementos from vacations. Even if a substantial contrast exists between this small-scale, personal imagery and the colorful, large-scale, and, at the same time, bizarre collages, in their relation to each another they are testament to my own involvement. I'm becoming aware that, as a member of our society, I too am part of this racially inscribed system—even if I don't want to be. Viewed from a distance, the overall image may appear pleasant and good —but at a micro level, such impressions begin to disintegrate. (MF)

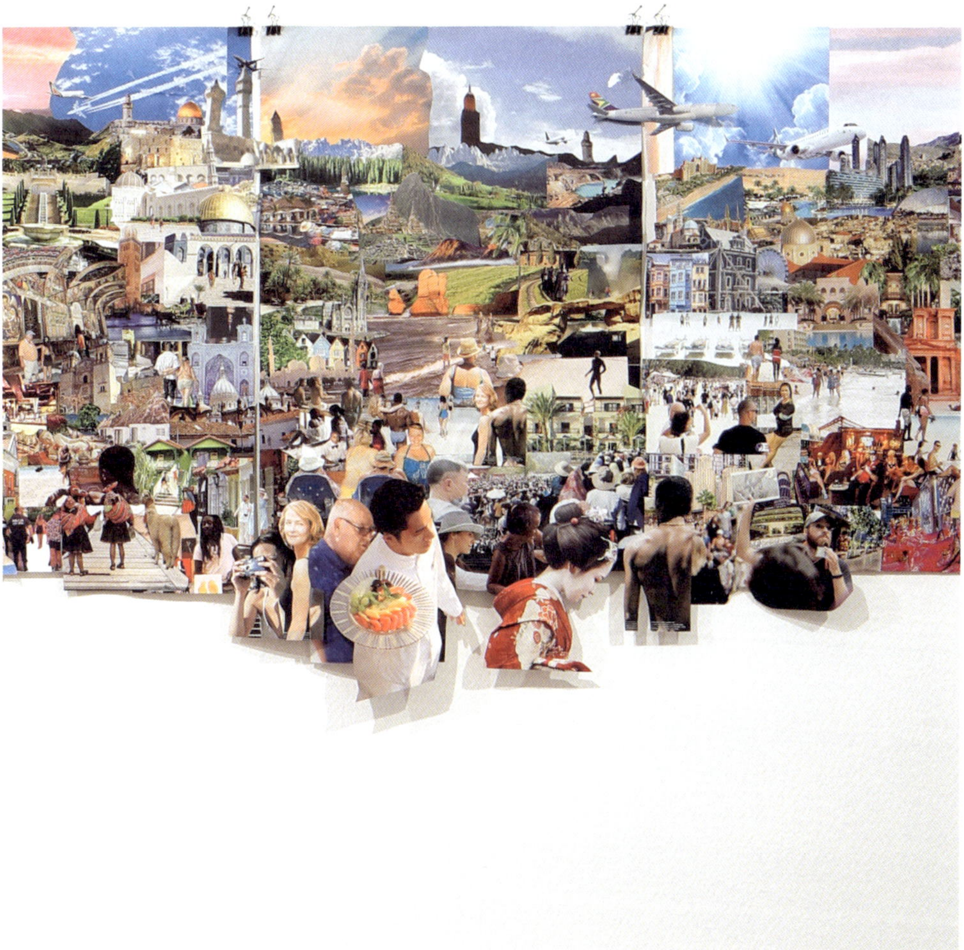

Paradies?, 2021

PIA GEISREITER

1996 Schrobenhausen, DE – Salzburg, AT

Comics gehörten schon immer zu meinem Leben. Sie führten mich in eine andere Welt. Eine Welt voller Fantasie und spannender Abenteuer. Eine Welt zum Träumen. Doch dieses Comicbild weckt ein reines Gefühlschaos in mir. Meine Hände sind schwarz verschmiert, Tränen fließen, Unverständnis taucht auf und eine große Wut breitet sich in mir aus ... Ich will das rassistische Bild unkenntlich machen. Ich versuche es immer wieder. Trotzdem bleibt es da, unscheinbar, aber es ist noch da. (PG)

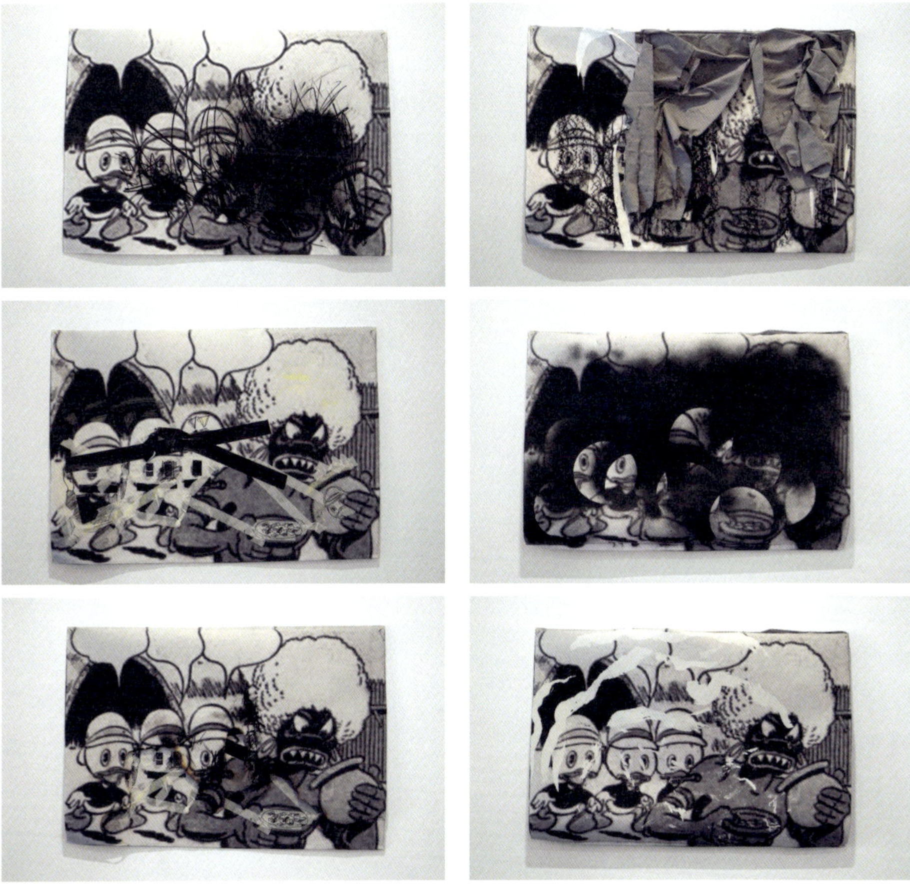

Gefühlschaos, 2020/21

PIA GEISREITER

1996 Schrobenhausen, DE—Salzburg, AT

Comics have always been a part of my life. They have introduced me to another world. A world full of fantasy and exciting adventures. A world to dream about. But this particular comic image awakens mixed emotions in me. My hands are smeared with black, tears flow, incomprehension emerges, and a deep anger spreads within me ... I want to efface the racist image. I keep trying. Yet it remains, inconspicuous, but it's still there. (PG)

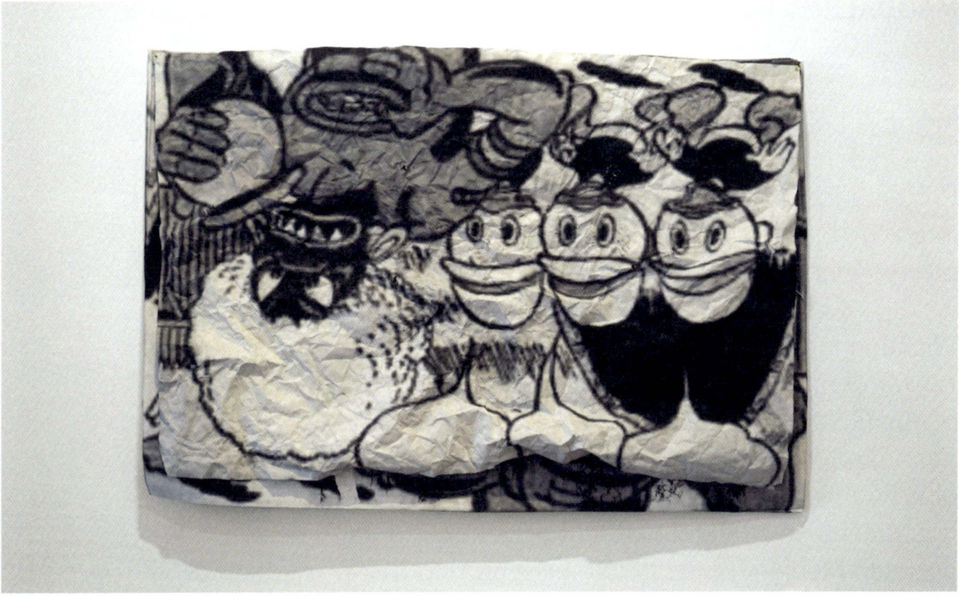

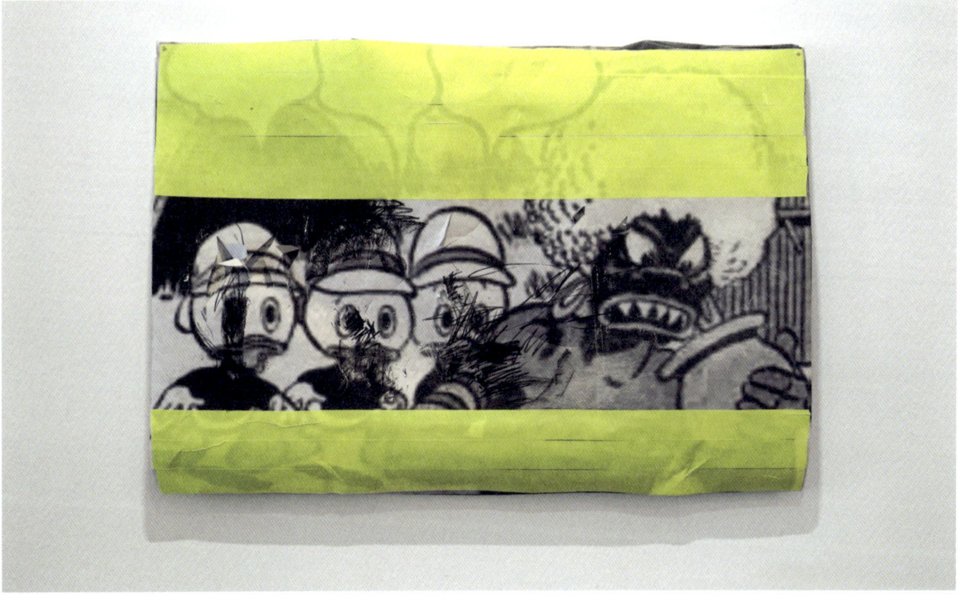

Gefühlschaos, 2020/21

MAGDALENA HELLER

1993 Vöcklabruck, AT – Salzburg, AT

Meine Arbeit versteht sich als Reaktion auf den politischen Aktivismus in den sozialen Medien. Die weltweiten Black-Lives-Matter-Proteste fanden auch dort statt. User:innen wurden aufgefordert, ihre Plattform für den Kampf gegen Rassismus zu nutzen und diverse Inhalte mit ihren Follower:innen zu teilen.

Wichtige Informationen können in sozialen Medien schnell verbreitet werden; zudem haben die Nutzer:innen das Gefühl, sich für etwas Gutes einzusetzen. Der Druck, diese Inhalte zu teilen, ist dennoch für viele unangenehm. Die Installation, die bewusst die oberflächliche Ästhetik sozialer Medien aufgreift, behandelt genau dieses ambivalente Gefühl gegenüber dem Aktivismus in sozialen Medien. Eine digitale Erweiterung der Installation bildet ein Instagram-Account, der für den Zeitraum der Ausstellung aktiv betrieben wird und anschließend inaktiv als Relikt zurückbleibt.
(MH)

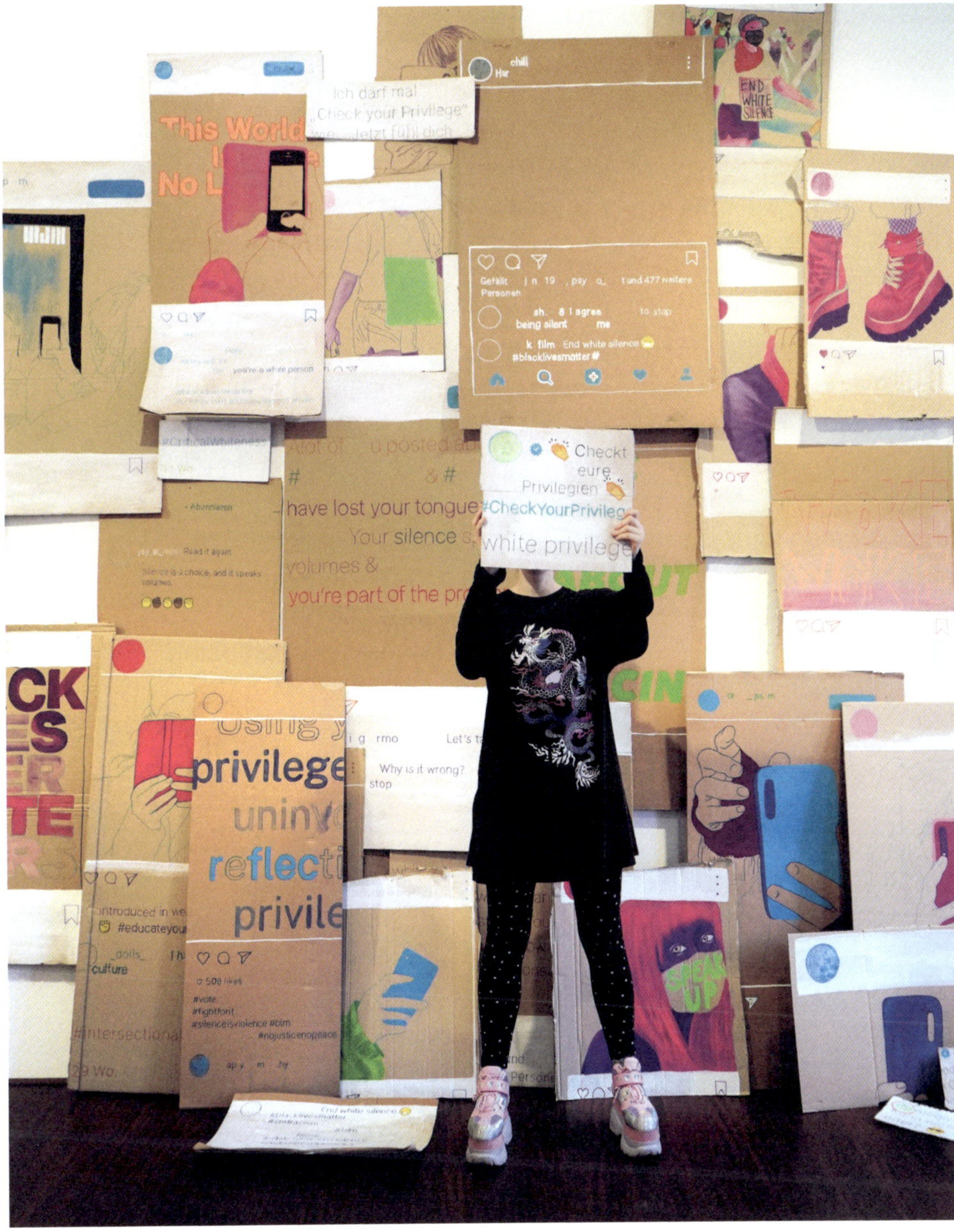

#bitteteilen, 2021

MAGDALENA HELLER

1993 Vöcklabruck, AT—Salzburg, AT

My work can be understood as a reaction to political activism on social media. This is where the worldwide "Black Lives Matter" protests also took place. Users were asked to use their platform to fight racism and to share a variety of content with their followers.

Important information can be disseminated rapidly on social media. In addition, the users then have the feeling that they are in-volved in a good cause. The pressure to share this content nevertheless remains uncomfortable for many. The installation, which consciously adopts the superficial aesthetics of social media, addresses exactly this ambivalent feeling toward activism on social media. The creation of an Instagram account (@pleaseshareartproject) is a digital extension of the installation that will be active for the duration of the exhibition and then remain as an inactive relic of the installation. (MH)

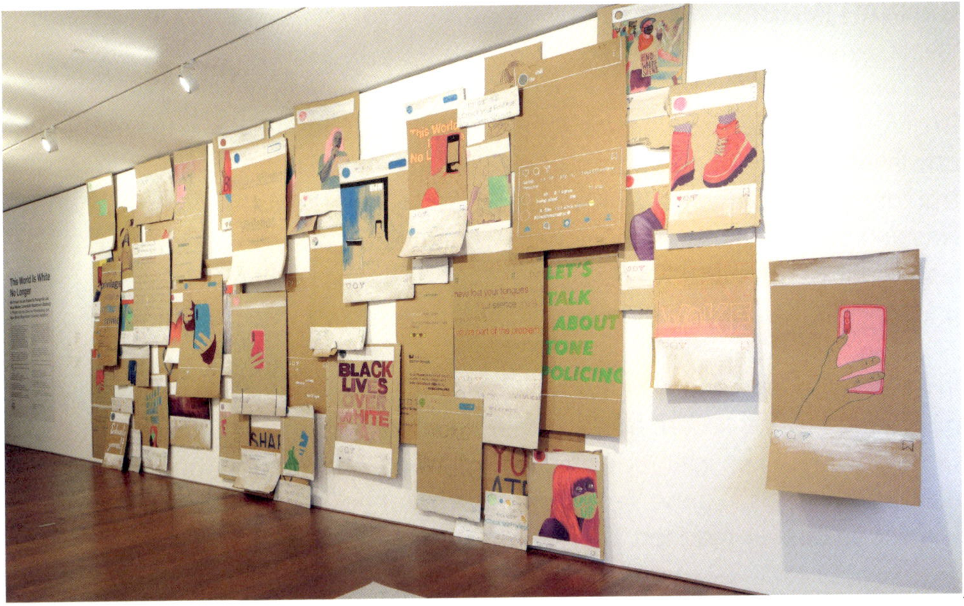

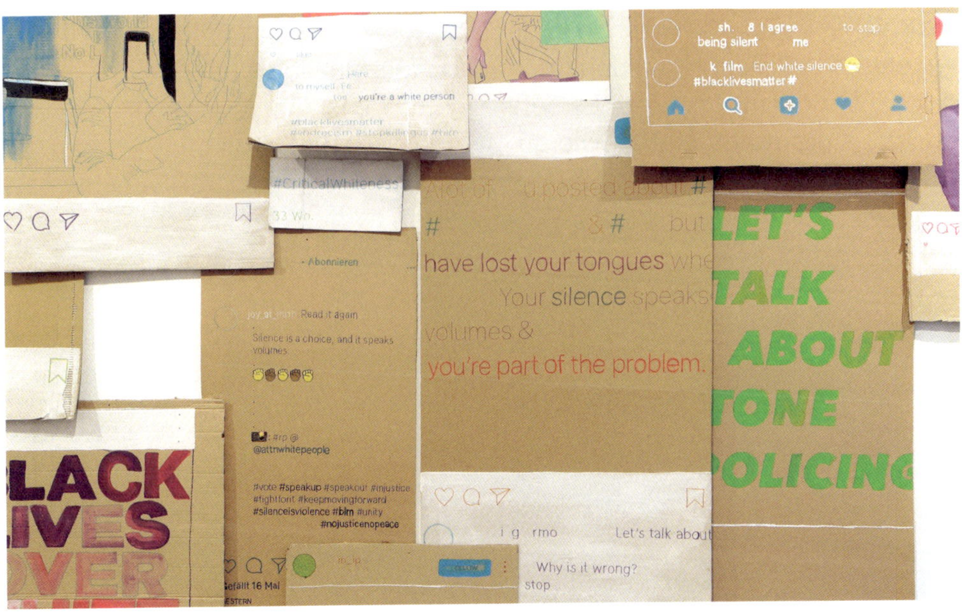

#bitteteilen, 2021

HANNAH IMHOFF

1997 München, DE – Salzburg, AT

Darf ich als *Weiße* zu Rassismus arbeiten? Es fühlt sich falsch, unwissend, anmaßend und ungerechtfertigt an. Aber ich tue es trotzdem. Ihr lest meine Worte hier, weil ich weder glaube, dass Rassismus nur ein amerikanisches Problem ist, noch, dass Rassisten nur Rechte und Nazis sind – sondern Menschen wie du und ich. Als *Weiße* habe ich die Wahl, hin- oder wegzuschauen.

In Anlehnung an Adrian Pipers *My Calling (Card) #1* formuliere ich mit meinen *Visitenkarten* einen Fingerzeig auf unsere rassistische Gesellschaft. Mein Ziel ist es, einen Raum zu öffnen, um über *weiße* Privilegien, eigene Verfehlungen, Unsicherheit und darüber, wie wir es besser machen können, zu sprechen.

Drei Kreishälften. Deine Assoziationen? Deine Position im Raum. Was siehst du? Deine Position in der rassistischen Gesellschaft. Wo stehst du? Dein Handlungsraum. Was tust du? Ich kann dir dieses Werk nicht erklären. Es setzt sich aus uns zusammen, auch aus dir: wo du stehst, wie du dich positionierst, was du wahrnimmst, welche Spuren du hinterlässt (HI)

Lieber Mensch,

ich bin *weiß.*

Du auch? Falls ja, dann bist du dir dessen wahrscheinlich die meiste Zeit deines Lebens nicht bewusst. Weder wenn du dich um einen Job oder eine Wohnung bewirbst, noch wenn du durch eine Ausstellung läufst und von anderen *Weißen* umgeben bist. Und es geht nicht nur dir so. Wenn wir scheitern oder Ablehnung erfahren, müssen wir uns nicht fragen, ob das nicht passiert wäre, wären wir nicht *weiß*. Wir werden auch nie gebeten, für alle *weißen* Menschen zu sprechen. Leider führt all das dazu, dass unsere *weißen* Privilegien für uns unsichtbar bleiben und es uns an Einfühlungsvermögen und Respekt für Menschen of Color fehlt. Eine Haltung, die Rassismus nicht beenden wird. Ein Verhalten, das ich nicht länger unterstützen will.

Ich gehe davon aus, dass wir uns all dessen nicht ausreichend bewusst sind. Deshalb verteile ich diese Karte.

Mit freundlichen Grüßen,

Dear Friend,

I am *white*.

You too? If you are, I am sure you will not realize it most of the time during your life. Not when applying for a job or a flat, nor when walking through an exhibition and being almost exclusively surrounded by *whites.* And it is not just you. If we fail or experience rejection we never have to worry if it would have been different had we not been *white.* Also, we are never asked to speak for all *white* people. Unfortunately, all of this ensures that our *white* privileges remain invisible to us and that we lack the ability to empathize with and respect people of color. This will not end racism. A behavior that I no longer want to support.

I assume that we are often not aware enough of all of this. I am therefore distributing this card.

Sincerely yours,

Visitenkarten (Erinnerung an mich selbst), 2020/21

HANNAH IMHOFF

1997 Munich, DE—Salzburg, AT

Am I, being *white*, permitted to do work about racism? It feels wrong, ignorant, presumptuous, and unjustified. But I do it anyway. You are reading my words here because I neither believe that racism is just an American problem, nor that racists are merely right-wing or Nazis—but people like you and me. Being *white*, I have the choice of either looking, or looking away.

Based on Adrian Piper's *My Calling (Card) #1*, I'm using my own *Calling Cards* to highlight our racist society. My aim has been to open a space in which to talk about *white* privilege, our own failings, insecurities, and how we could do better.

Three halves of a circle. Your associations? Your position in space. What do you see? Your position in racist society. Where do you stand? The extent of your space for action? What are you doing? I can't explain this work to you. It is being assembled from us, including you: Where you stand, how you position yourself, what you are able to perceive, what traces you leave behind. (HI)

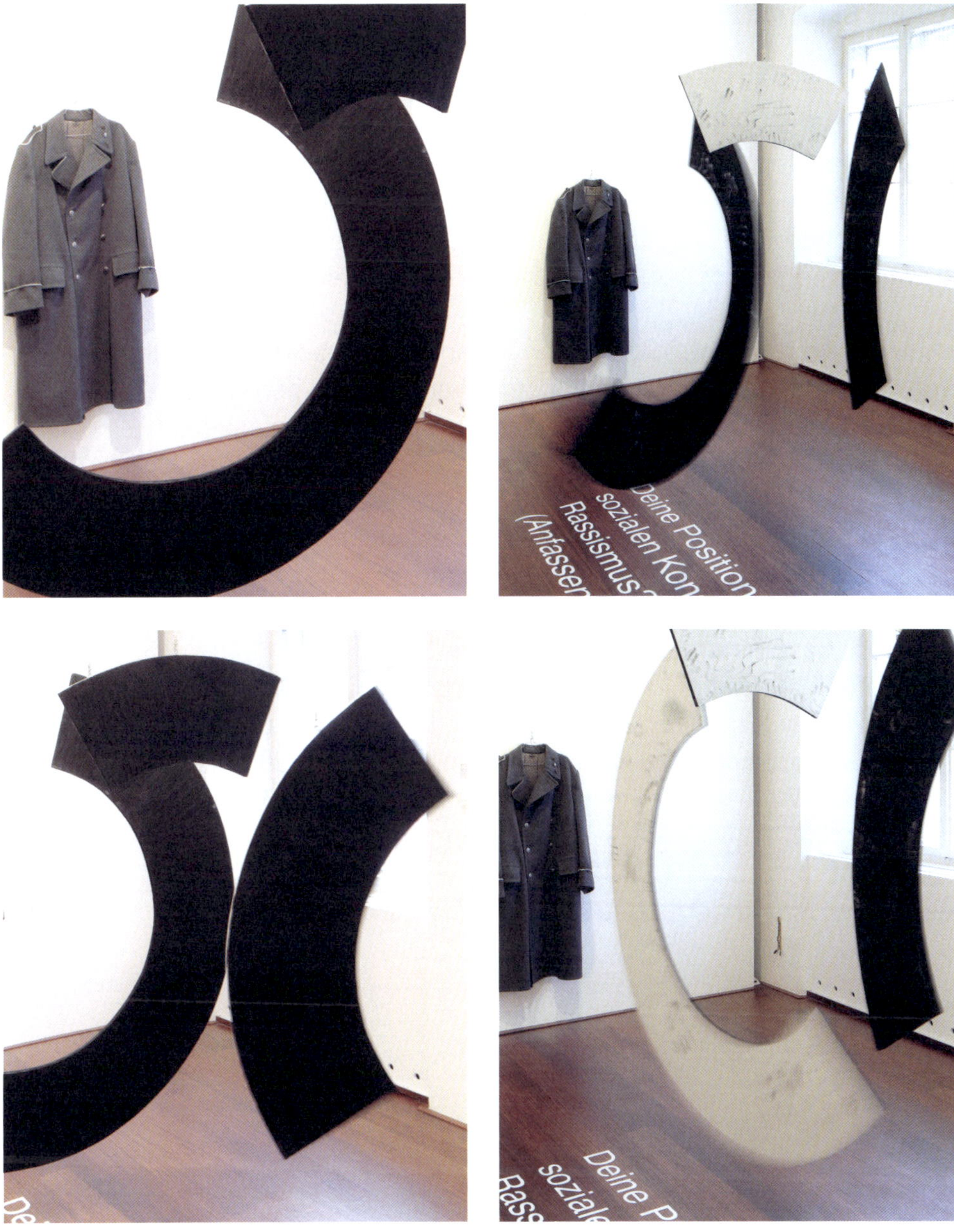

Rassistische Gesellschaft (Eine Problemdarstellung mit offenem Ende), 2020

AGNES ELENA KERN

Salzburg, AT

Wo es Zivilisation gibt, gibt es Graffiti. Damit erreicht man Menschen ungefiltert in der Außenwelt – vor tausend Jahren schon und heute immer noch. Ist einmal etwas dort, hat man weder Ahnung davon noch Einfluss darauf, wer es sehen wird. Im öffentlichen Raum wird täglich diskutiert, gerufen und gefordert.

In meiner Arbeit ist gleichzeitig ein Perspektivenwechsel möglich. Weg von der Straße und hinein in die Wohnzimmer derer, über deren Existenz draußen diskutiert wird. Über ihre Daseinsberechtigung, ihre Zukunft. Die gezeigten Personen erfahren aus veschiedenen Gründen Diskriminierung in der Gesellschaft: aufgrund ihrer Hautfarbe, ihrer Sexualität, ihrer geschlechtlichen Identität, ihrer Art zu lieben oder auch aufgrund ihrer Art, ihren Körper zu gestalten. Im Alltag der Pandemie kümmern sie sich um den Haushalt, bekämpfen die Langeweile, vertiefen Beziehungen und sind einfach Mensch. Ohne die Vergleichswerte der Gesellschaft ist jeder Mensch für sich Mensch, wertvoll und lebendig. Oder wie die Straße es ausdrücken würde: „Wir sind doch alle Hurensöhne Gottes." Die Welt ist so wenig weiß, wie sie schwarz ist. Sie ist alles dazwischen, ist grau, ist bunt. (AEK)

Mit: André, Iris, Robert, Josef, Kirsten, Alex, Phillip, Constantin und Luisa

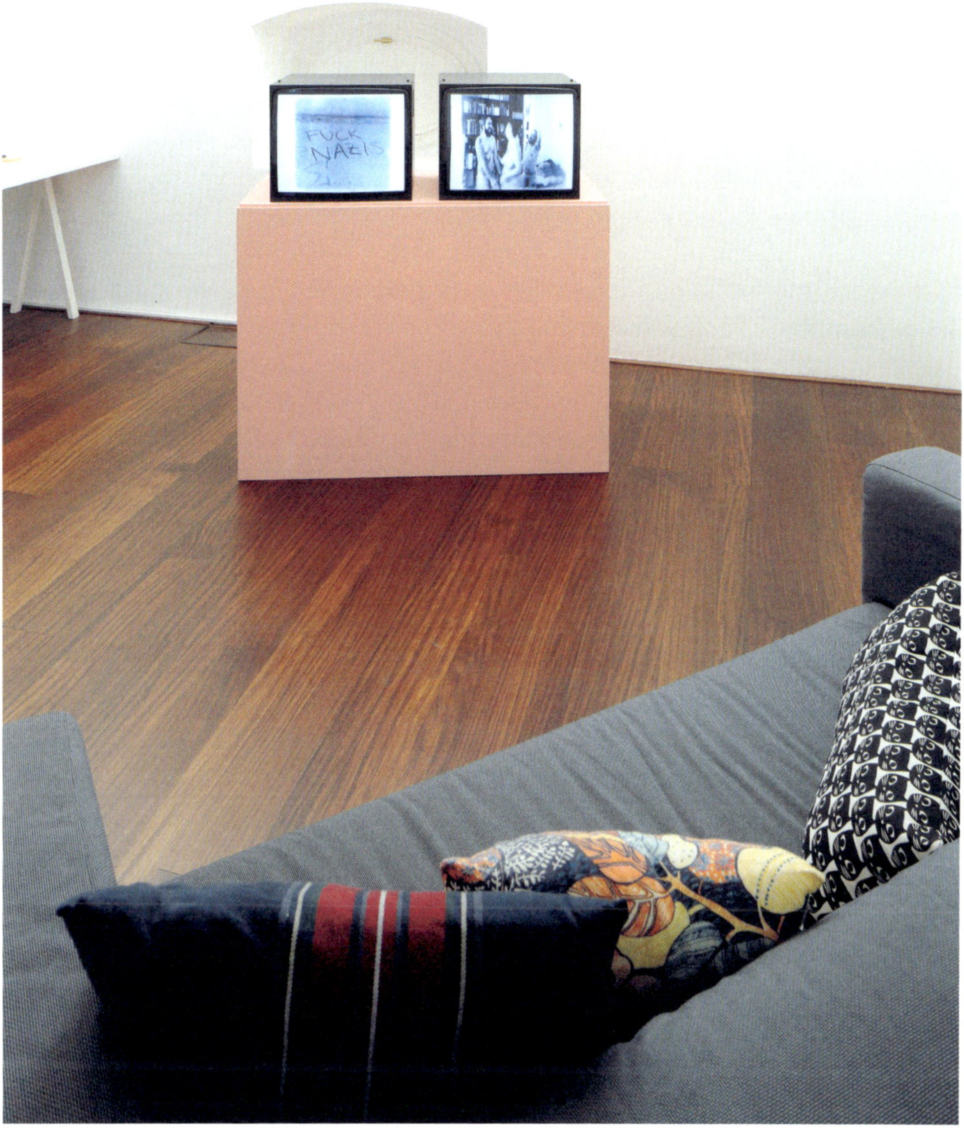

~~Schwarz.Weiß.~~ Grau.Bunt., 2021

AGNES ELENA KERN

Salzburg, AT

Where there is civilization, there is also graffiti, an unfiltered means of reaching people in the wider world—a phenomena that existed a thousand years ago and one that is still in existence today. Once something is there, you have no idea or control in terms of who will see it. Discussions, calls, and demands are an everyday occurrence in public space.

In my work, a change of perspective is, at the same time, possible. Away from the street and into the living rooms of those whose existence is being discussed in the outside world. Their right to be, their future. The people being depicted experience social discrimination for various reasons: Because of the color of their skin, their sexuality, their gender identity, the way they love, or because of the way in which they choose to shape their bodies. During the everyday life of the pandemic, they have been taking care of household chores, fighting boredom, deepening relationships, and are simply being human. Beyond society's comparative values, every person is human, valuable, and vibrant. Or as the street would put it: "We are all God's sons-of-a-bitch." The world is no more white than it is black. It's everything in between, it's gray, it's colorful.
(AEK)

With: André, Iris, Robert, Josef, Kirsten, Alex, Phillip, Constantin, and Luisa

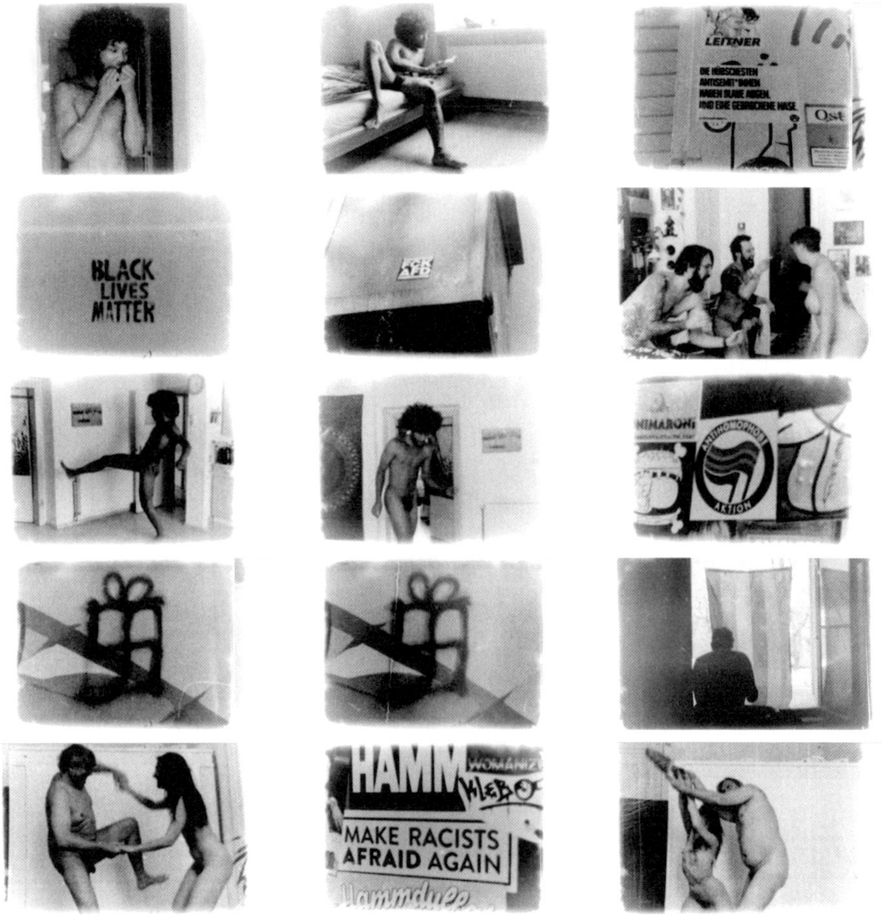

~~Schwarz.Weiß.~~ Grau.Bunt., 2021

VERA KERN

1994 Wien, AT – Salzburg, AT

Meine Arbeit setzt sich damit auseinander, wie auf der Social-Media-Plattform Instagram Rassismus thematisiert wird. Dort ist es leicht, sich seine eigene Welt zu kreieren, abhängig davon, wem man folgt und was man postet. Besonders eindringlich ist für mich dort der Kontrast zwischen oberflächlichen Inhalten und jenem Content, dessen Verfasser:innen Menschen informieren, für Rechte eintreten, Solidarität zeigen. Um das Verhältnis dieser zwei Mengen sichtbar zu machen, habe ich den visuell größtmöglichen Kontrast gewählt und meinen persönlichen Instagram-Konsum vom 7. Januar 2021 in Abstraktion übersetzt. Dahinter stehen Fragen nach Alibihandlungen und besten ersten Schritten, aber auch das Zugeständnis, noch zögerlich vor der Entwicklung zu stehen, die von einer passiven, zuhörenden zu einer aktiven Haltung führt. (VK)

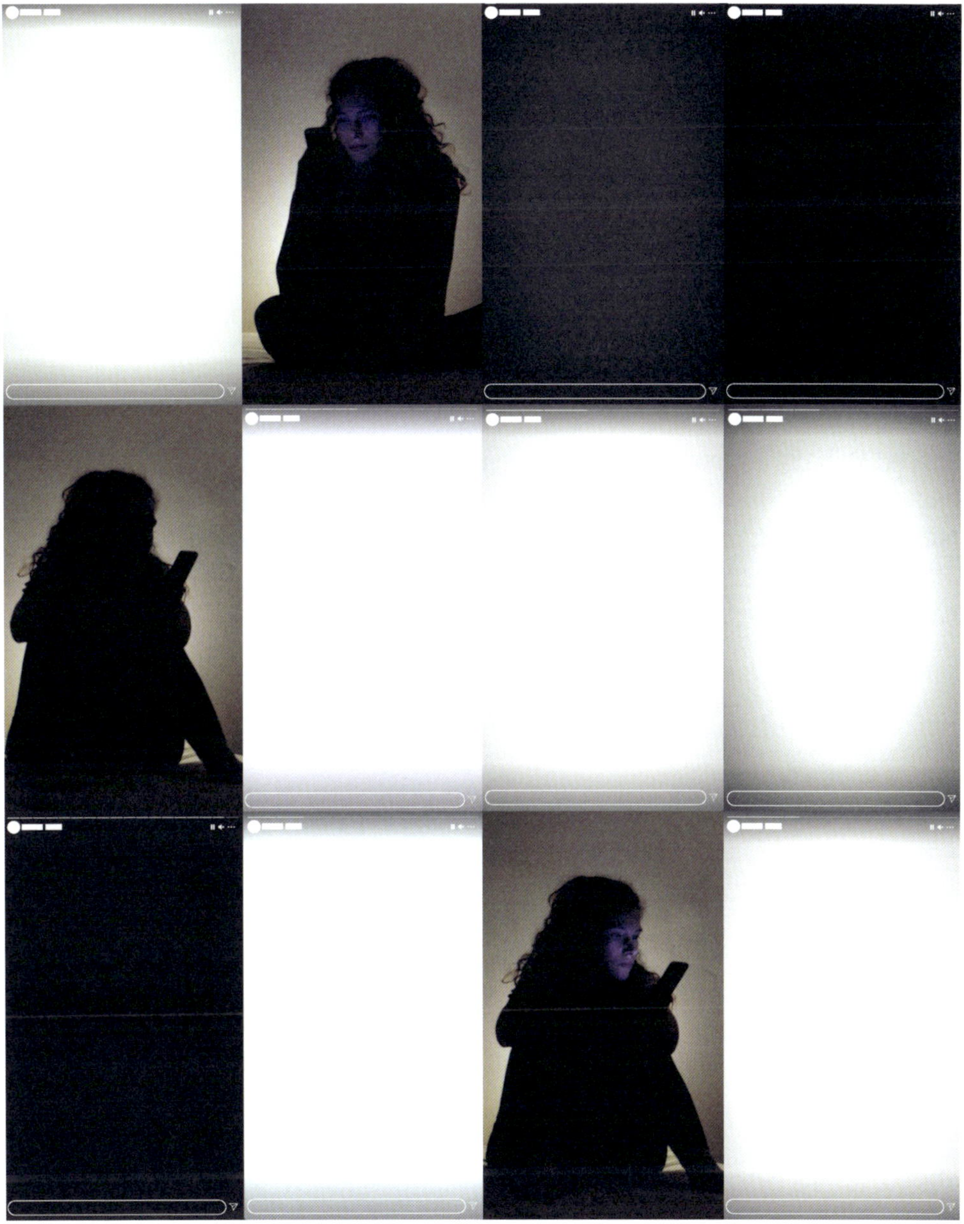

07-01-21, 2021

VERA KERN

1994 Vienna, AT—Salzburg, AT

My work examines how racism is addressed on the social media platform Instagram, where it is easy to create your own world, depending on who you follow and what you post. For me, the contrast between superficial content and content whose authors inform people, stand up for rights, and display solidarity is particularly trenchant. In order to make the relation between these two quantities visible, I have chosen the greatest possible visual contrast and translated my personal Instagram consumption from January 7, 2021 into abstraction. There are questions lying behind this concerning alibi activities and the best first steps, but also an admission of some hesitancy regarding developments that lead from passive listening to an active attitude. (VK)

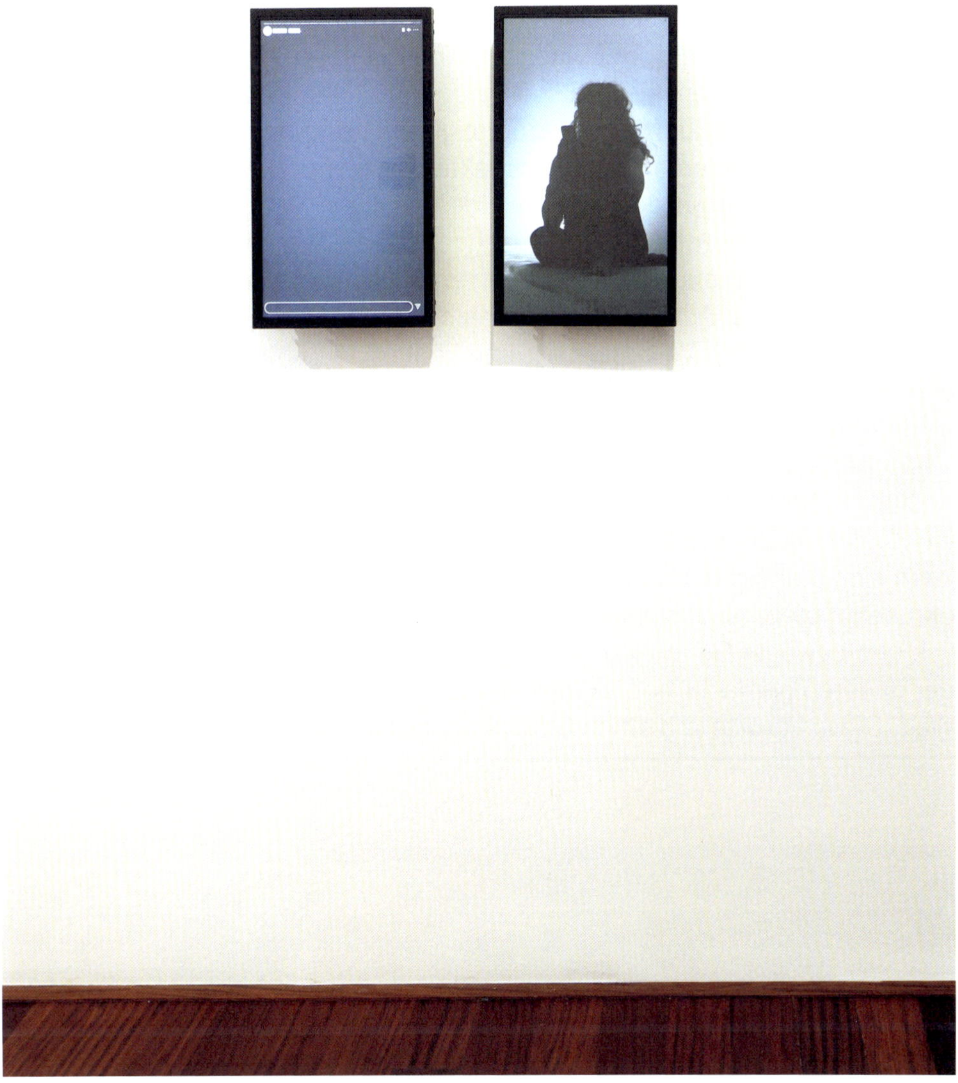

07-01-21, 2021

KEVIN KLINGER

1992 Salzburg, AT – Salzburg, AT

In dieser Arbeit geht es um eine kritische Selbstreflexion und um die Frage nach Exklusion und Inklusion in der Gesellschaft. Was mich dazu inspiriert hat, mit Video zu arbeiten, ist die Tatsache, dass darin das Gegenwärtige, das Vergangene und im weitesten Sinne sogar das Zukünftige zusammengeführt sind. Mit dem Aufnehmen eines Moments, einer Perspektive oder gar einer Sichtweise wird das Dargestellte im Raum des digitalen Mediums festgehalten. Das Bewegtbild kann zwar nachbearbeitet und verstellt werden und damit die Wirklichkeit verzerren, aber die Perspektive bleibt dieselbe. Auch wir Menschen sind eine Abbildung der Gegenwart und des Vergangenen und können mit unserer Sprache, unseren Worten und Taten die Zukunft beeinflussen. Ohne einen bewussten Eingriff werden die Filme – genauso wie wir Menschen – immer dieselben bleiben. Eingeschlossen in einem Kasten, werden wir unreflektiert „abgespielt“, tagein, tagaus. Wer die Konfrontation mit seinen Rassismen zu umgehen versucht, kann sich ständig mit unschuldiger Unwissenheit herausreden und behaupten, nicht rassistisch zu sein. Wenn man sich nie ehrlich und bewusst Gedanken über Herkunft, Hautfarbe und Kultur der anderen gemacht hat, läuft man nicht vorurteilsfrei durch die Welt. Diese Vorurteile bleiben für einen einfach verborgen. (KK)

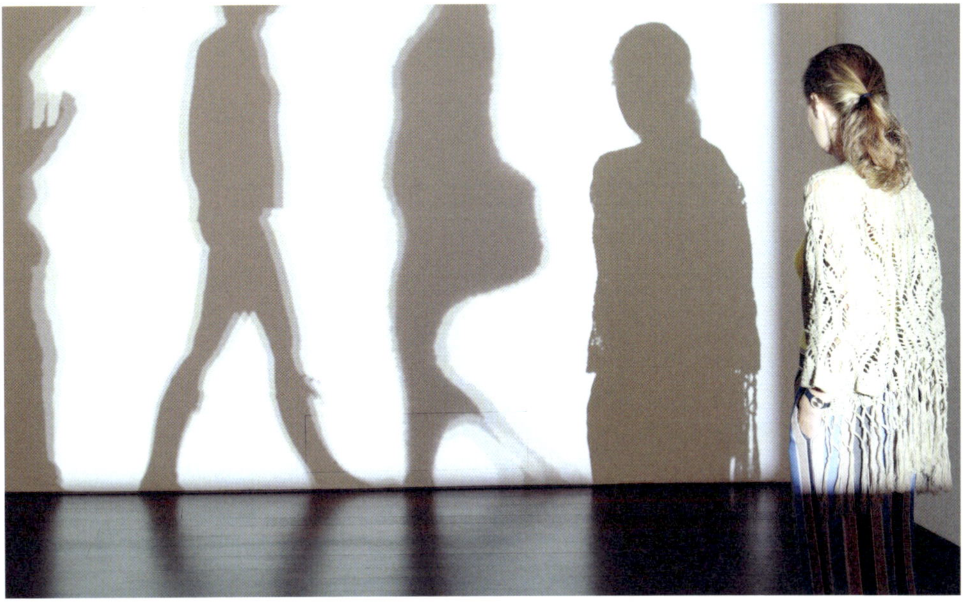

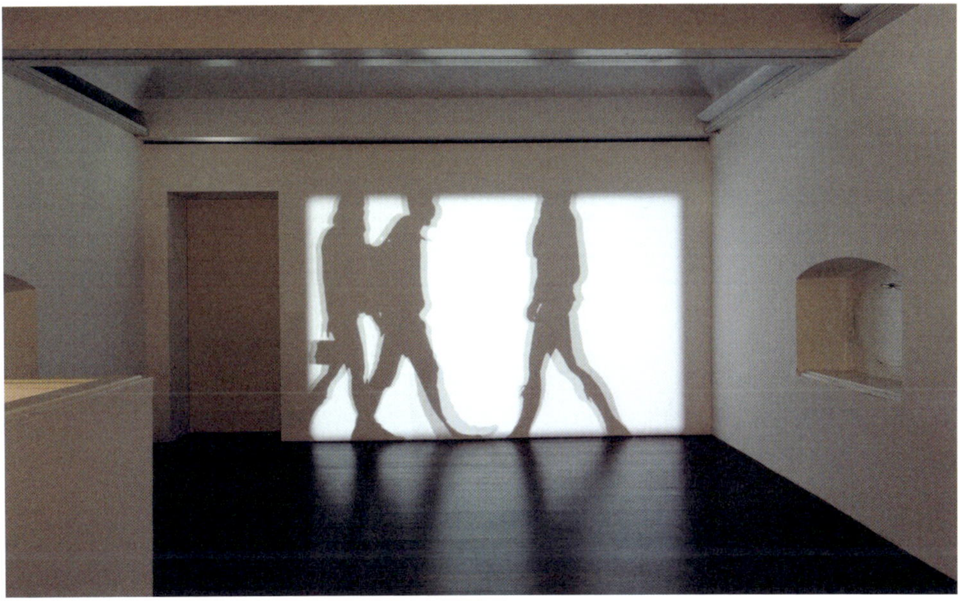

Exit the Box, 2020

KEVIN KLINGER

1992 Salzburg, AT—Salzburg, AT

This work concerns critical self-reflection together with questions of exclusion and inclusion in society. What inspired me to work with video is the fact that it merges the present, the past, and in the broadest sense even the future. By capturing a moment, a perspective, or even a point of view, what is being represented is captured within the space of the digital medium. The moving image can be reworked and manipulated, distorting reality accordingly, but the perspective nevertheless remains the same. We humans are likewise a representation of the present and what is past, and are able to influence the future through our language, our words, and actions. Without conscious intervention, films—just like we humans—will always remain the same. Enclosed within a box, we are continually "played back" without any further thought, day in, day out. Those who try to avoid confrontation with their own racism can constantly excuse themselves through innocent ignorance and claim not to be racist. If you have never honestly and consciously thought about origins, skin color, and the culture of others, you are not proceeding through the world without prejudice. Such prejudices simply remain concealed from you. (KK)

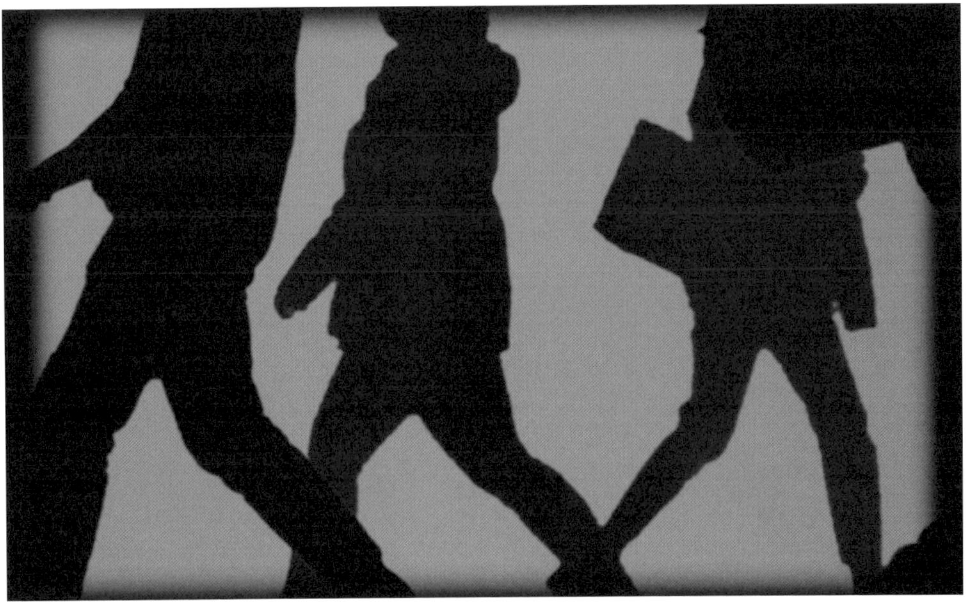

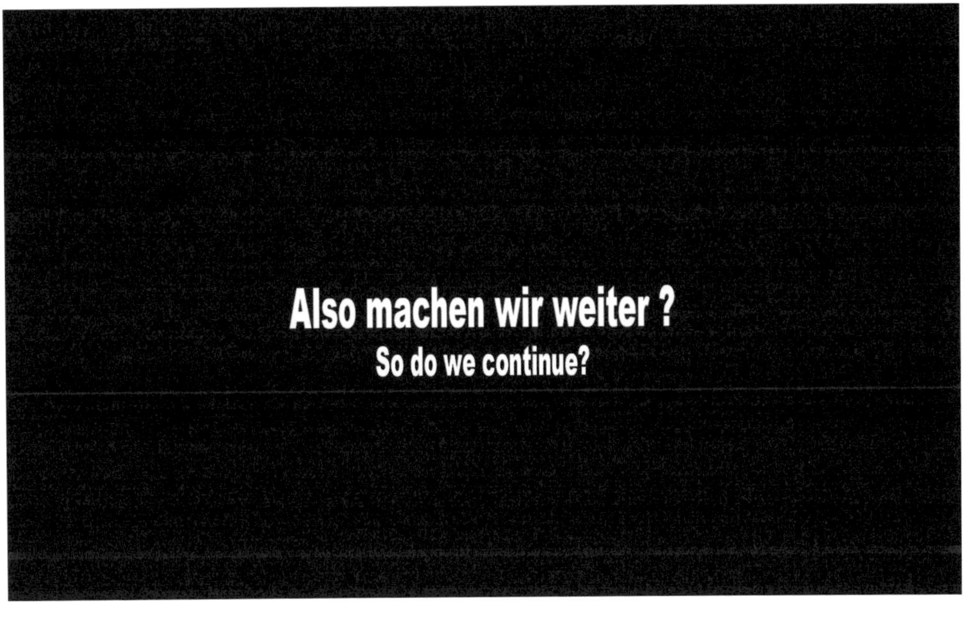

Exit the Box, 2020

LEONIE MIRJAM LINDINGER

2000 Richterswil, CH – Salzburg, AT

Im Zentrum meiner Arbeit stehen gesammelte Fotos. Ich fragte Freunde und Freundinnen aus Asien und Europa, ob sie mir zu den vier Begriffen „Augen“, „Haut“, „Sprache“ und „Farbe“ Fotos zuschicken könnten. So bekam ich über hundert Fotografien aus:

Deutschland: Bremen, Frankfurt am Main
Philippinen: Manila, Laguna
Korea: Yangpyeong
Schweden: Bettna, Malmö
Schweiz: Bern, Zürich
USA: San Francisco

Warum wählte jemand genau dieses Bild? Welche Bedeutung hat es für die Person? Diese Fragen bleiben unbeantwortet. Die Geschichte, die in dem Videoessay entsteht, ist assoziativ und fragmentarisch. Meine eigene Perspektive ist die einer 20-jährigen weißen Europäerin. Durch die Arbeit mit dem Bildmaterial anderer Menschen eröffneten sich für mich weitere Perspektiven. Die gewählten Textfragmente sind unabhängig von den Bildern entstanden.

In einem Gespräch über Rassismus kam die Frage „Do you think this will change soon?“ auf. Eine andere Person fragte: „How soon is soon?“ Auch die Arbeit an diesem Videoessay erlebe ich als offene Frage, die bestehen bleibt. (LML)

"How
Soon
Is Soon ?"

Leonie Lindinger

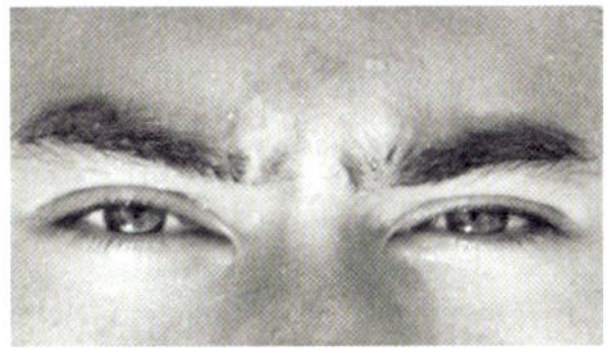

AUGENH

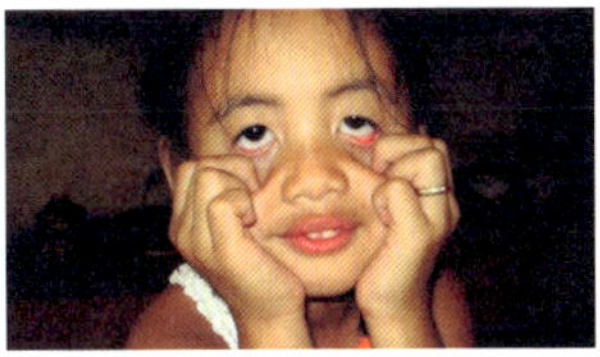

HAUT

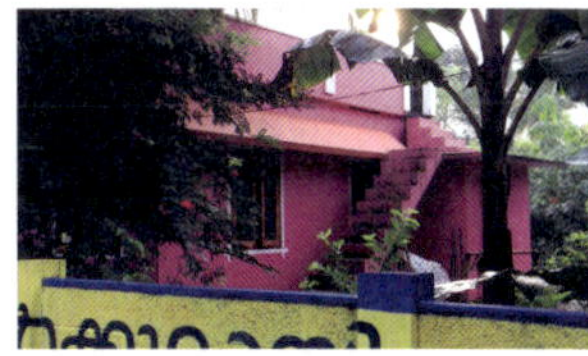

SPRACHE

– Lucas Weber LAGUNA PH
BREMEN DE
– Maxine Alip LAGUNA PH
⇝ SALZBURG AT
– Karin Baumeler ZÜRICH CH
⇝ INDIEN

FARBE

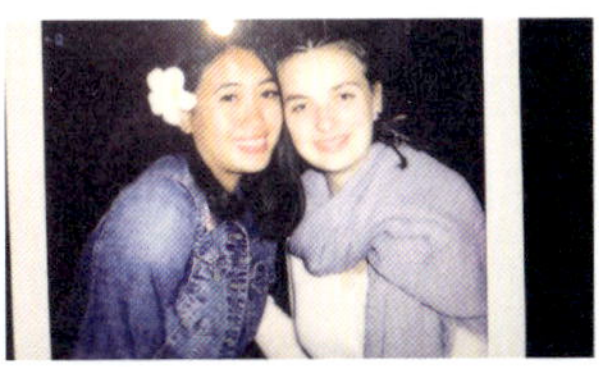
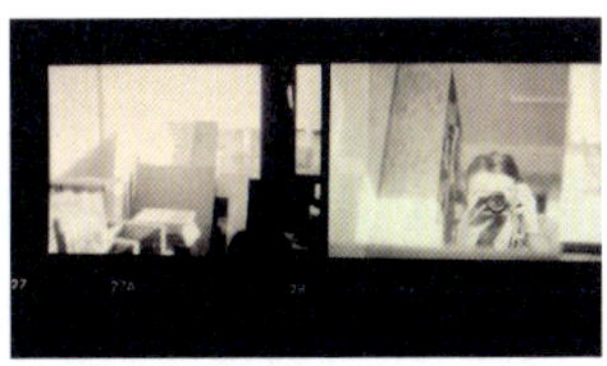
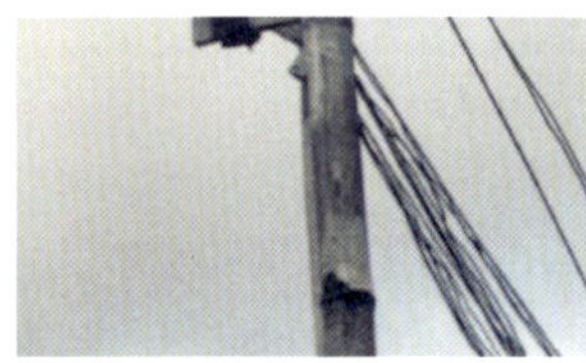
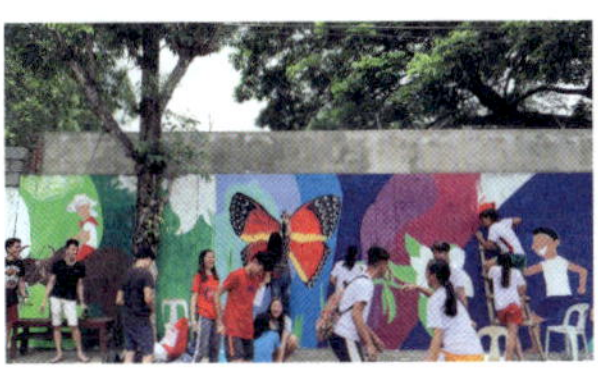
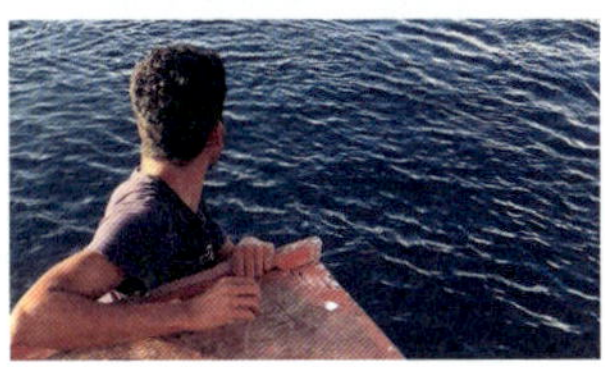
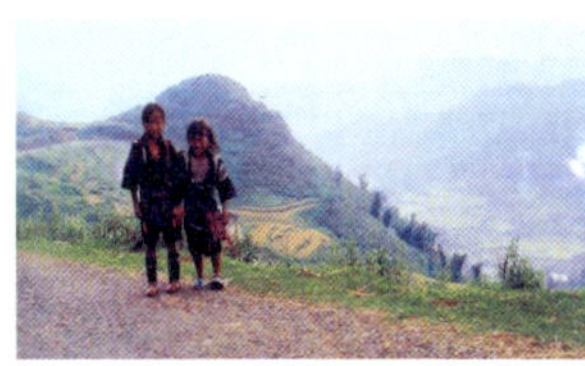
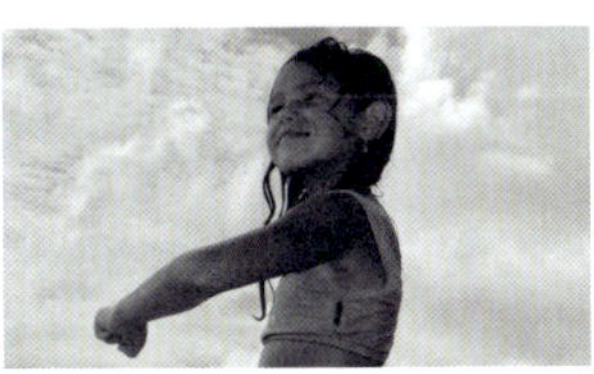
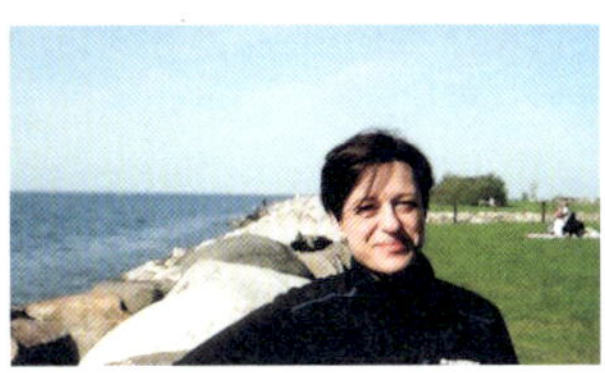
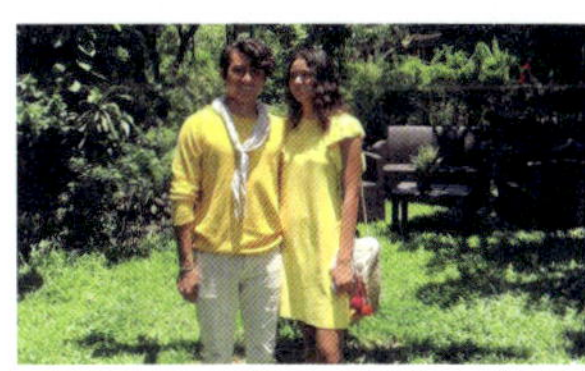

How Soon Is Soon?, 2020/21

LEONIE MIRJAM LINDINGER

2000 Richterswil, CH—Salzburg, AT

Collected photographs are at the center of my work. I asked friends from Asia and Europe if they could send me photographs relating to the four terms "eyes," "skin," "language," and "color." As a result, I obtained over a hundred photographs from:

Germany: Bremen, Frankfurt am Main
The Philippines: Manila, Laguna
Korea: Yangpyeong
Sweden: Bettna, Malmö
Switzerland: Bern, Zürich
USA: San Francisco

Why did someone choose a particular image? What would its significance be to that person? Such questions remain unanswered. The story that emerges in the video essay is associative and fragmentary. My own perspective is that of a 20-year-old *white* European woman. Working with other people's imagery has opened up additional perspectives for me. The selected text fragments were produced independently of the imagery.

In a conversation about racism, the question "Do you think this will change soon?" came up. Another person asked: "How soon is soon?" I've experienced working on this video essay as a question that likewise remains open. (LML)

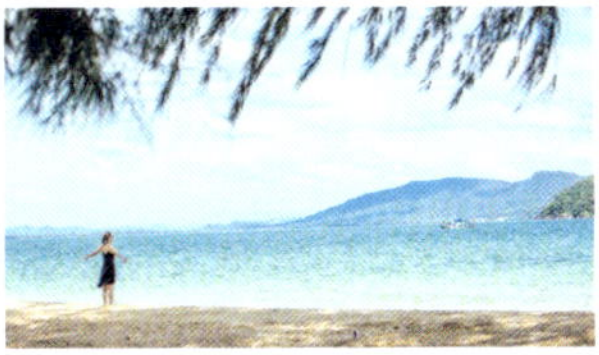

- Jessica Lee Seul — LAGUNA PH, YANGPYEONG KOR
- Beatrice Roth-Wyss — BERN CH ↝ VIETNAM
- Maxine Hayes Mejia — LAGUNA PH, MALMÖ SE
- Ronja Rühmkorff — FRANKFURT DE ↝ KAMBODSCHA/VIETNAM

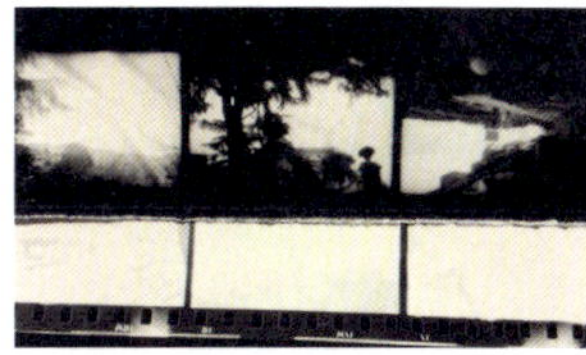

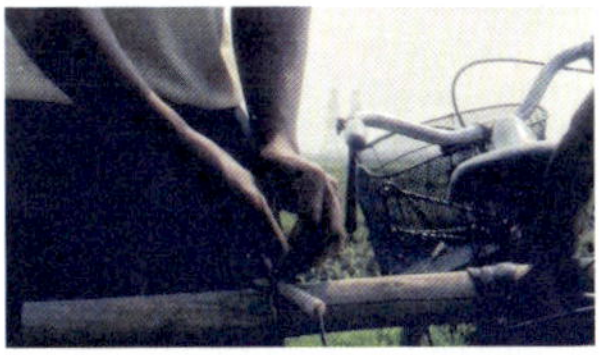

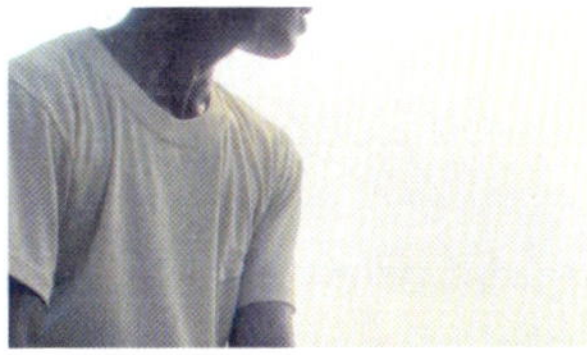

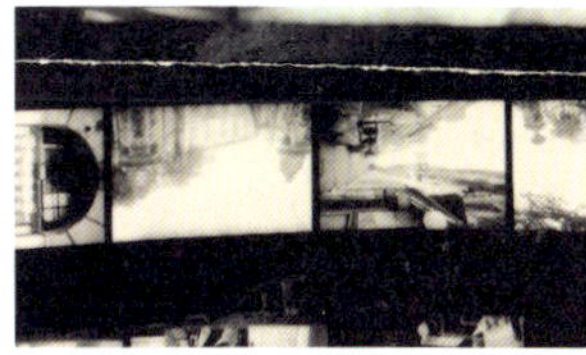

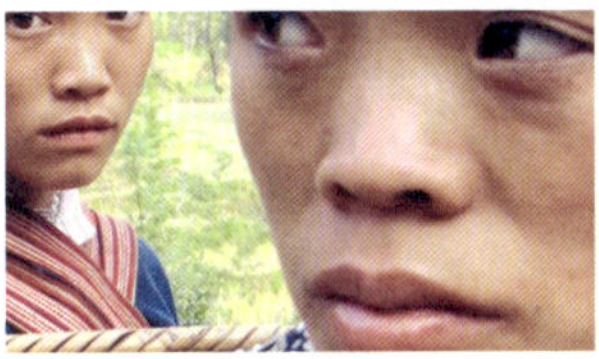

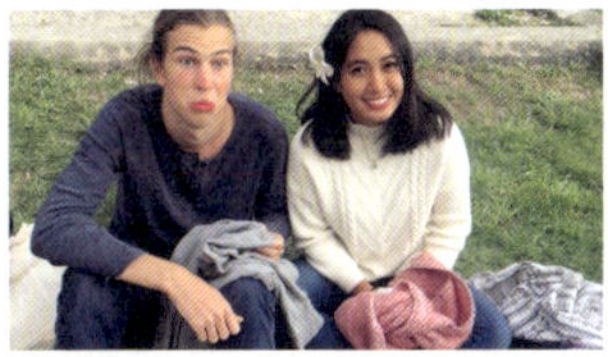

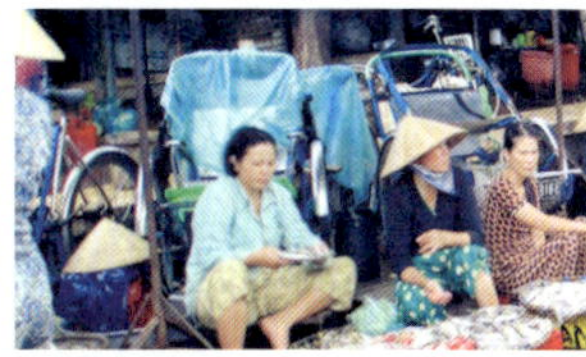

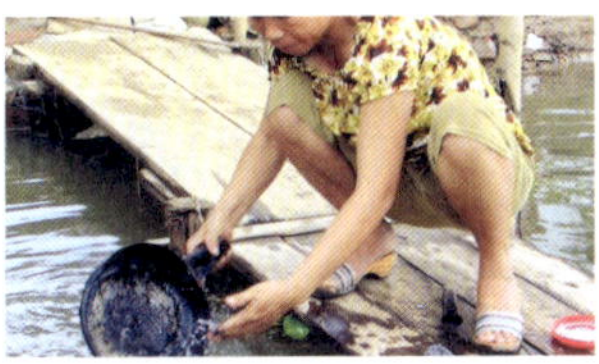

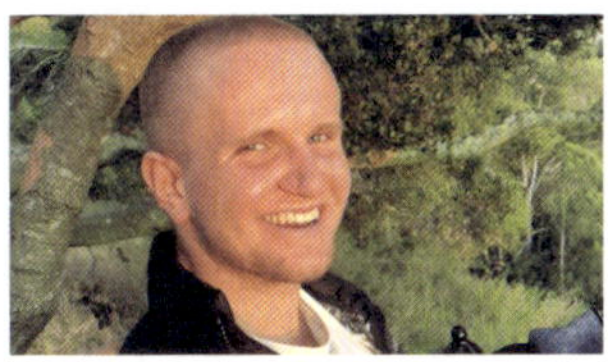

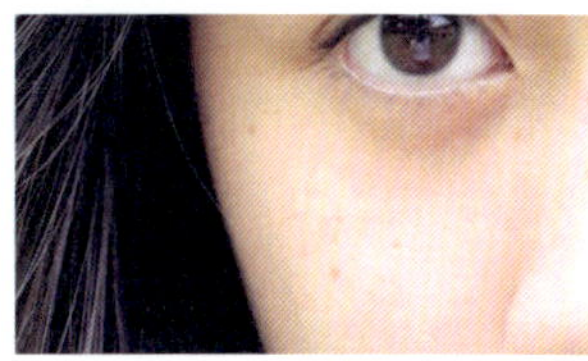

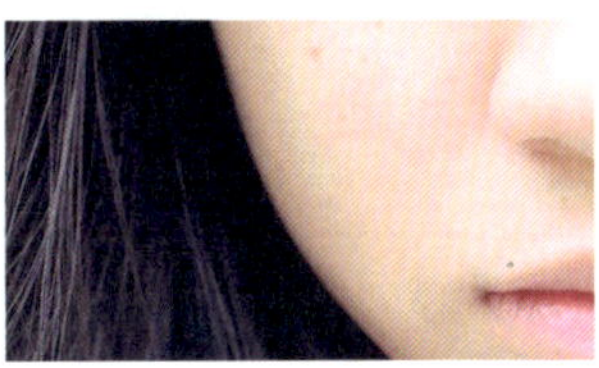

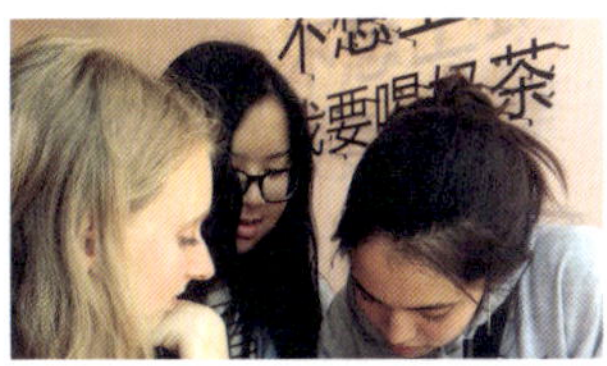

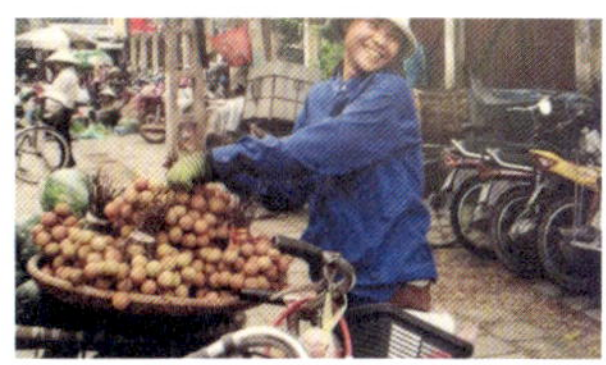

- Lukas Edelberg — SAN FRANCISCO USA, SCHAFFHAUSEN CH
- Johnnessa Rito — MANILA PH

Beatrice, Ronja, Maxine

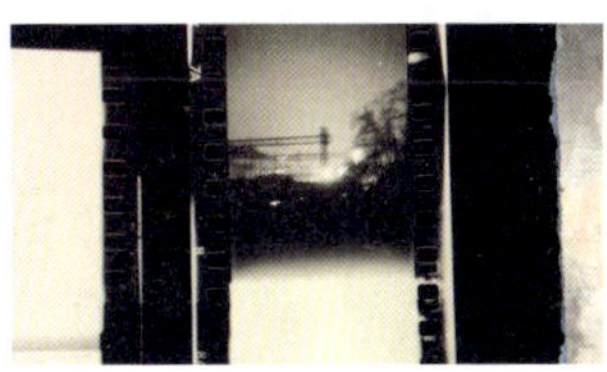

How Soon Is Soon?, 2020/21

CHARLOTTE PANN

1990 Salzburg, AT – Salzburg, AT

Die Projektionsfläche Kinoleinwand als Bildträger und Interaktionsbereich zwischen Film und Betrachter:in: Zu sehen sind gezeichnetes Filmmaterial sowie Found-Footage-Filmsequenzen, bestehend aus Handyaufnahmen, Bildern aus Überwachungskameras oder filmischen Dokumenten von Polizei-Körperkameras.

Im Fokus stehen Eric Garner, Charles Kinsey, Walter Scott, die Amokfahrt von Charlottesville, Menschen in Deutschland, Österreich, Großbritannien und der Schweiz, die sich ihren Lebensraum nicht mit „Fremden" teilen wollen und dies auch kundtun. Egal ob hier oder dort, wir alle teilen uns ein und denselben Handlungsraum. Ein Raum, der uns alle umspannt, uns vernetzt und uns so betroffen macht. Hier passieren Konflikt und Eskalation – und hier können Lösung und Konsens stattfinden. Das eigene Beteiligtsein steht so außer Frage, die eigene Ausrichtung – Hinwendung oder Abwendung – wird zur persönlichen Entscheidung. (CP)

CHARLOTTE PANN

1990 Salzburg, AT—Salzburg, AT

The cinema screen as a conveyor of imagery and site of interaction between film and viewer: On display is drawn film materials as well as sequences of found film footage consisting of cell phone recordings, images from surveillance cameras, as well as documentary footage from police body cameras.

The focus is on Eric Garner, Charles Kinsey, Walter Scott, the car rampage in Charlottesville, as well as people in Germany, Austria, Great Britain, and Switzerland who do not want to share their living space with "foreigners" and wish to make this known. It doesn't matter whether it's here or there, we all share one and the same space in which to act. A space encompassing us all, connecting us, and affecting us all. This is where conflict and escalation happen—and where resolution and consensus can also occur. Individual involvement is beyond question, and individual orientation—either turning toward or away—becomes a personal decision. (CP)

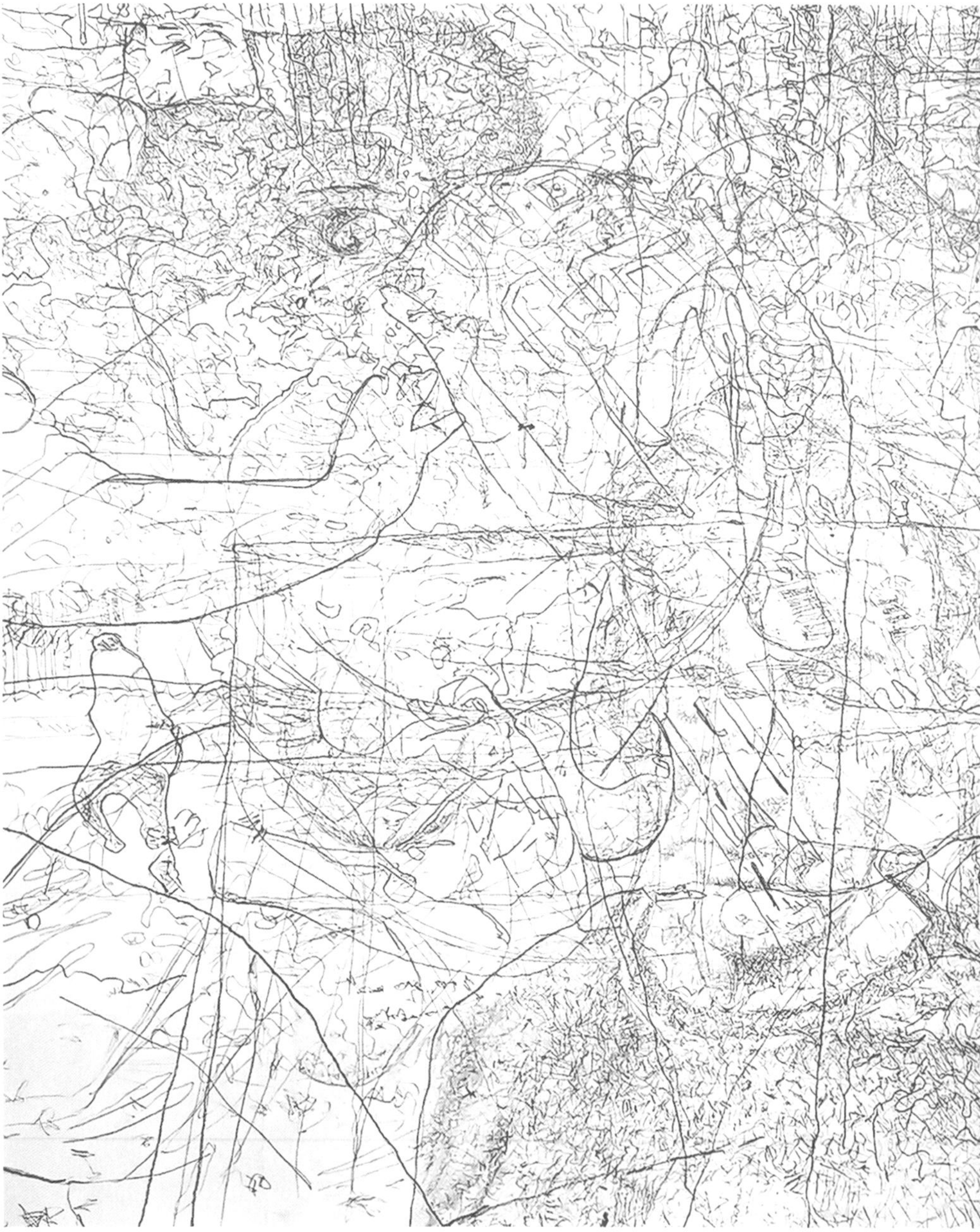

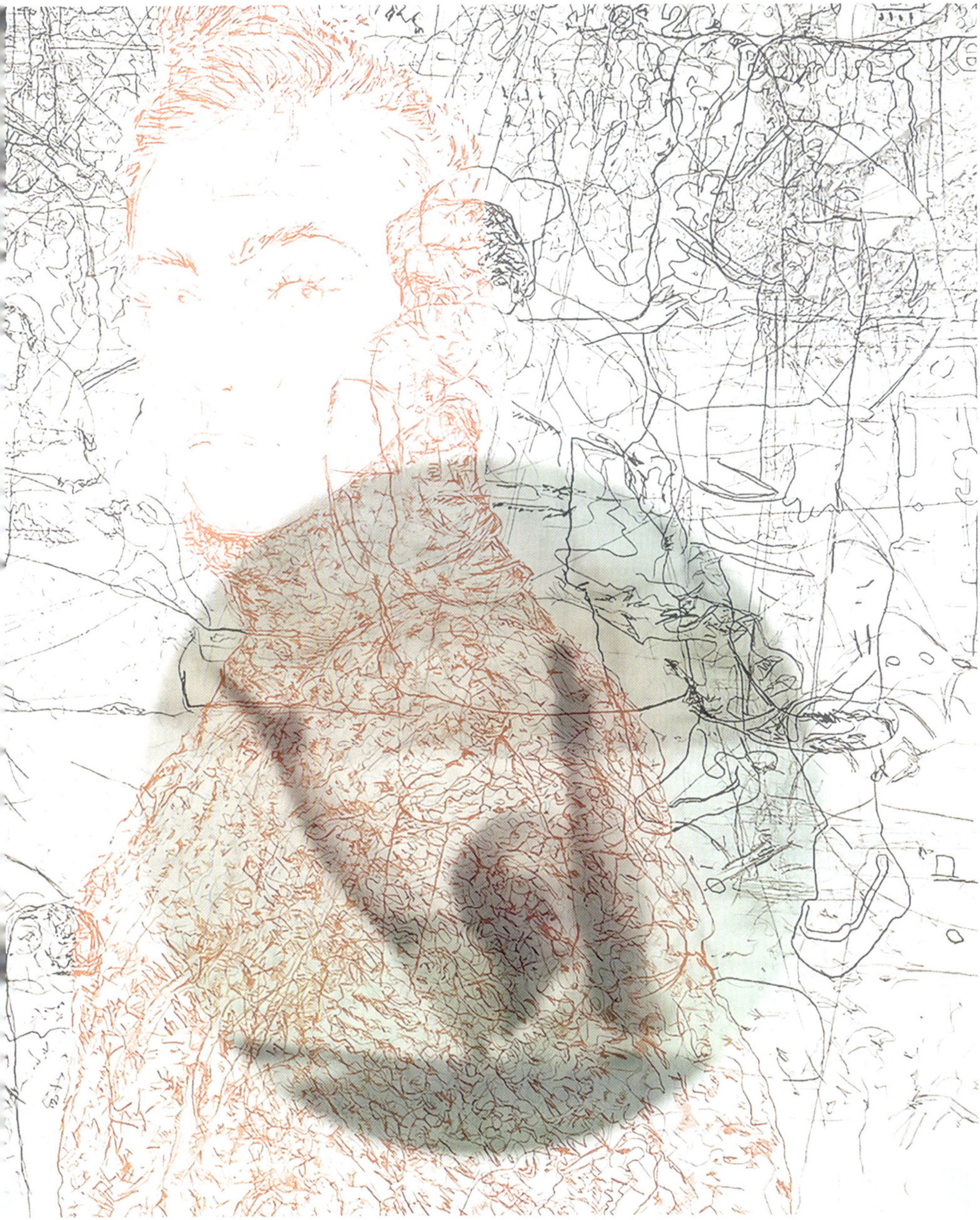

AUTOKINO, 2021

SABINE REISENBÜCHLER

1977 Salzburg, AT – Salzburg, AT

In meinem Video geht es um das Erbe, das in uns allen und in der gesamten Menschheitsgeschichte liegt. Die DNA erzählt über unsere Herkunft. Welche Geschichte tragen wir mit uns?

Es gab Zeiten ohne den patriarchalen Anspruch auf Besitznahme von Natur, Tieren und Menschen. Licht und Schatten führen uns und sollen von diesen Zeiten erzählen. Die Natur gibt uns eine Idee, wie es wohl gewesen sein könnte. Keine bessere oder schlechtere Herkunft, kein besserer oder schlechterer Schatten. Die Schatten sind dieselben, unterscheiden sich nur in ihrer Form und im Grad ihrer Dunkelheit. Um den Schatten zu sehen, braucht es Licht. Schattenspiele lassen vieles erahnen und erzählen Geschichten, nur das Licht bringt uns das Erkennen. Doch lassen wir uns nicht zu sehr blenden. Zu schnell gefällte Urteile, Kategorisierungen in Hell und Dunkel, Gut und Böse. Grauabstufungen erzählen von einem Dazwischen, das sich nicht einzuordnen vermag. In diese Welt der Zwischentöne entführt die Musik von Tanya Tagaq mit ihren Kehlkopfgesängen. Sie selbst ist Aktivistin, die sich unter anderem gegen Rassismus und für indigene Landrechte und indigenes Kulturgut einsetzt. Indem ich auf ihr Werk verweise, honoriere ich ihre Aktivität als Künstlerin. Genauso beziehe ich mich auf bell hooks, die sich in ihrer Arbeit mit Rassismus, Feminismus und Klassismus beschäftigt und diese Themen sehr umfangreich in ihren Büchern behandelt. Dabei geht sie immer von der eigenen Erfahrung der Grenzüberschreitung aus: Mit dem Übertritt in eine andere Klasse kann eine neue Freiheit erlangt werden. Ich möchte also von einem Erbe erzählen, das in uns allen schlummert und das wir nicht außer Acht lassen dürfen. (SR)

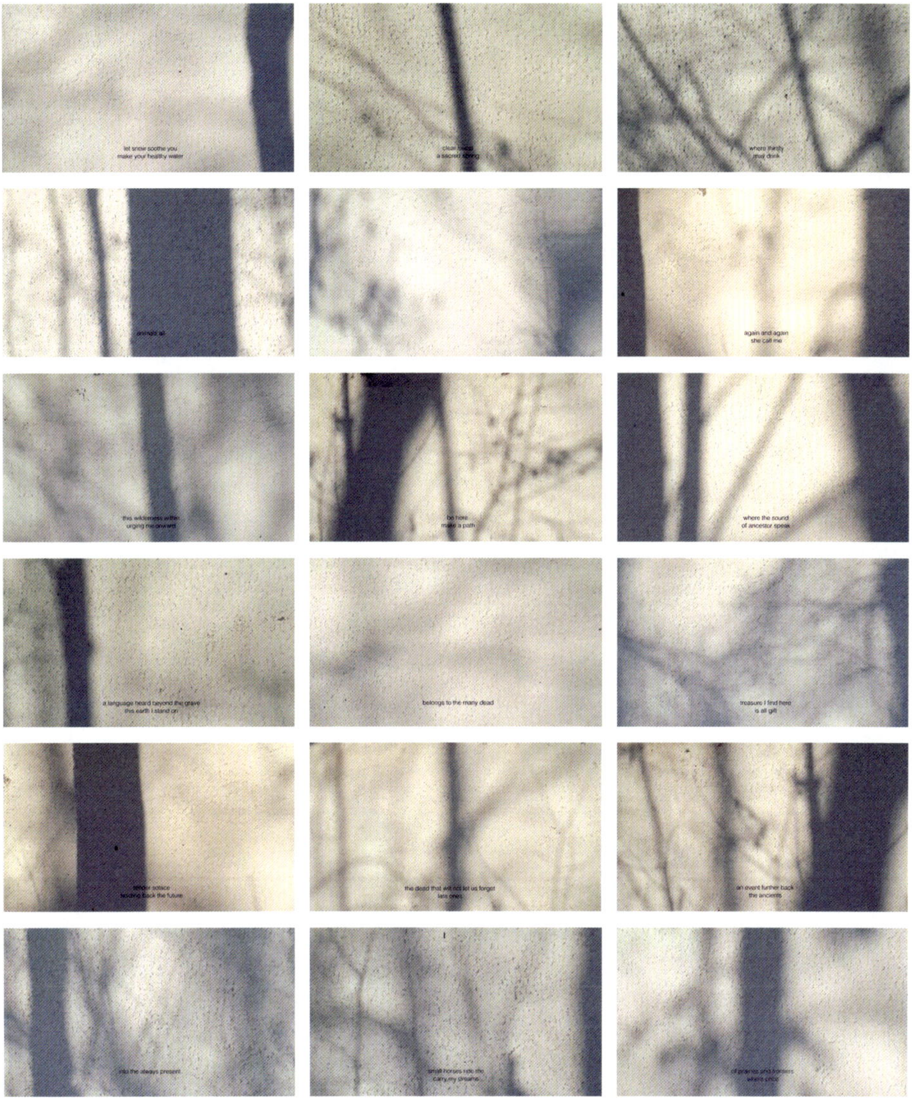

Appalachian Heritage – Shatter Your Hearts with Rain, 2021

SABINE REISENBÜCHLER

1977 Salzburg, AT—Salzburg, AT

My video concerns the heritage lying within all of us and throughout human history. DNA tells us about our origins. What is the history that we carry within us?

There were times that forwent any patriarchal right to take possession of nature, animals, and people. Light and shadow guide us, telling of such times. Nature provides us with an idea of how it might have been. No superior or inferior origins, no better or worse shadows. The shadows are the same, differing only in their form and degree of darkness. To see shadow, you need light. A play of shadows suggests much and narrates stories, but only light provides us with insight. But let's not be too dazzled. Judgments made too quickly, categorizations of light and dark, good and bad. Gray zones tell of something in between that cannot be classified. Tanya Tagaq's music of throat singing conveys the listener into such a world of nuances. She is herself an activist who campaigns against racism and for indigenous land rights as well as indigenous cultural assets, among other issues. In referencing her work, I'm seeking to honor her activities as an artist. I also make reference to bell hooks, who addresses racism, feminism, and classism in her work and confronts such matters extensively in her books. In doing so, she always begins with her own experience of crossing borders: In crossing to another class, a new freedom can be acquired. Consequently, I want to tell of a heritage that lies dormant in all of us, one that we must not ignore. (SR)

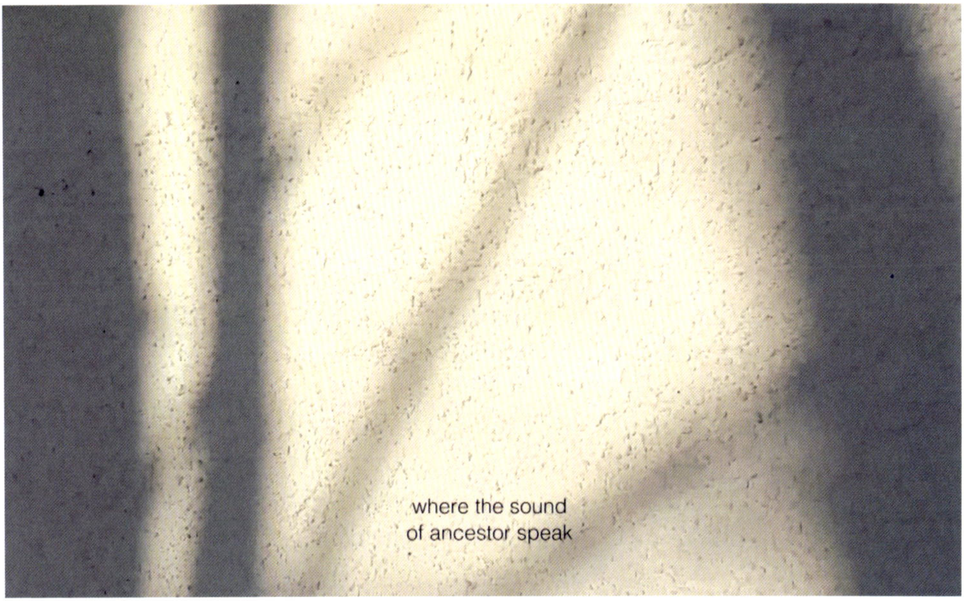

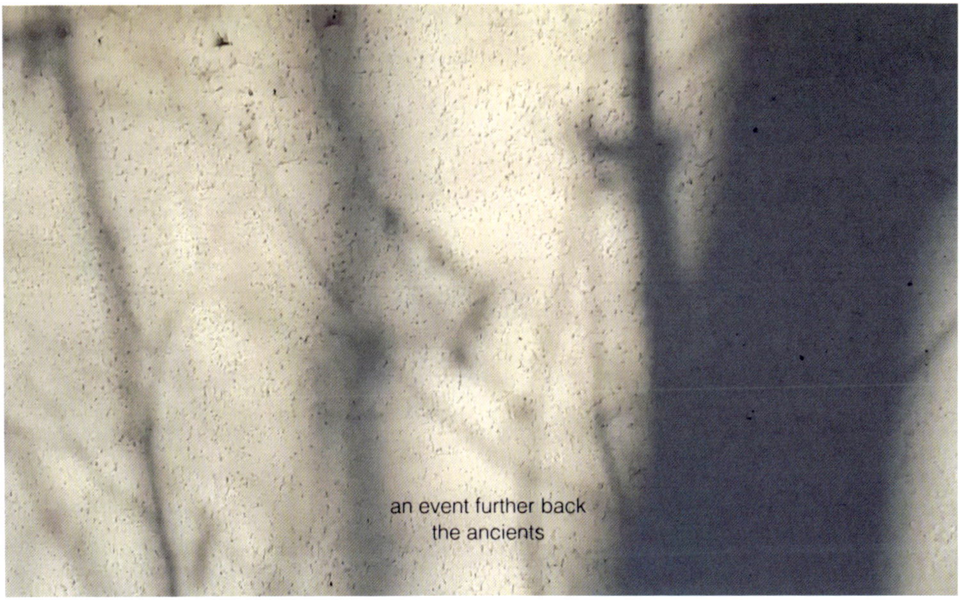

Appalachian Heritage – Shatter Your Hearts with Rain, 2021

EVA-MARIA SCHITTER

1993 Oberndorf, AT – Salzburg, AT

Hierarchisch, rassistisch, diskriminierend. So lässt sich das System beschreiben, in dem wir leben. Ich war mir lange nicht bewusst, dass ich als weiße Europäerin trotz meiner scharfen und expliziten Ablehnung rassistischer Handlungsweisen dennoch Teil dieses Gliederungsprinzips bin. Die Bettlerin, die vor der Eingangstüre meines Wohnhauses sitzt, ist jene Person, die mir durch ihre Präsenz in unmittelbarster Form vor Augen führt, wie sehr ich in diese wüsten Strukturen eingewoben bin. Die Erkenntnis darüber ist keine angenehme. Ich setze mich in meiner Arbeit dem Unbehagen, dem schlechten Gewissen und den Schuldgefühlen aus, die ich empfinde, wenn ich an ihr vorübergehe oder von meinem Zimmer auf sie herabschaue.

„Ich schaue hin und ich fühl mich schuldig und schlecht – jedes Mal, wenn ich mit zwei Fingern den Digitalzoom meines Smartphones auf sein Maximum aufdrehe, damit ich sie möglichst groß auf den Fotos abbilden kann. Ich schaue hin, bedauere ihre Situation und unternehme nichts. Ich schaue nur."
(EMS)

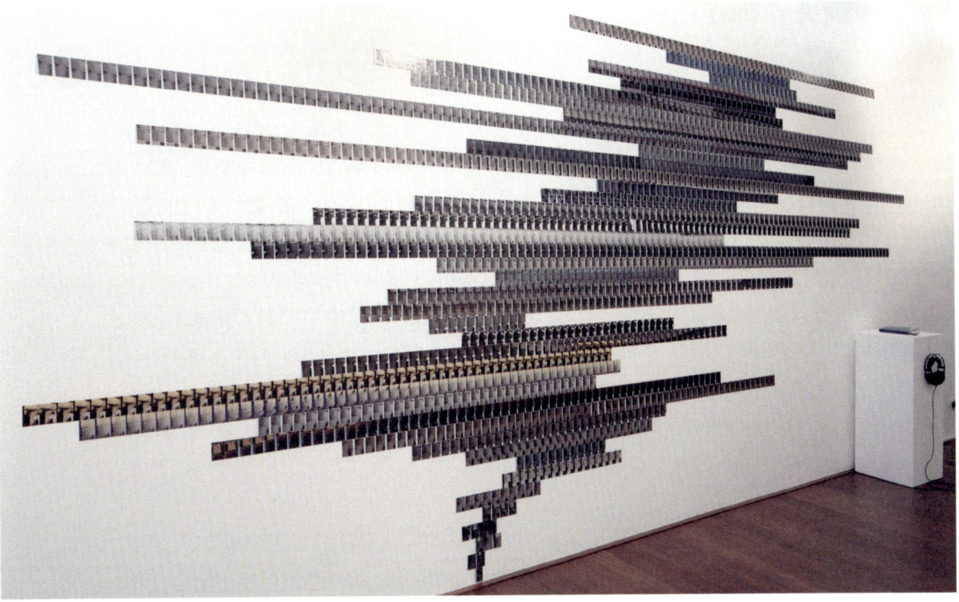

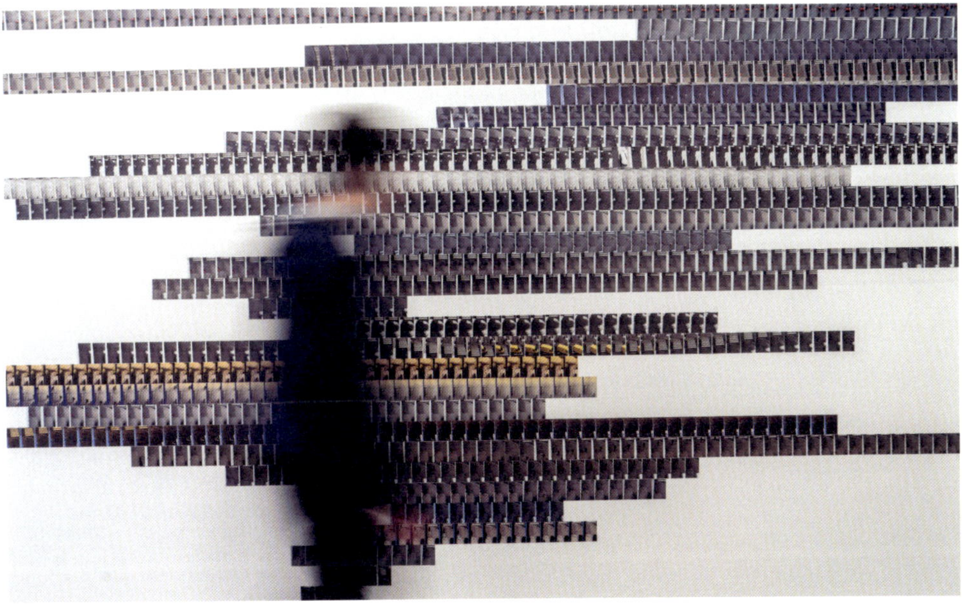

Ich über mich über ihr über sie, 2020/21

EVA-MARIA SCHITTER

1993 Oberndorf, AT—Salzburg, AT

Hierarchical, racist, discriminatory. This is how we could describe the system in which we live. For a long time, I was unaware that, as a *white* European woman, despite my strict and explicit rejection of racist behavior, I was still a part of this structure. The beggar sitting in front of the door to my building is the person who, through her presence, demonstrates to me in the most direct form how much I am woven into these tangled structures. Such a realization is not a pleasant one. In my work, I expose myself to the discomfort, bad conscience, and guilt that I feel when I walk past her or look down on her from my room.

"I look and I feel guilty and bad—every time I use two fingers to turn the digital zoom of my smartphone up to its maximum so that I can capture her as large as possible in the photographs. I look, regret her situation, and do nothing. I'm just looking." (EMS)

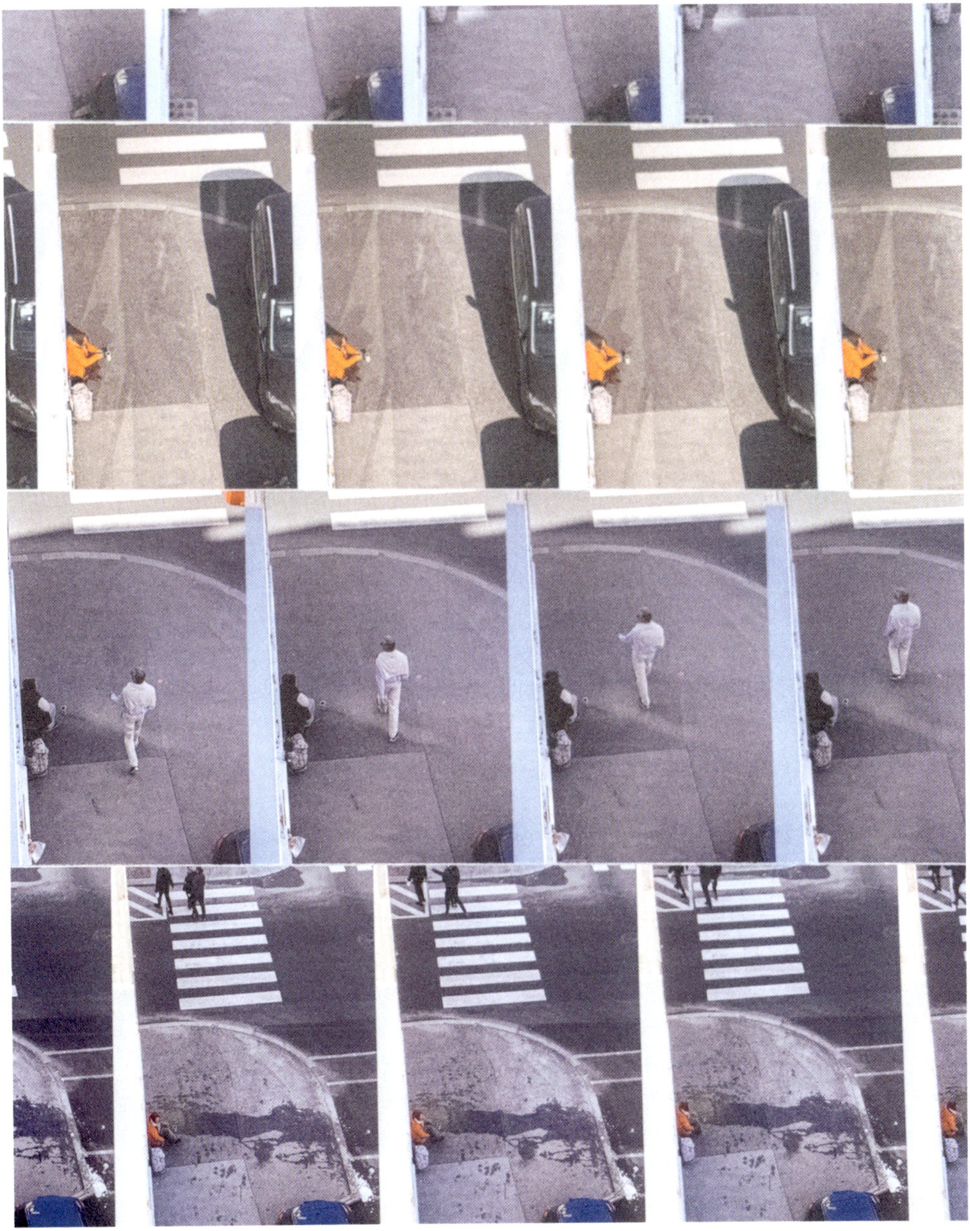

Ich über mich über ihr über sie, 2020/21

SCULPTING FEMINISM READING GROUP

Gegründet 2020 in Salzburg, AT

Das Vorlesen (vor einer Zuhörer:innenschaft laut zu lesen und umgekehrt auch Zuhörende:r zu sein) ist der Aspekt, der im Zentrum der Aktivitäten der Sculpting Feminism Reading Group steht. Das gemeinsame Lesen erzeugt eine Atmosphäre, die emotionaler ist, als wenn allein gelesen wird. Durch die individuelle Stimme, den Akzent, die Intonation sowie die eigene Lesegeschwindigkeit machen die Lesenden die Texte physisch erfahrbar und fügen ihnen eine persönliche Komponente hinzu.

Das ganze Jahr hindurch haben wir in einem hybriden Setting gelesen: Nur ein einziges Mal, zu Beginn des Wintersemesters, hatten wir die Möglichkeit, uns an der Universität – im realen Raum – zu treffen. Danach waren wir auf Online-Meetings beschränkt, auch wenn sich gelegentlich einige der Teilnehmenden einen Raum oder den Bildschirm teilten (an der Uni, bei sich zu Hause). Über die diversen Lockdowns hinweg war und ist die Gruppe ein sicherer und vertrauter Raum, um einander zu begegnen und im Anschluss an die Lesungen gemeinsam die Veränderungen zu diskutieren, die in der Gesellschaft zurzeit vor sich gehen – in Zusammenhang mit dem Virus, aber auch unabhängig davon. Gemeinsam erschaffen wir Zusammenhalt und Vertrautheit und freuen uns darüber, einander regelmäßig zu sehen.

Jeden Mittwoch von 18 bis 18:45 Uhr wurden von einer/einem oder mehreren Teilnehmenden via Videokonferenz Texte vorgelesen, ausgewählt aus unserer immer länger werdenden feministischen Leseliste. Die Museumsbesucher:innen waren eingeladen, vor Ort teilzunehmen und in der Franz-West-Lounge zuzuhören oder sich online zuzuschalten. Im Anschluss an jeden Mittwochabend waren die gelesenen und aufgenommenen Texte für die darauffolgende Woche im Rahmen der Ausstellung zu hören.
(SFRG)

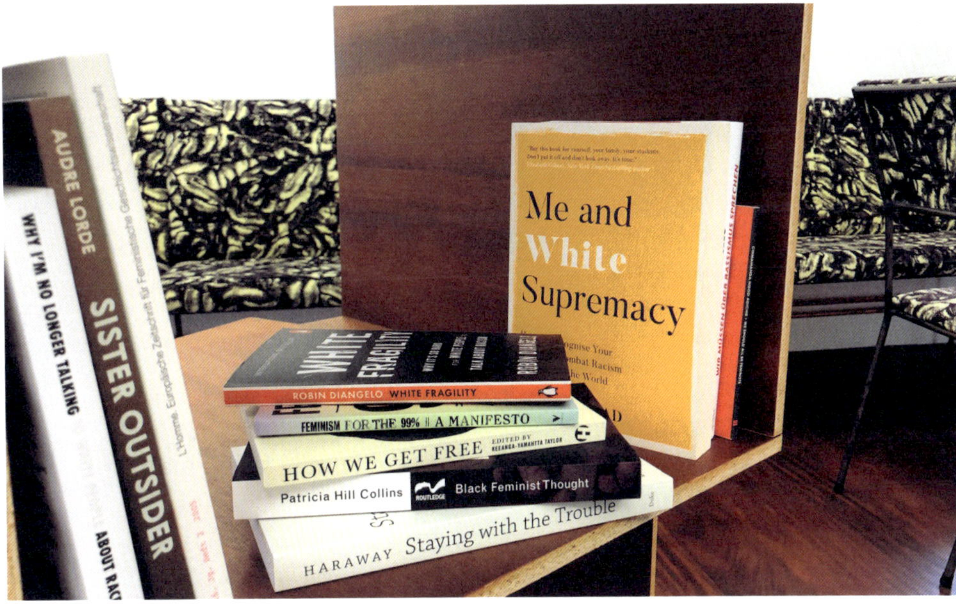

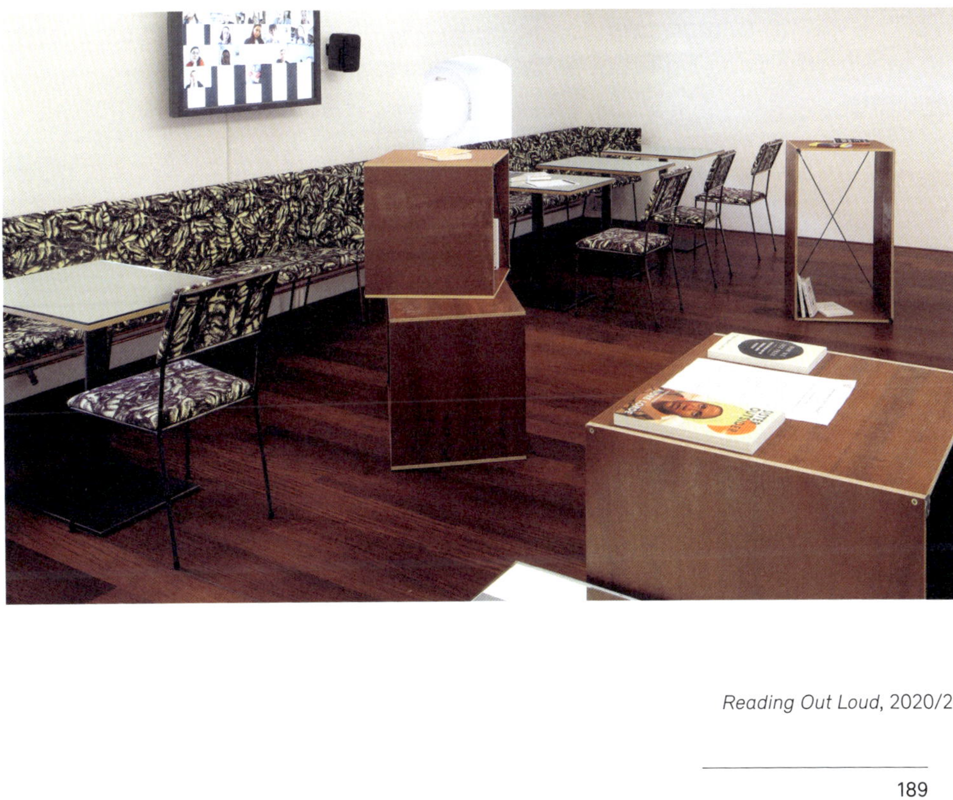

Reading Out Loud, 2020/21

SCULPTING FEMINISM READING GROUP

Founded 2020 in Salzburg, AT

Reading out loud (as well as listening and being listened to) is the core work of the Sculpting Feminism Reading Group. This sets up a more emotional atmosphere than reading alone. Each reader, through their different voices, accents, tonalities, and speeds of reading, adds something physical, as well as personal, to the chosen texts.

Throughout the year, we have performed in a hybrid setting: We only met once, at the beginning of the fall semester, in real space. From then, we were limited to Zoom, but occasionally some members of the group would share a room and a Zoom window (at the university or at their homes). During the various lockdowns, the group was, and still is, a safe and intimate space to meet and, following the readings, discuss the changes that are happening in society, both related and unrelated to the virus. We are creating togetherness and mutual empathy, pleased to come together regularly.

Every Wednesday from 6 to 6:45 p.m., one or more members of the group read texts, chosen from an expanding feminist reading list, via Zoom. Visitors to the museum were invited to participate on-site from the Franz West Lounge or to join online. Following each Wednesday evening, the read and recorded texts were available to listen to for the following week as part of the exhibition.
(SFRG)

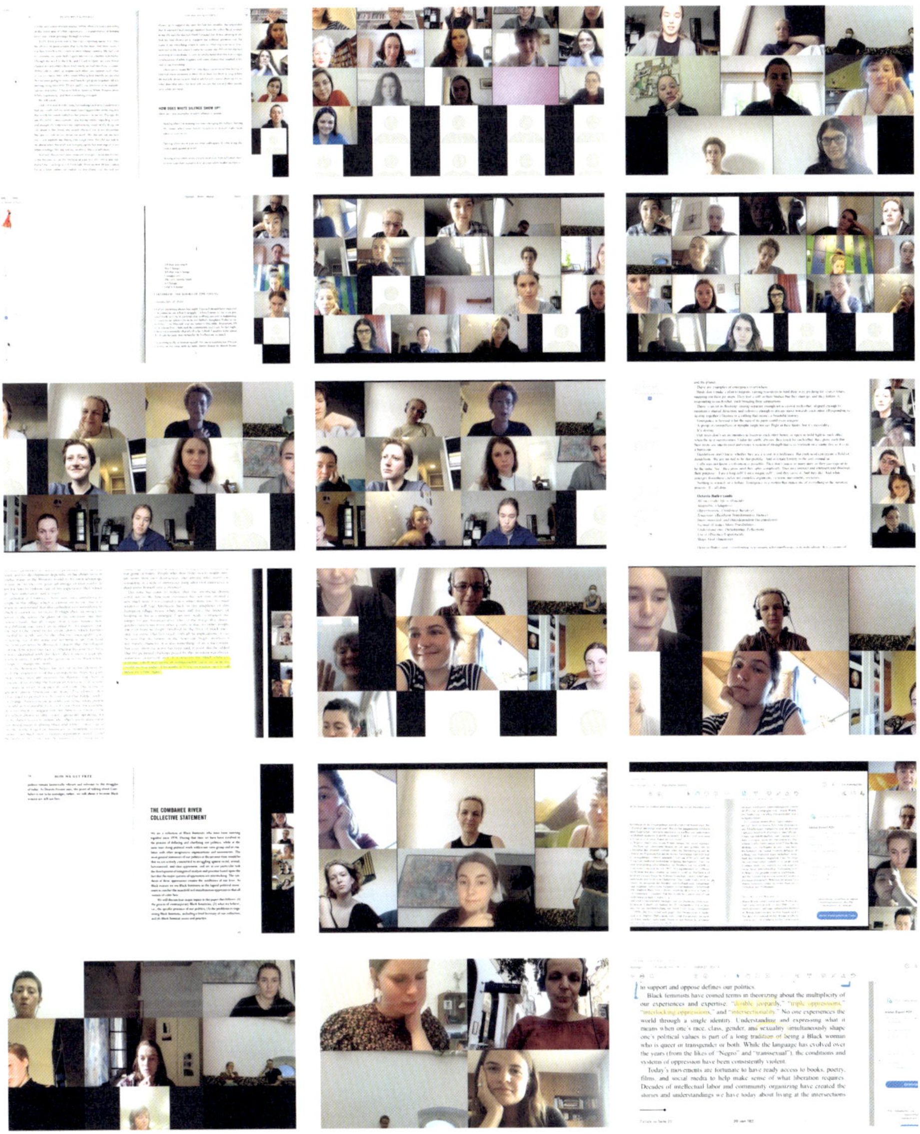

Reading Out Loud, 2020/21

LESELISTE / READING LIST SCULPTING FEMINISM READING GROUP

- Chimamanda Ngozi Adichie, *Mehr Feminismus. Ein Manifest und vier Stories*, Frankfurt am Main: Fischer, 2016.
- Chimamanda Ngozi Adichie, *We Should All Be Feminists*, London: Fourth Estate, 2014.
- Susan Arndt et al., Hg. / eds., *Mythen, Masken und Subjekte. Kritische Weißseinsforschung in Deutschland*, 4. Aufl. / 4th ed., Münster: Unrast, 2020.
- Cinzia Arruzza, Tithi Bhattacharya, Nancy Fraser, *Feminism for the 99%. A Manifesto*, London, New York: Verso, 2019.
- James Baldwin, „Stranger in the Village", in: James Baldwin, *Collected Essays*, New York: The Library of America, 1998, S. / pp. 117–129.
- Adrienne Maree Brown, *Emergent Strategy. Shaping Change, Changing Worlds*, Chico, Edinburgh: AK Press, 2017.
- Octavia E. Butler, *Parable of the Sower*, London: Headline, 2019.
- Octavia E. Butler, *Kindred*, London: Headline, 2018.
- Charlene A. Carruthers, *Unapologetic. A Black, Queer, and Feminist Mandate for Radical Movements*, Boston: Beacon Press, 2018.
- Combahee River Collective, „A Black Feminist Statement (United States, 1977)", in: *The Essential Feminist Reader*, Hg. / ed. Estelle B. Freedman, New York: The Modern Library, 2007, S. / pp. 325–330.
- Angela Davis, *Freiheit ist ein ständiger Kampf*, Münster: Unrast, 2016.
- Robin DiAngelo, *White Fragility. Why It's So Hard for White People to Talk About Racism*, London: Allen Lane, 2019.
- Reni Eddo-Lodge, *Warum ich nicht länger mit Weißen über Hautfarbe spreche*, 4. Aufl. / 4th ed., Stuttgart: Tropen, 2020.
- Reni Eddo-Lodge, *Why I'm No Longer Talking to White People about Race*, London: Bloomsbury, 2018.
- Bernardine Evaristo, *Girl, Woman, Other*, London: Hamish Hamilton, 2019.
- Brigitte Fuchs, Gabriele Habinger, Hg. / eds., *Rassismen & Feminismen. Differenzen, Machtverhältnisse und Solidarität zwischen Frauen*, Wien / Vienna: Promedia, 1996.
- Roxane Gay, *Hunger. A Memoir of (My) Body*, New York: HarperCollins, 2017.
- Hanna Hacker, „Nicht weiß weiß nicht. Übergänge zwischen Critical White-

ness Studies und feministischer Theorie“, in: *L’Homme. Europäische Zeitschrift für feministische Geschichtswissenschaft: Whiteness*, Bd. / vol. 16, Nr. / no. 2 (2005), S. / pp. 13–27.

- Donna J. Haraway, *Unruhig bleiben. Die Verwandtschaft der Arten im Chthuluzän*, Frankfurt am Main, New York: Campus, 2018.
- Donna J. Haraway, *Staying with the Trouble. Making Kin in the Chthulucene*, Durham, London: Duke University Press, 2016.
- Alice Hasters, *Was weiße Menschen nicht über Rassismus hören wollen, aber wissen sollten*, München: hanserblau, 2019.
- Patricia Hill Collins, *Black Feminist Thought. Knowledge, Consciousness, and the Politics of Empowerment*, London, New York: Routledge 2009.
- bell hooks, *Talking Back. Thinking Feminist, Thinking Black*, New York, London: Routledge, 2015.
- bell hooks, *Feminism Is for Everybody. Passionate Politics*, London: Pluto Press, 2000.
- Belinda Kazeem, „Energie Sparen!“, in: *Conzepte*, 2011, http://www.conzepte.org/home.php?il=51&l=deu (03.12.2021).
- Audre Lorde, *Sister Outsider. Essays and Speeches*, Berkeley: Crossing Press, 2007.
- Layla F Saad, *Me and White Supremacy. How to Recognise Your Privilege, Combat Racism and Change the World*, London: Quercus, 2020.
- Keeanga-Yamahtta Taylor, Hg. / ed., *How We Get Free. Black Feminism and the Combahee River Collective*, Chicago: Haymarket Books, 2017.
- Sojourner Truth, „Ain’t I a Woman? – May 29, 1851“, in: *Iowa State University. Archives of Women’s Political Communication*, o. J. / n. d., https://awpc.cattcenter.iastate.edu/2017/03/21/aint-i-a-woman-may-291851/ (03.12.2021).

THIS WORLD IS EGO NO LONGER

Salzburg, AT

Es werden hier eigene Erfahrungen sowie Beobachtungen von Gewaltphänomenen in Bereichen aufgegriffen, die meist unberührt bleiben. Das Thema Gewalt an Personen, die nicht der „gängigen Norm“ entsprechen, zieht sich durch die Arbeit; beleuchtet werden tabuisierte öffentliche und private Räume in Österreich. Sie erzählen zum Beispiel von Covid-Folgeerscheinungen, von zugesperrten Krankenhausabteilungen, von tagtäglichen Diskriminierungen an Menschen, die aufgrund von psychiatrisch-medizinisch oder psycho(logisch)-therapeutisch bedingten Stigmatisierungen in unserer Gesellschaft behindert werden. Abgerundet wird die Arbeit von ganz persönlichen, kraftvollen Überlebensstrategien durch Kunst und Liebe zu den Tieren. (twiENl)

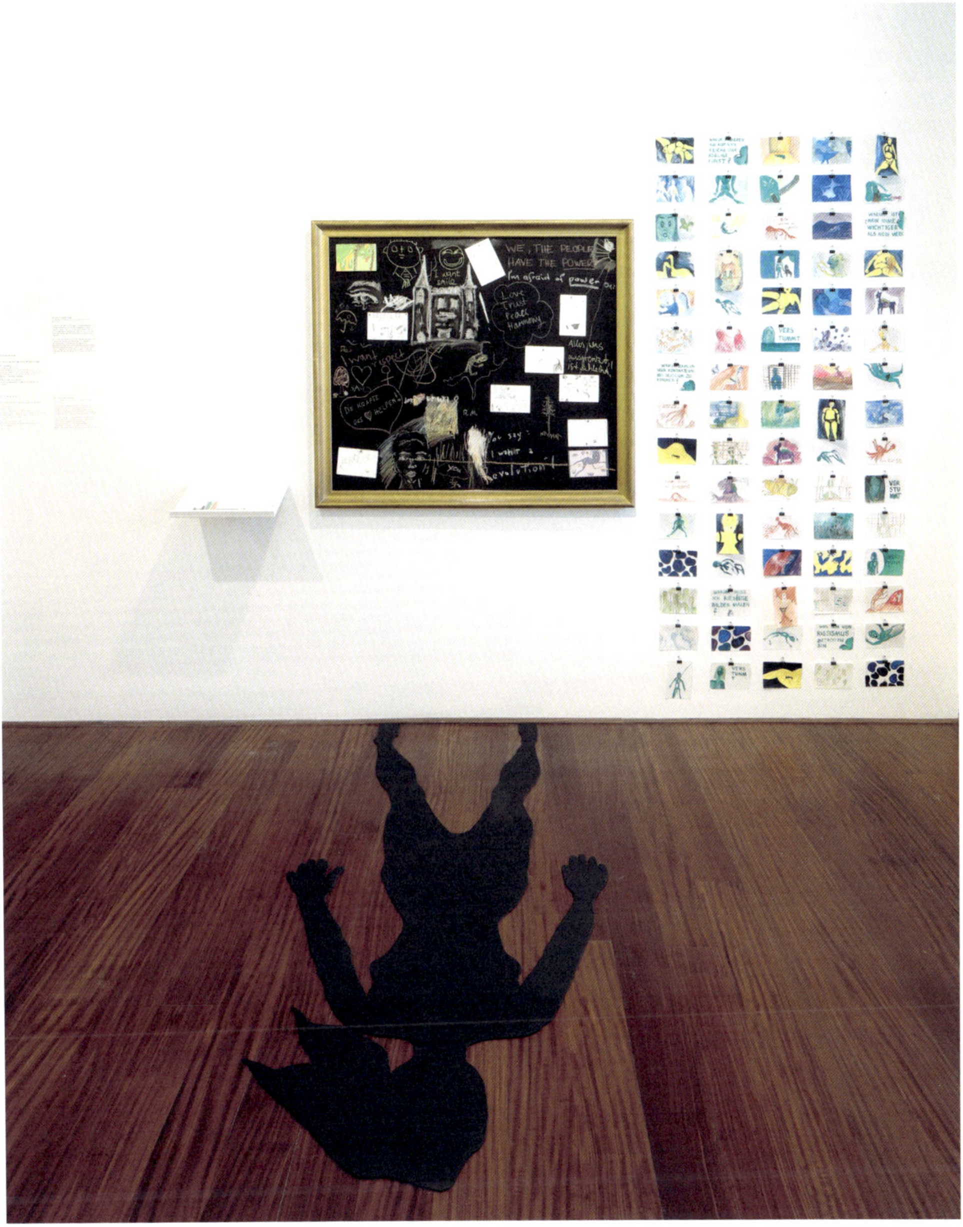

this (art) world is Ego No longer and never will be again, 2020/21

THIS WORLD IS EGO NO LONGER

Salzburg, AT

Here personal experiences as well as observations of violent phenomena in areas that mostly remain unexamined are addressed. The issue of violence against people who don't correspond to "prevailing norms" permeates the work; light is shed on public and private spaces that remain taboo in Austria. They tell, for example, of the after-effects of Covid, locked hospital departments, and everyday discrimination against people who are impeded in our society due to psychiatric/medical or psycho(-logical) therapeutic stigmatization. The work is rounded off by very personal, powerful survival strategies involving art and a love of animals.
(twiENl)

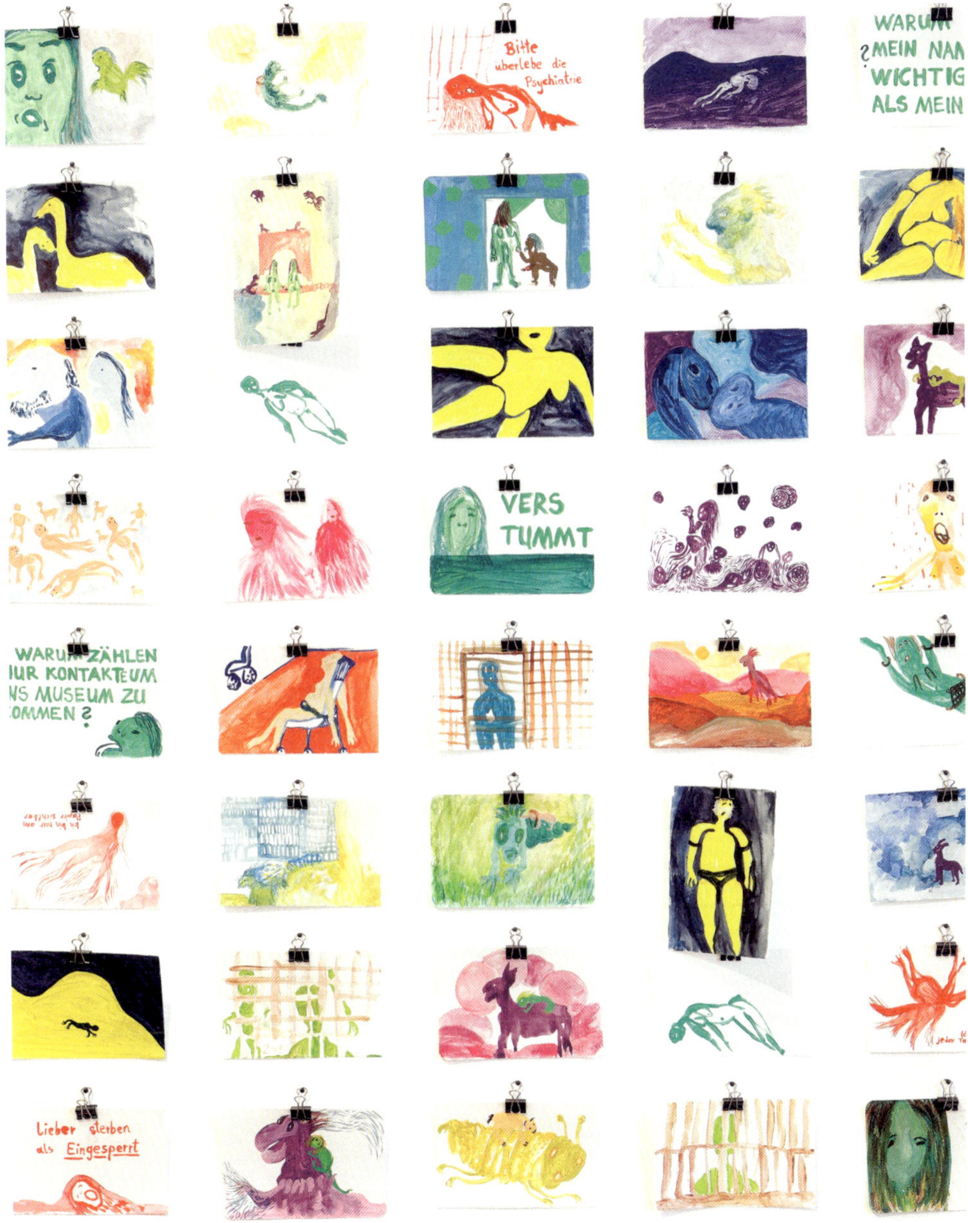

this (art) world is Ego No longer and never will be again, 2020/21

ANGELIKA WIENERROITHER

1986 Bad Ischl, AT – Salzburg, AT

Utopia beschäftigt sich mit einer Welt, in der eine Woman of Color an der Macht ist. Zwei Protagonistinnen, Mirjam Helminger und Christine Bayer-Borrero, erzählen in einem Gespräch von ihrem gesellschaftlichen Idealzustand. Auf den Fotografien tragen sie die Kostüme von König:innen. Sie erscheinen mit Dingen und Symbolen, die ihnen Macht verleihen. Zudem zeigen die Bilder Zwischenmomente, in denen die Protagonistinnen von ihrer perfekten Welt träumen. Ihre Gedanken hat Christine auch auf Karteikärtchen visualisiert. Um zu erfahren, wie sich Macht vielleicht anfühlt, hat die Künstlerin selbst einen Offiziersmantel angezogen.

An der Wand hängt eine Fotografie, die zerrissen ist. Sie zeigt Ida Wells-Barnett (1862–1931). Die Frauenrechtsaktivistin wurde als Sklavin geboren, sechs Monate nach ihrer Geburt wurde die Sklaverei abgeschafft. Als Journalistin argumentierte sie, dass Lynchmorde an People of Color in den USA keine Taten von Extremisten waren, sondern dazu dienten, das gesellschaftliche System zu erhalten.

Der Untertitel *Why can't we just get along?* bezieht sich auf eine Aussage von Rodney King. Die Polizei von Los Angeles prügelte 1991 auf den Afroamerikaner ein – und löste damit Unruhen und Proteste aus. In einem Interview sprach sich King später gegen Gewalt aus und fragte, ob wir nicht einfach miteinander auskommen können. (AW)

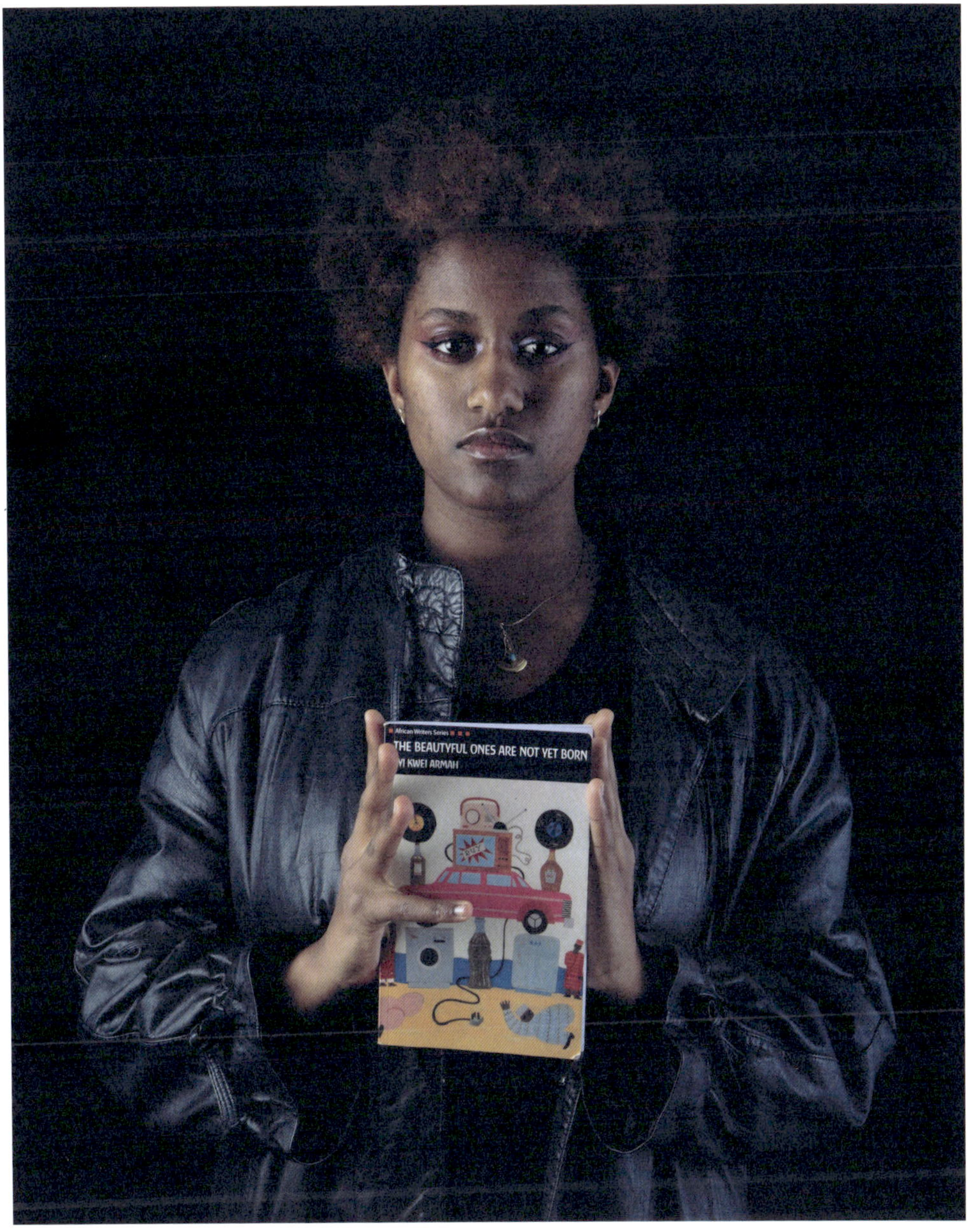

Utopia (Why can't we just get along?), 2021

ANGELIKA WIENERROITHER

1986 Bad Ischl, AT—Salzburg, AT

Utopia concerns a world in which a woman of color is in power. Two protagonists, Mirjam Helminger and Christine Bayer-Borrero, talk about how they would rule if they were in charge. In the photographs they are wearing the costumes of kings. They are depicted with items and symbols that invest them with power. In addition, the imagery shows moments in between, in which the protagonists dream of their perfect world. Christine also visualized her thoughts on index cards. To find out what power might feel like, the artist wore an officer's coat.

A photograph hangs on the wall that is torn. It shows Ida Wells-Barnett (1862–1931). The women's rights activist was born a slave; however, slavery was abolished just six months after her birth. As a journalist, she argued that the lynchings of people of color in the United States were not the acts of extremists—but that they served to preserve the social system.

The subtitle *Why can't we just get along?* refers to a statement by Rodney King. The Los Angeles police had beaten the African-American in 1991—resulting in riots and protests. In an interview, King later spoke out against violence, asking if we couldn't all just get along with each other. (AW)

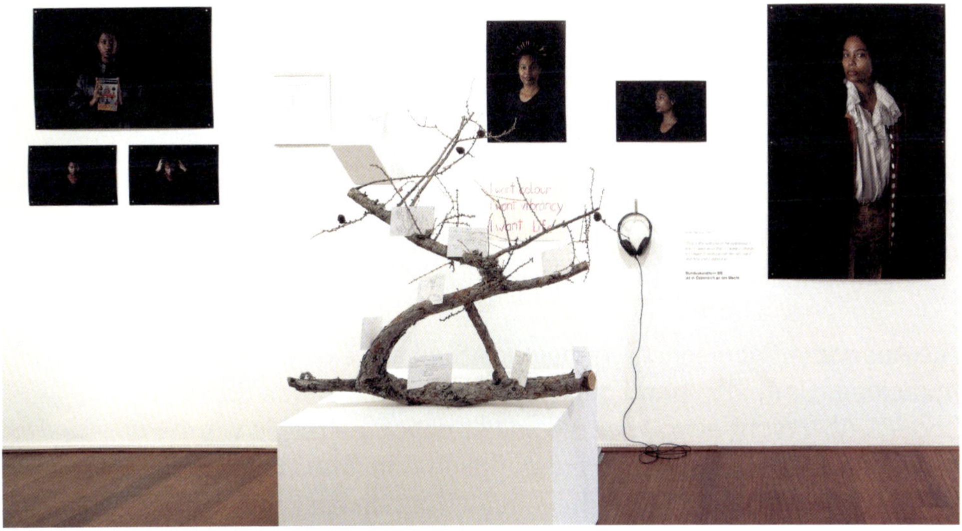

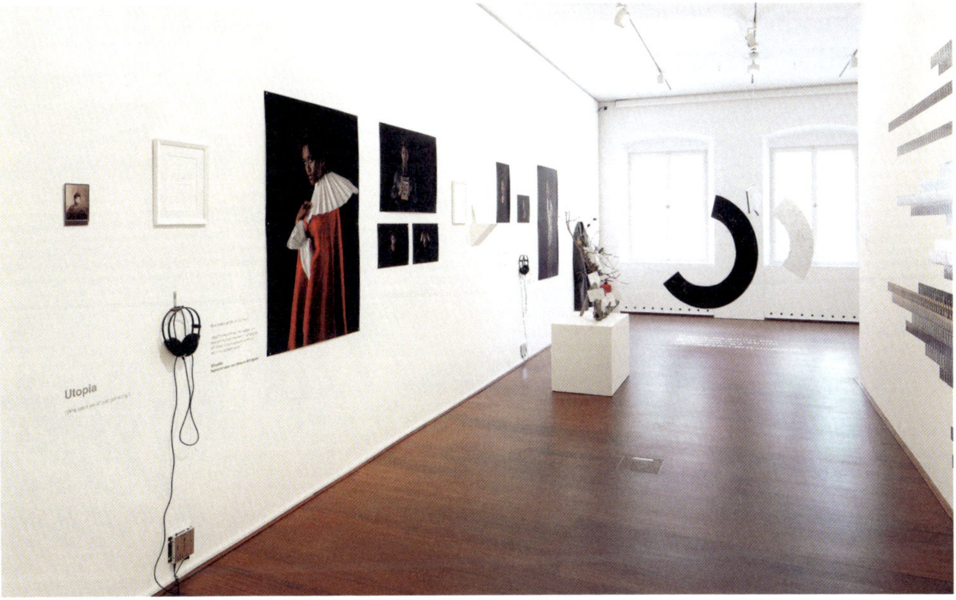

Utopia (Why can't we just get along?), 2021

JUDITH ZAUNSCHIRM

Salzburg, AT

Was kann ich aus meiner Position – als weiße Studentin in einer kleinen österreichischen Stadt – überhaupt zu einem Thema wie Rassismus öffentlich sagen oder zeigen, ohne in irgendeiner Weise das Leid anderer für eigene Zwecke zu nutzen oder Aktivismus vorzutäuschen? Diese und ähnliche Fragen führten zu Anfangsschwierigkeiten bei meiner persönlichen künstlerischen Auseinandersetzung mit dem Thema.

Als Ausweg entschied ich, in meiner Arbeit die einzige Person in meinem Umfeld in den Fokus zu nehmen, die etwas dazu zu sagen hat – nicht etwa, weil sie selbst davon betroffen wäre, sondern weil sie beruflich beinahe täglich damit beschäftigt ist. Sie ist Polizistin und ihre Erzählungen zeichnen ein komplexes subjektives Bild. Stellt man ihrem Einzelfall öffentlich zugängliche Informationen (Zeitungsartikel, Statistiken etc.) zur Seite, wird das Bild noch vielschichtiger. (JZ)

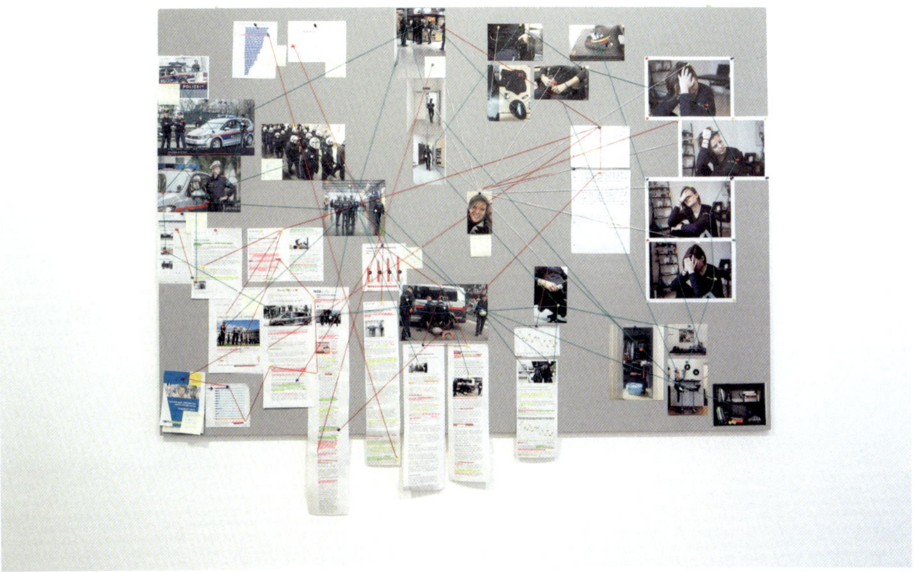

Ein ungelöster Fall, 2020/21

JUDITH ZAUNSCHIRM

Salzburg, AT

What can I possibly say or display in public from my position—as a *white* student in a small Austrian city—concerning an issue such as racism without in any way using the suffering of others for my own purposes, or pretending it is activism? This and similar questions led to initial difficulties in my individual examination of the subject in terms of my artistic practice.

As a way out, I decided to focus my work on the only person in my immediate environment who would have something to say about it—not because she is herself affected, but because she has to deal with it professionally on an almost daily basis. She is a police officer and her stories paint a complex subjective picture. In adding publicly available information (newspaper articles, statistics, etc.) to her individual case, the picture becomes even more complex. (JZ)

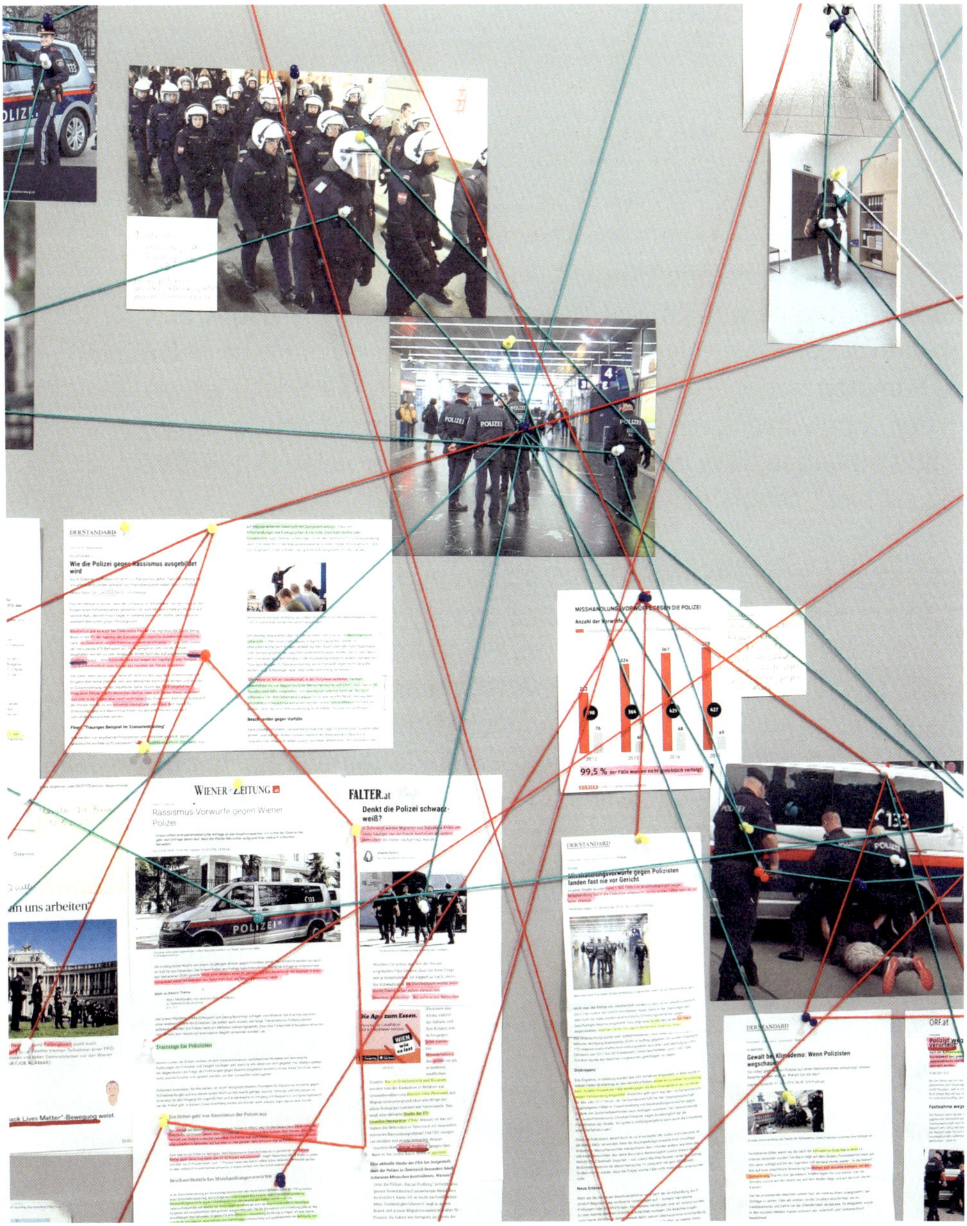

Ein ungelöster Fall, 2020/21

MARIJA ŽIVOJINOVIĆ

2000 Salzburg, AT

Mit der Aussage „I don't see color" wird, obwohl wir es gut meinen, auch die Botschaft vermittelt, dass wir die Kämpfe und Schwierigkeiten von People of Color nicht sehen. Anstatt also zu sagen, „I don't see color", sage ich, „ich sehe deine Hautfarbe, ich sehe deine Kämpfe und Hürden". Ich sehe das Privileg, das einige haben und andere nicht, aufgrund ihrer Hautfarbe. Diese Arbeit zeigt eine von vielen Schwierigkeiten, mit denen People of Color zu kämpfen haben – auch wenn es eine so triviale Sache ist wie in der Lage zu sein, ein passendes Make-up im lokalen Drogeriemarkt zu finden. Das ist nur ein Beispiel für die vielen Privilegien, die wir nicht sehen wollen.

Ich war auf einer Shopping-Tour, als ich mich in einem Drogeriemarkt wiederfand, auf der Suche nach nichts Bestimmten. Da ich immer gerne auschecke, was es für neue Produkte am Make-up-Markt gibt, fand ich mich vor verschiedenen Marken wieder, um etwas zu kaufen, das ich eigentlich nicht einmal brauchte. Während ich mich umsah und neue Produkte testete, fiel mir der signifikante Unterschied zwischen dem Angebot für *weiße* Menschen und dem Angebot für People of Color auf. Ich ging von Regal zu Regal und wurde immer frustrierter beim Anblick der geringen Auswahl, die geboten wurde. Das Verhältnis erschien mir absurd, doch ich realisierte schnell, dass dieses Verhältnis auch in anderen Bereichen unseres Lebens zutrifft. Ich realisierte, dass wir manchmal so blind gegenüber Dingen in unserer eigenen Umgebung sind, wenn sie uns selbst nicht betreffen, dass wir uns nicht einmal die Mühe machen, auch andere Perspektiven heranzuziehen. Wir sehen nicht über unsere eigene Hautfarbe hinaus. Wir sehen nicht die Schwierigkeiten, die dahinterliegen. Diese Arbeit entstand mit der Absicht, ein Licht auf unsere verschiedenen Erfahrungen zu werfen und die eigene Ignoranz herauszufordern. (MŽ)

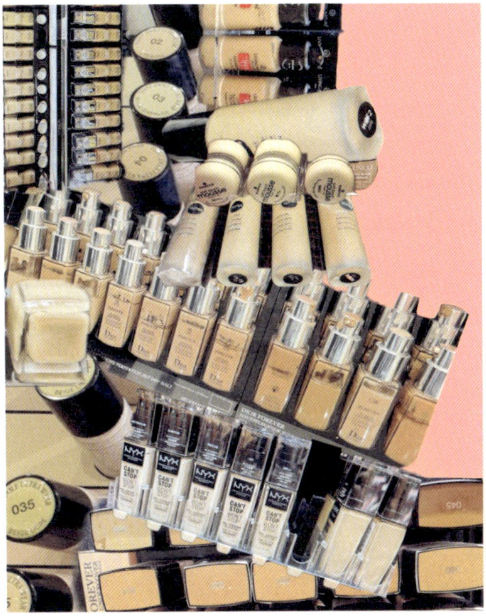

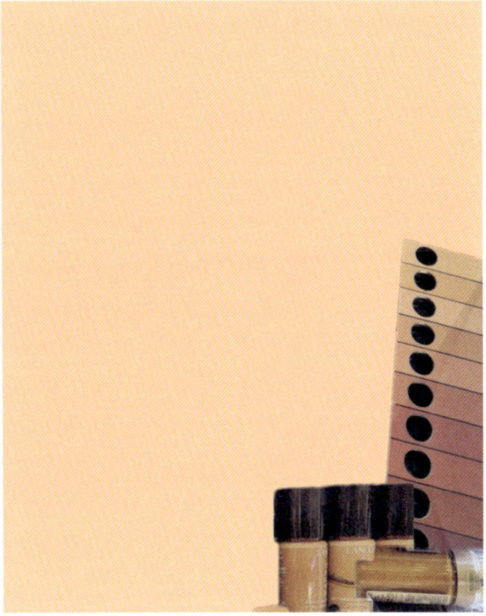

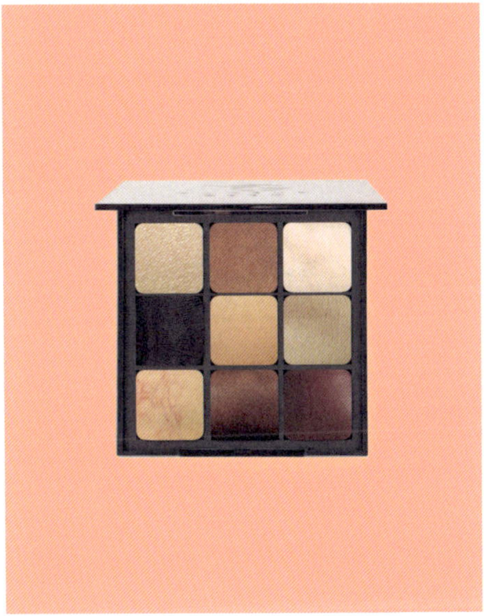

I See Color, 2021

MARIJA ŽIVOJINOVIĆ

2000 Salzburg, AT—Salzburg, AT

By saying "I don't see color," although we might mean well, we also convey the message that we don't see the struggles and difficulties of People of Color. So instead of saying, "I don't see color," I say, "I see your color, I see your struggle, and I see your hardships." I see the privilege that some have and some don't because of their appearance. This work depicts one of the many struggles that People of Color face, even if it might be such a trivial thing like finding your matching foundation make-up at your local drugstore. That is one example of our many privileges that we turn a blind eye to.

I was out shopping when I found myself in a drugstore looking for nothing of importance. Since I always check out what is new on the make-up market, I found myself standing in front of various different brands, looking to buy something that I don't really need. As I kept looking and testing out new products, I noticed the significant difference between the range of shades for *white* people and the range of shades for People of Color. I kept walking from display to display and with every make-up stand I passed, I grew more frustrated. The ratio seemed so absurd, and I quickly realized that it also applied to various other aspects of our lives. I realized that sometimes we are so blind to the circumstances that don't affect us specifically, that we don't bother to look any other way. We don't see beyond our own skin color. We don't see the struggle that lies beneath. This work came into being with the intention of shining a light on the different experiences we face and to challenge our own ignorance. (MŽ)

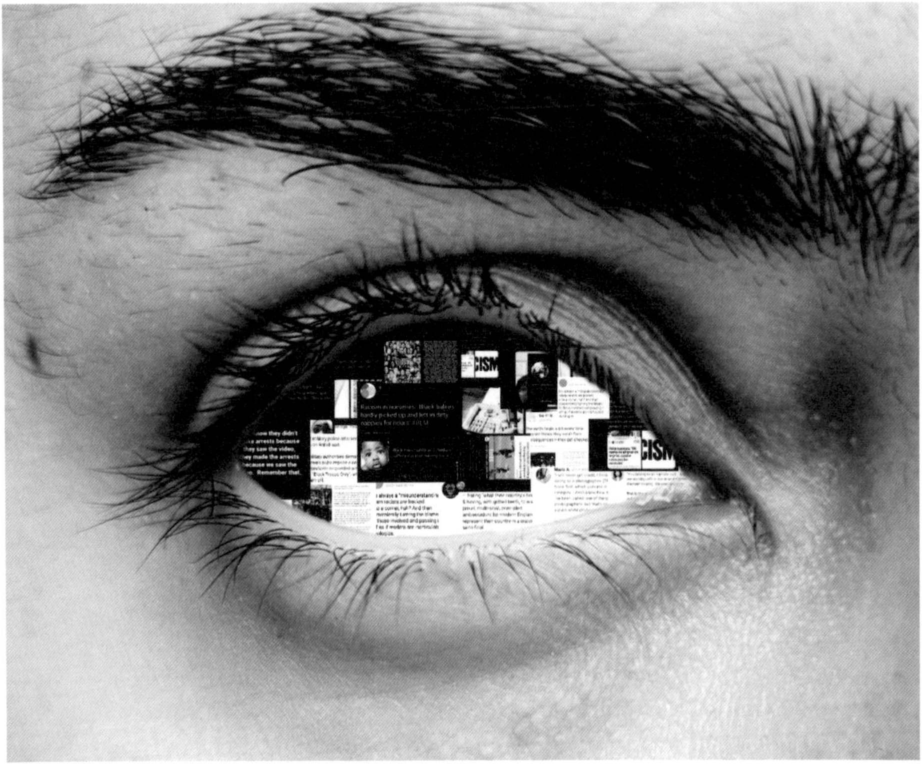

I See Color, 2021

MEIN *WEISSES* ÖSTERREICH

Farid Hafez

Haben wir in Österreich ein Problem mit Rassismus? Nicht erst seit mehr als 50.000 Menschen im Juni 2020 in Wien für Black Lives Matter auf die Straße gegangen sind, sträuben sich die Menschen hierzulande, mit Rassismus in Verbindung gebracht zu werden. Rassismus sei ein Problem der Rechten, denken viele in der Alpenrepublik. Rassismus wird mit völkisch-rassischem Denken gleichgesetzt, oftmals in Form einer bewussten ideologischen Einstellung. Das ist alles richtig. Aber es ist nicht die ganze Wahrheit. In den 1960er-Jahren sagte James Baldwin in einer Diskussion: „Was weiße Menschen tun müssen, ist in ihrem eigenen Herzen herauszufinden, warum es überhaupt notwendig war, einen ‚N***er' zu haben. Denn ich bin kein N***er, ich bin ein Mensch. Aber wenn Sie denken, dass ich ein N***er bin, bedeutet das, dass Sie ihn brauchen. [...] Sie, Ihr weißen Menschen, habt ihn erfunden und Sie müssen herausfinden, warum. Und die Zukunft dieses Landes hängt davon ab, ob es in der Lage ist, diese Frage zu stellen oder nicht."

Tatsächlich hängt nicht nur die Zukunft der Vereinigten Staaten davon ab. In gewissem Sinne hängt die Zukunft unserer Welt davon ab, inwiefern Menschen in privilegierten Machtpositionen die Fähigkeit aufbringen können und *wollen*, genau diese Frage in all ihren Variationen zu stellen. Für Österreich: Warum wurden „diese Juden" erfunden? Warum wurden „diese nicht-deutschsprachigen Burgenlandkroaten und Kärntner Slowenen" gebraucht? Warum brauchen wir heute „die Muslime"? Denn, wie schon Jean-Paul Sartre mit Blick auf den Antisemitismus gesagt hat: „Wenn es keinen Juden gäbe, würde der Antisemit ihn erfinden." Konjunkturen von Rassismen, sei es gegenüber Rom:nja, Muslim:innen oder anderen Gruppen, sagen wenig oder nichts über deren reale Verhältnisse aus. Sie sagen aber viel über die Wünsche und Ängste der *weißen* Dominanzgesellschaft aus, die mit Hilfe von Projektionen erst diese Figuren des „Anderen" schafft.

Vielerorts im Globalen Norden sind Bewegungen in Richtung einer Auseinandersetzung mit der eigenen rassistischen Ordnung wahrnehmbar. Diese Bewegungen setzen sich oft auch mit den historischen Voraussetzungen aktueller Verhältnisse auseinander. In Österreich ist eine solche kritische Reflexion

MY *WHITE* AUSTRIA

Farid Hafez

Do we have a problem with racism in Austria? It's not just since more than 50,000 people took to the streets in Vienna for Black Lives Matter in June 2020 that people in this country don't want to see themselves associated with racism. Racism is a right-wing problem, many in the Alpine republic think. Racism is equated with an ethno-racist thinking, often in the form of a conscious ideological attitude. That is all true. But not the whole truth. In the 1960s, James Baldwin said in a discussion, "What white people have to do is try to find out in their own hearts why it was necessary to have a 'n***er' in the first place, because I'm not a n***er, I'm a man. But if you think I'm a n***er, it means you need him. [...] If I'm not the n***er here and you, the white people, invented him, then you've got to find out why. And the future of the country depends on that, whether or not it's able to ask that question."

In fact, it's not just the future of the United States that depends on it. In a sense, the future of our world depends on the extent to which people in privileged positions of power can and will muster the ability to ask precisely this question in all its variations. For Austria: Why were "these Jews" invented? Why were "these non-German-speaking Burgenland Croats and Carinthian Slovenes" needed? Why do we need "the Muslims" today? Because, as Jean-Paul Sartre already said with regard to anti-Semitism: "If the Jew did not exist, the anti-Semite would invent him." Conjunctures of racism, be it against Roma, Muslims, or other groups, say little or nothing about their real conditions. But they say a lot about the desires and fears of the *white* dominant society, which creates these figures of the "other" by means of projections.

In many places in the Global North, movements toward a confrontation with their own racist order are perceptible. These movements often also deal with the historical preconditions of current conditions. In Austria, such critical reflection is scarce. Not only that Austria, due to its victim myth in relation to National Socialism, only began very late to deal with this not yet long ago period of its own history. In countries like Austria, National Socialism is still kept out of its connection with global racism and regarded as a phenomenon

Mangelware. Nicht nur, dass Österreich aufgrund seines Opfermythos in Bezug auf den Nationalsozialismus erst sehr spät begann, sich mit diesem noch nicht lange zurückliegenden Abschnitt der eigenen Geschichte zu beschäftigen. In Ländern wie Österreich wird der Nationalsozialismus bis heute aus seinem Zusammenhang mit dem globalen Rassismus herausgehalten und als für sich stehendes Phänomen betrachtet. Dass etwa die Nürnberger Rassengesetze Anleihe bei den US-amerikanischen Rassengesetzen nahmen, die wiederum ohne den transatlantischen Handel mit versklavten Afrikaner:innen nicht zu denken sind, wird oft ausgeblendet. Genau das hat dazu geführt, dass nach 1945 Diskriminierungen auf gesetzlicher Ebene fortgesetzt und Volksgruppen keine Rechte eingeräumt wurden. Struktureller Rassismus wurde nie als solcher anerkannt. Und das ist auch heute noch der Fall.

Österreich ist geprägt von einer Dominanz *weiß*-deutschsprachig-heteronormativ-katholischer Identitätskonstruktionen, die alles „Andere" einmal mehr, einmal weniger ausgrenzen. Die Kolonialgeschichte der Monarchie wird heruntergespielt oder gar nicht erst zur Kenntnis genommen. Die Verflechtung von Nationalsozialismus und globaler rassistischer Ordnung wird nicht thematisiert. Und so ist es auch nicht überraschend, dass damit auch der Rassismus kein Thema ist. Nirgendwo wird dies deutlicher als in der deutschen Sprache. Vergleichen wir diese etwa mit der englischen Sprache, so wird der Mangel an Vokabular deutlich, um überhaupt über das Thema Rassismus sprechen zu können. Begriffe wie *racialization*, *whiteness* oder *safe spaces* sind nicht Teil unseres Sprachgebrauchs. Uns fehlen also die Worte, um diese Missstände zu benennen.

All dies verfestigt die Strukturen der Dominanzgesellschaft, die oft – wenn auch nicht nur – entlang *weiß*-deutschsprachig-heteronormativ-katholischer Identitätsmarker konstruiert sind. Wenn *Weiß*-Sein nicht thematisiert wird, kann auch die Dominanz *weißer* Menschen in den Räumen der Macht – von der parlamentarischen Volksvertretung über die Lehrerschaft in Schulen bis hin zu akademischen Institutionen – in ihrer hegemonialen Position nicht in Frage gestellt werden. In dieser Hinsicht sollte es nicht verwundern, dass Rassismus kaum Thema ist; weder in der Politik, wo Rassismus immer wieder gang und gäbe ist, noch in der Bildungslandschaft, auch wenn nicht-*weiße* Deutschsprachige inzwischen einen großen Teil der Schülerschaft ausmachen.

in its own right. The fact that the Nuremberg Race Laws, for example, borrowed from the U.S. Race Laws, which in turn are unthinkable without the transatlantic trade in enslaved Africans, is often ignored. This is precisely what led to the continuation of discrimination at the legal level after 1945 and the denial of rights to ethnic groups. Structural racism was never recognized as such. And this is still the case today.

Austria is characterized by a dominance of *white*-German-speaking-heteronormative-Catholic identity constructions that exclude everything "other" to a greater or lesser extent. The colonial history of the monarchy is downplayed or not even acknowledged. The intertwining of National Socialism and the global racist order is not addressed. And so it is not surprising that racism is thus not an issue either. Nowhere is this more evident than in the German language. If we compare it with the English language, for example, the lack of vocabulary to be able to talk about the topic of racism at all becomes clear. Terms like racialization, *whiteness*, or safe spaces are not part of our language usage. We therefore lack the words to even name these grievances.

All of this solidifies the structures of the dominant society, which are often—though not only—constructed along *white*-German-speaking-heteronormative-Catholic identity markers. If *whiteness* is not thematized, the dominance of *white* people in the spaces of power—from parliamentary representation to teachers in schools to academic institutions—cannot be challenged in their hegemonic position either. In this respect, it should not be surprising that racism is hardly an issue—neither in politics, where racism is always commonplace, nor in the educational landscape, even though non-*white* German-speaking people now make up a large proportion of students.

For the question of racism is, at its core, a question of power, affecting all sites of symbolic, cultural, economic, and political power centers. The question of power also raises an epistemological question: How many other views are allowed alongside the dominant views? It also raises a political power question: How much space is given to those, usually from poorer backgrounds, who have to fight for a place in society? One of the most obvious answers to Baldwin's question quoted above seems to me to be the fear of losing these unspoken privileges. The privileges of a largely *white*-German-

Denn die Frage des Rassismus ist im Kern eine Frage der Macht, die alle Orte symbolischer, kultureller, wirtschaftlicher und politischer Machtzentren betrifft. Die Frage der Macht wirft auch eine epistemologische Frage auf: Wie viele andere Sichtweisen werden neben den dominanten Sichtweisen zugelassen? Sie wirft auch eine politische Machtfrage auf: Wie viel Raum wird denjenigen eingeräumt, die sich – in der Regel aus ärmeren Verhältnissen – einen Platz in der Gesellschaft erkämpfen müssen? Eine der offensichtlichsten Antworten auf Baldwins oben zitierte Frage scheint mir die Angst vor dem Verlust dieser unausgesprochenen Privilegien zu sein. Die Privilegien einer weitgehend *weiß*-deutschsprachig-heteronormativ-katholischen Identität in diesem Land, die um den Verlust ihrer Hegemonie und Dominanz bangt.

Wie kann diese hegemoniale Dominanz überwunden werden? Es wird nichts geschehen, wenn nicht zuerst die eigenen *weißen* Privilegien einer kritischen Selbstreflexion unterzogen werden. Diese Anstrengung bedeutet letztlich, die „Anderen" als gleichwertig anzuerkennen. Und diese Anerkennung nicht-*weiß*-deutschsprachig-heteronormativ-katholischer Menschen muss dazu führen, ihnen den gleichen Raum zu geben, den dominante Lebensstile heute als Normalität genießen. Dieser Weg, der sicherlich nicht schmerzlos ist, wird den Privilegierten Opfer abverlangen. Machträume müssen verkleinert werden, Privilegien abgebaut werden. Auf diesem Weg werden Räume der Auseinandersetzung mit dem Eigenen nötig sein, aber auch Räume der Allianz und Kooperation mit den „Anderen" sowie Räume, die den „Anderen" überlassen werden.

speaking-heteronormative-Catholic identity in this country that fears for the loss of its hegemony and dominance.

How can this hegemonic dominance be overcome? Nothing will happen unless one's own white privilege is first subjected to critical self-reflection. This effort ultimately means recognizing the "others" as equals. And this recognition of non-*white*-German-speaking-heteronormative-Catholic people must lead to giving them the same space that dominant lifestyles enjoy today as normality. This path, which is certainly not painless, will require sacrifice on the part of the privileged. Spaces of power will have to be reduced, privileges will have to be dismantled. On this path, spaces of confrontation with one's own will be necessary, but also spaces of alliance and cooperation with the "others" as well as spaces that are left to the "others."

„THIS WORLD IS WHITE NO LONGER". EINE REFLEXION ÜBER DIE AUSSTELLUNG

Dženeta Karabegović

Das Video, das die letzten Minuten von George Floyds Leben am 25. Mai 2020 dokumentierte, wurde auf der ganzen Welt gesehen und löste Wut, Proteste und Selbstreflexion über die Notwendigkeit antirassistischer Ansätze für unser tägliches Leben und die Strukturen um uns herum aus. Black Lives Matter als politische und soziale Bewegung gewann weltweit immer mehr an Zugkraft, da die Menschen begannen, sich offener mit dem systemischen Rassismus in ihrer Gesellschaft auseinanderzusetzen – in den Medien, in öffentlichen Diskussionen, durch Proteste, mit ihren Eltern und Familienmitgliedern und über Grenzen hinweg. Dabei brachten sie nicht nur ihren Wunsch nach Veränderung zum Ausdruck, sondern auch das Streben, Verhaltensweisen zu ändern und zu korrigieren, die sie selbst erlernt hatten und die in der Gesellschaft systemisch und tief verwurzelt sind.

Österreichische Kolleg:innen fragten mich nach meinen Gedanken. Wir diskutierten den Fall und die Rolle von Black Lives Matter in einem Kurs über soziale Bewegungen, den ich 2021 an der Universität Salzburg hielt. Auch Studierende in Bosnien und Herzegowina, die ich zu ganz anderen Themen unterrichtete, erkundigten sich danach, wobei jede:r von ihnen detaillierte Kenntnisse über die Proteste und die Umstände hatte sowie Überlegungen zu den möglichen Auswirkungen der Ereignisse auf die amerikanische Gesellschaft und darüber hinaus anstellte. Im April 2021 wurden der Prozess, die Beratungen und die begrüßenswerten Schuldsprüche für den ehemaligen Polizeibeamten von Minneapolis, Derek Chauvin, wegen Mordes und Totschlags im Zusammenhang mit dem Tod von George Floyd nicht nur in den Vereinigten Staaten, sondern auch in der ganzen Welt verfolgt. Diese Momentaufnahmen zeigen den transnationalen Charakter von Black Lives Matter und den Wunsch und die Offenheit, eine gerechtere Gesellschaft nicht nur anzuerkennen, sondern auch anzustreben; eine Gesellschaft, die berücksichtigt, dass *weiße* Vorherrschaft und Rassismus nach wie vor in vielen gesellschaftlichen Strukturen und Praktiken verankert sind und daher reformiert, geändert oder ganz abgebaut werden müssen.

"THIS WORLD IS WHITE NO LONGER." A REFLECTION ON THE EXHIBITION

Dženeta Karabegović

The video documenting the last minutes of George Floyd's life on May 25, 2020, was seen around the world and sparked anger, protests, and self-reflection on the need for anti-racist approaches to our daily lives and the structures around us. Black Lives Matter as a political and social movement gained traction around the world as people began to more openly address systemic racism in their society—in the media, in public discussions, through protest, with their parents and family members, and across borders. In doing so, they expressed not only their desire for change, but also their desire to change and correct behaviors that they themselves had learned and that are systemic and deeply rooted in our society.

Austrian colleagues asked me for my thoughts. We discussed the case and the role of Black Lives Matter in a course on social movements that I gave at the University of Salzburg in 2021. Students in Bosnia and Herzegovina, for whom I taught on very different topics, also inquired about it, each demonstrating detailed knowledge of the protests and the circumstances, as well as reflections on the potential impact of the events on American society and beyond. In April 2021, the trial, deliberations, and the welcome guilty verdicts for former Minneapolis police officer Derek Chauvin for murder and manslaughter in the death of George Floyd were followed not only in the United States but also around the world. These snapshots demonstrate the transnational nature of Black Lives Matter and the desire and openness to not only recognize but also strive for a more just society—one that takes into account that *white* supremacy and racism remain embedded in many social structures and practices and therefore need to be reformed, changed, or dismantled altogether.

"This world is white no longer, and it will never be white again." James Baldwin's words continue to resonate as we are in a social moment where the "great deal of will power involved in the white man's naïveté" is shifting toward enlightenment, toward ways to confront racism head-on. Together, we are opening our eyes to the fact that the world was not *white* to begin with.

„Diese Welt ist nicht mehr weiß, und sie wird nie wieder weiß sein." James Baldwins Worte klingen nach wie vor nach, denn wir befinden uns in einem gesellschaftlichen Moment, in dem sich die „große Willenskraft, die mit der Naivität des weißen Mannes verbunden ist", in Richtung Aufklärung verlagert, hin zu Möglichkeiten, dem Rassismus frontal zu begegnen. Gemeinsam öffnen wir unsere Augen für die Tatsache, dass die Welt von Anfang an nicht *weiß* war.

Gerechtigkeit ist noch lange nicht erreicht und lässt sich nicht von heute auf morgen oder durch eine Reihe von Urteilen in einem einzigen Land verwirklichen. Vielmehr befinden wir uns in einem mühsamen Prozess der Rechenschaftslegung, der Reflexion, der Selbstbeobachtung und der aktiven Schritte zu einem dauerhaften Wandel. Dies wird auch weiterhin auf verschiedenen Ebenen der Gesellschaft, zwischen Einzelpersonen und Institutionen, über staatliche und nichtstaatliche Strukturen, Verfahren und Strategien auf lokaler, nationaler, regionaler und internationaler Ebene geschehen. Der öffentliche Diskurs, so langsam er sich auch anfühlen mag, bewegt sich dennoch in Richtung eines stärkeren Bewusstseins, einer stärkeren Anerkennung, einer Änderung der Verhaltensweisen und der Gewährleistung von Gerechtigkeit.

Das ist es, was die Ausstellung *This World Is White No Longer* im Museum der Moderne Salzburg in Zusammenarbeit mit Studierenden der Universität Mozarteum so außergewöhnlich und zeitgemäß machte. Ich sah sie als eine Antwort darauf, durch neue Medien und Fotografie Rassismus und Ungleichheit in unserer unmittelbaren Umgebung, in unserem täglichen Leben, anzuprangern und aufzugreifen. Die Ausstellung zeigte, wie verletzlich junge Künstler:innen und künftige Kunstpädagog:innen sind, wenn es darum geht, sich mit Themen des Antirassismus in einer Umgebung auseinanderzusetzen, die weit von den Vereinigten Staaten entfernt, aber dennoch relevant ist – in Salzburg, Österreich, Europa. Ihre künstlerischen Antworten waren maßvoll, manchmal zaghaft, in anderen Momenten selbstbewusster, immer in dem Bewusstsein, dass sie an der Schwelle zum Wandel stehen, auch wenn dieser Wandel nur schrittweise erfolgt. Die Werke luden die Besucher:innen dazu ein, ihre eigenen Reaktionen und Handlungen während der Ausstellung zu überdenken und zu hinterfragen, im Unbehagen zu schwelgen, bevor sie versuchen, in eine gerechtere Richtung weiterzugehen.

Justice is far from being achieved and cannot be accomplished overnight or through a series of verdicts in a single country. Rather, we are in an arduous process of accountability, reflection, introspection, and active steps toward lasting change. This will continue to happen at different levels of society, among individuals and institutions, through governmental and non-governmental structures, procedures, and policies at the local, national, regional, and international levels. Public discourse, however slow it might feel, is nonetheless moving toward greater awareness and recognition, changing behaviors, and ensuring justice.

This is what made the exhibition *This World Is White No Longer* at the Museum der Moderne Salzburg in collaboration with students from the Mozarteum University exceptional and timely. I saw it as a response to call out and address racism and inequality in our immediate environment, in our daily lives, through new media and photography. The exhibition showed how vulnerable young artists and future art educators are when it comes to addressing issues of anti-racism in an environment that is far from the United States, but still relevant—in Salzburg, Austria, Europe. Their artistic responses were measured, sometimes tentative, at other moments more confident, always aware that they are on the threshold of change, even if that change is incremental. The pieces invited visitors to consider and question their own reactions and actions throughout the exhibition, to simmer in discomfort before attempting to move forward in a more equitable direction.

In talking with the students and browsing the exhibition, it became clear to me that there was also a duality inherent in the works. On the one hand, the students took a proactive and very public step toward exposing the world around them by expressing the need for anti-racist approaches in society, thus recognizing their own active role in this process as artists, educators, citizens, and human beings. On the other hand, they questioned their legitimacy in these processes, the authenticity of their voices to others, including those of people of color. Through the exhibition, they opened up these conversations, exposed their vulnerabilities, and broke down barriers, especially among *white* people and in public spaces, to show the potential of anti-racism on the local level and the need for all of us to participate. The exhibition was thus a challenge and a necessity, revealing yet welcome.

Im Gespräch mit den Studierenden und beim Durchstöbern der Ausstellung wurde mir klar, dass den Werken eine Dualität innewohnt. Auf der einen Seite haben die Studierenden einen proaktiven und öffentlichen Schritt unternommen, um die Welt um sie herum zu entlarven, indem sie die Notwendigkeit antirassistischer Ansätze in der Gesellschaft zum Ausdruck brachten und so ihre eigene aktive Rolle in diesem Prozess als Künstler:innen, Pädagog:innen, Bürger:innen und Menschen erkannten. Andererseits hinterfragten sie ihre Legitimität in diesen Prozessen, die Authentizität ihrer Stimmen gegenüber anderen, einschließlich derjenigen von People of Color selbst. Durch die Ausstellung eröffneten sie diese Gespräche, legten ihre Verwundbarkeit offen, bauten Barrieren ab, vor allem bei *weißen* Menschen und im öffentlichen Raum, um das Potenzial des Antirassismus auf lokaler Ebene und die Notwendigkeit der Beteiligung von uns allen zu zeigen. Die Ausstellung war somit eine Herausforderung und eine Notwendigkeit, entblößend und doch willkommen.

THIS WORLD IS WHITE NO LONGER
Ein Projekt mit der Klasse für Fotografie und Neue Medien, Universität Mozarteum Salzburg
Museum der Moderne Salzburg, Rupertinum
24. April – 10. Oktober 2021
Akt 1: 24. April – 20. Juni 2021
Akt 2: 24. Juni – 22. August 2021
Akt 3: 26. August – 10. Oktober 2021

THIS WORLD IS WHITE NO LONGER
A Project with the Class for Photography and New Media, Mozarteum University Salzburg
Museum der Moderne Salzburg, Rupertinum
April 24—October 10, 2021
Act 1: April 24—June 20, 2021
Act 2: June 24—August 22, 2021
Act 3: August 26—October 10, 2021

Presented by GENERALI

Werkliste | List of Works

Die Werke sind nach Künstler:innen alphabetisch gereiht.

Works are listed by artist in alphabetical order.

ALBA MALIKA BELHADJ MERZOUG
2000 Salzburg, AT – Salzburg, AT
2000 Salzburg, AT—Salzburg, AT

NichTS, 2020/21
Projektion
200 × 80 cm
Courtesy of the artist

NichTS, 2020/21
Projection
200 × 80 cm
Courtesy of the artist

MELANIE FORSTHUBER
2000 Grieskirchen, AT – Salzburg, AT
2000 Grieskirchen, AT—Salzburg, AT

Paradies?, 2021
Fünfteilige Collage, je ca. 70 – 86 × 50 cm
Inkjet-Drucke, Reiseprospekt-Ausschnitte;
Pinnwand, chromogene Abzüge, Postkarten
Reißnägel, 60 × 90 cm
Courtesy of the artist

Paradies?, 2021
Collage in five parts, each approx. 70–86 × 50 cm
Inkjet prints, cuttings from travel brochures
Pin board, chromogenic prints, postal cards
pins, 60 × 90 cm
Courtesy of the artist

PIA GEISREITER
1996 Schrobenhausen, DE – Salzburg, AT
1996 Schrobenhausen, DE—Salzburg, AT

Gefühlschaos, 2020/21
„Umgekehrter Kalender"
Zeichnung auf Inkjet-Druck
Kohle, Stoff, Schnitte, Klebeband

rbeiten, je 74 × 108 cm
ırtesy of the artist

fühlschaos, 2020/21
ngekehrter Kalender" ("Inverted calendar")
wing on inkjet print
arcoal, fabric, cuts, adhesive tape
vorks, each 74 × 108 cm
ırtesy of the artist

GDALENA HELLER
93 Vöcklabruck, AT – Salzburg, AT
93 Vöcklabruck, AT—Salzburg, AT

itteteilen, 2021
tallation
ryl und Permanentmarker auf Karton
tagram-Profil @pleaseshareartproject
ße variabel
urtesy of the artist

itteteilen, 2021
rylic and permanent marker on
rdboard
tagram handle @pleaseshareartproject
nensions variable
urtesy of the artist

NNAH IMHOFF
97 München, DE – Salzburg, AT
97 Munich, DE—Salzburg, AT

ssistische Gesellschaft (Eine Problem-
rstellung mit offenem Ende), 2020
eiteilige Skulptur
errholz, Nylonschnur, Schrauben, Acryl,
eide, Kohle, Klebebuchstaben
0 × 150 cm
ourtesy of the artist

Rassistische Gesellschaft (Eine Problem-darstellung mit offenem Ende), 2020
Sculpture in three parts
Plywood, nylon cord, screws, acrylic, chalk, charcoal, adhesive letters
150 × 150 cm
Courtesy of the artist

Visitenkarten (Erinnerung an mich selbst), 2020/21
Visitenkarten, Digitaldruck auf Leinen-papier
5,5 × 8,5 cm
Courtesy of the artist

Visitenkarten (Erinnerung an mich selbst), 2020/21
Calling cards, digital print on linen paper
5.5 × 8.5 cm
Courtesy of the artist

AGNES ELENA KERN
Salzburg, AT
Salzburg, AT

~~Schwarz.Weiß.~~ Grau.Bunt., 2021
2 Filme, Super-8, digitalisiert
Zweikanal-Video (schwarz-weiß, ohne Ton)
3:56 Min.
Courtesy of the artist

~~Schwarz.Weiß.~~ Grau.Bunt., 2021
2 films, Super-8, digitized
Two-channel video (black and white, no sound)
3:56 min.
Courtesy of the artist

VERA KERN
1994 Wien, AT – Salzburg, AT
1994 Vienna, AT—Salzburg, AT

07-01-21, 2021
Zweikanal-Video (Farbe, ohne Ton)
21:24 Min.
Tinte auf Papier, 14,8 × 21 cm
Laserkopien, 14,8 × 21 cm
Courtesy of the artist

07-01-21, 2021
Two-channel video (color, no sound)
21:24 min.
Ink on paper, 14.8 × 21 cm
Laser copies, 14.8 × 21 cm
Courtesy of the artist

KEVIN KLINGER
1992 Salzburg, AT – Salzburg, AT
1992 Salzburg, AT—Salzburg, AT

Exit the Box, 2020
Video (HD, Graustufen, Ton)
17:36 Min.
Courtesy of the artist

Exit the Box, 2020
Video (HD, grayscale, sound)
17:36 min.
Courtesy of the artist

LEONIE MIRJAM LINDINGER
2000 Richterswil, CH – Salzburg, AT
2000 Richterswil, CH—Salzburg, AT

How Soon Is Soon?, 2020/21
Video (Farbe, Ton)
7 Min.
Courtesy of the artist

How Soon Is Soon?, 2020/21
Video (color, sound)
7 min.
Courtesy of the artist

CHARLOTTE PANN
1990 Salzburg, AT – Salzburg, AT
1990 Salzburg, AT—Salzburg, AT

AUTOKINO, 2021
„Loop“
Zeichnung und Videoprojektion
Grafit und Farbstift auf Papier
Video (Farbe, ohne Ton), 7 Sequenzen
je 30 Sekunden
187 × 288 cm
Courtesy of the artist

AUTOKINO, 2021
"Loop"
Drawing and video projection
Pencil and colored pencil on paper
Video (color, no sound), 7 sequences each
30 seconds
187 × 288 cm
Courtesy of the artist

SABINE REISENBÜCHLER
1977 Salzburg, AT – Salzburg, AT
1977 Salzburg, AT—Salzburg, AT

Appalachian Heritage – Shatter your Hearts with Rain, 2021
Video (Farbe, Ton)
Text: bell hooks
Musik: Tanya Tagaq
2:29 Min.
Courtesy of the artist

Appalachian Heritage – Shatter your Hearts with Rain, 2021
Video (color, sound)
Lyrics: bell hooks
Music: Tanya Tagaq
2:29 min.
Courtesy of the artist

-MARIA SCHITTER
3 Oberndorf, AT – Salzburg, AT
3 Oberndorf, AT—Salzburg, AT

über mich über ihr über sie, 2020/21
ografisches Mural
et-Drucke, Notizbuch
kanal-Audio (Stereo), 6:11 Min.
) × 600 cm
urtesy of the artist

über mich über ihr über sie, 2020/21
otographic mural
et prints
ebook, 29,6 × 21 cm
e-channel audio (stereo), 6:11 min.
) × 600 cm
urtesy of the artist

ULPTING FEMINISM READING GROUP
gründet 2020 in Salzburg, AT
unded 2020 in Salzburg, AT

ading Out Loud, 2020/21
tallation: Lara Schnepf, Zoe Vitzthum,
drea Lumplecker, Marie Gruber
leo (Farbe, Sound)
cherregale, Bücher
öße variabel
urtesy of the artists

ading Out Loud, 2020/21
stallation: Lara Schnepf, Zoe Vitzthum,
drea Lumplecker, Marie Gruber
deo (color, sound)
okshelves, books
mensions variable
urtesy of the artists

eading Out Loud, 2020/21
eading Performance
esende: Rebecca Naß, Elena Lengauer,
Dustin Waskow, Zoe Vitzthum, Charlotte Lang, Lara Schnepf, Benita Kogler, Hannah Imhoff, Marie Gruber, Caterina Mayer, Linda Kudla, Lena Ortner, Christina Jaques, Andrea Lumplecker, Ruth Berleth, Milena Keser, Leonie Zangerl u. a.
Courtesy of the artists

Reading Out Loud, 2020/21
Reading performance
Readers: Rebecca Nass, Elena Lengauer, Dustin Waskow, Zoe Vitzthum, Charlotte Lang, Lara Schnepf, Benita Kogler, Hannah Imhoff, Marie Gruber, Caterina Mayer, Linda Kudla, Lena Ortner, Christina Jaques, Andrea Lumplecker, Ruth Berleth, Milena Keser, Leonie Zangerl et al.
Courtesy of the artists

THIS WORLD IS EGO NO LONGER
Salzburg, AT
Salzburg, AT

this (art) world is Ego No longer and never will be again, 2020/21
Interaktive Installation
4 Inkjet-Drucke, je 120 × 84 cm
7 Aquarelle auf Papier, je 24 × 32 cm bzw. 32 × 24 cm
75 Aquarelle auf Papier, je 10,5 × 14,8 cm bzw. 14,8 × 10,5 cm
18 Inkjet-Drucke, je 10,5 × 14,8 cm bzw. 14,8 × 10,5 cm
Tafel, Rahmen, Tafelkreide, Sperrholz
Künstlerbuch
Schaukelstuhl, Sofa, Tisch, Bücher
Courtesy of the artist

this (art) world is Ego No longer and never will be again, 2020/21
Interactive installation
4 inkjet prints, each 120 × 84 cm

7 watercolors on paper, each 24 × 32 cm or 32 × 24 cm
75 watercolors on paper, each 10.5 × 14.8 cm or 14.8 × 10.5 cm
18 inkjet prints, each 10.5 × 14.8 cm or 14.8 × 10.5 cm
Chalkboard, frame, chalk, plywood
Artist's book
Rocking chair, couch, table, books
Courtesy of the artist

ANGELIKA WIENERROITHER
1986 Bad Ischl, AT – Salzburg, AT
1986 Bad Ischl, AT—Salzburg, AT

Utopia (Why can't we just get along?), 2021
Foto-Audio-Installation
3 Inkjet-Drucke je 30 × 45 cm, 1 Inkjet-Druck 60 × 40 cm, 1 Inkjet-Druck 60 × 90 cm, 2 Inkjet-Druck je 135 × 90 cm
Cihak & Zima, Ida B. Wells-Barnett, 1893/94, Ausdruck 2021, Inkjet-Druck, 15 × 10 cm, mit freundlicher Genehmigung von Hanna Holborn Gray Special Collections Research Center, University of Chicago Library
Zweikanal-Audio (Stereo), 16:03 Min. und 21:02 Min.
Text, Gouache auf Papier, 30 × 40 cm
Text, Schreibmaschine auf Papier, gerahmt, 35 × 30 cm
Text, Klebebuchstaben
Büchlein mit japanischer Bindung, 18 × 14 cm, Kubus 20 × 20 × 20 cm
Mantel, Kleiderbügel, Karteikärtchen, Ast
Courtesy of the artist

Utopia (Why can't we just get along?), 2021
Photo audio installation
3 inkjet prints each 30 × 45 cm, 1 inkjet print 60 × 40 cm, 1 inkjet print 60 × 90 cm, 2 inkjet prints each 135 × 90 cm
Cihak & Zima, Ida B. Wells-Barnett, 1893/94, print 2021, inkjet print 15 × 10 cm, courtesy the Hanna Holborn Gray Special Collection Research Center, University of Chicago Lib
Two-channel audio (stereo), 16:03 min. and 21:02 min.
Text, gouache on paper, 30 × 40 cm
Text, typewriter on paper, framed, 35 × 30
Text, adhesive letters
Booklet with Japanese stab binding, 18 × 14 cm, cube 20 × 20 × 20 cm
Coat, coat hanger, index cards, branch
Courtesy of the artist

JUDITH ZAUNSCHIRM
Salzburg, AT
Salzburg, AT

Ein ungelöster Fall, 2020/21
„Aktueller Stand einer künstlerischen Recherche"
Installation
Pinnwand, Inkjet-Drucke, Computerausdrucke, Notizen, Reißnägel, Faden
150 × 220 cm
Courtesy of the artist

Ein ungelöster Fall, 2020/21
"Aktueller Stand einer künstlerischen Recheche" ("Current state of an artistic research"
Installation
Pin board, inkjet prints, printouts, notes, pins, thread
150 × 220 cm
Courtesy of the artist

MARIJA ŽIVOJINOVIĆ
2000 Salzburg, AT – Salzburg, AT
2000 Salzburg, AT—Salzburg, AT

I See Color, 2021
Fotoserie

kjet-Drucke, je 80 × 60 cm
kjet-Druck, 110 × 136 cm
urtesy of the artist

ee Color, 2021
oto series
nkjet prints, each 80 × 60 cm
kjet print, 110 × 136 cm
urtesy of the artist

IMPRESSUM
COLOPHON

se Publikation erscheint anlässlich der Ausstellung / olished in conjunction with the exhibition

s World Is White No Longer
April – 10. Oktober 2021 / April 24—October 10, 2021
seum der Moderne Salzburg

esented by GENERALI

Ausstellung Teil I / Exhibition Part I:
This World Is White No Longer. Ansichten einer dezentrierten Welt / This World Is White No Longer: Views of a Decentered World
Kuratiert von / Curated by: Thorsten Sadowsky, Jürgen Tabor

Mit Werken von / With works by: Karo Akpokiere, Lothar Baumgarten, Danica Dakić, Forensic Architecture, Samuel Fosso, Charlotte Haslund-Christensen, Alfredo Jaar, Voluspa Jarpa, Belinda Kazeem-Kamiński, Adrian Piper, Lisl Ponger, Kara Walker

Ausstellung Teil II / Exhibition Part II:
This World Is White No Longer. Ein Projekt mit der Klasse für Fotografie und Neue Medien, Universität Mozarteum Salzburg / This World Is White No Longer: A Project with the Class for Photography and New Media, Mozarteum University Salzburg
Kuratiert von / Curated by: Stefanie Grünangerl, Jürgen Tabor
Lehrende / Teachers: Gregor Neuerer, Sigrid Langrehr, Michael Mauracher, Peter Schreiner

Mit Werken von / With works by: Alba Malika Belhadj Merzoug, Melanie Forsthuber, Pia Geisreiter, Magdalena Heller, Hannah Imhoff, Agnes Elena Kern, Vera Kern, Kevin Klinger, Leonie Mirjam Lindinger, Charlotte Pann, Sabine Reisenbüchler, Eva-Maria Schitter, Sculpting Feminism Reading Group, this world is Ego No longer, Angelika Wienerroither, Judith Zaunschirm, Marija Živojinović

Publikation / **Publication**
Herausgegeben von / Edited by Thorsten Sadowsky
für die Sammlung Generali Foundation – Dauerleihgabe am Museum der Moderne Salzburg / for the Generali Foundation Collection—Permanent Loan to the Museum der Moderne Salzburg
Museum der Moderne Salzburg
Mönchsberg 32
5020 Salzburg
Österreich / Austria
T +43 662 842220-0
www.museumdermoderne.at

Konzept, Redaktion / Concept, editing: Jürgen Tabor
Geleitwort von / Opening remarks by: Dietrich Karner
Vorwort von / Foreword by: Thorsten Sadowsky, Gregor Neuerer
Interview mit / with: Belinda Kazeem-Kamiński
Texte von / Texts by: Stefanie Grünangerl, Jürgen Tabor
Artist Statements von / by: Forensic Architecture; Alba Malika Belhadj Merzoug, Melanie Forsthuber, Pia Geisreiter, Magdalena Heller, Hannah Imhoff, Agnes Elena Kern, Vera Kern, Kevin Klinger, Leonie Mirjam Lindinger, Charlotte Pann, Sabine Reisenbüchler, Eva-Maria Schitter, Sculpting Feminism Reading Group, this world is Ego No longer, Angelika Wienerroither, Judith Zaunschirm, Marija Živojinović
Übersetzungen / Translations: Tim Beeby & Sabine Bürger (S. / pp. 123–200), Greg Bond (S. / pp. 15–107)
Lektorat / Copy editing: textstern, Ulrike Ritter (Deutsch / German), Daniel Ross (Englisch / English)
Gestaltung / Design: Annja Krautgasser
Bildbearbeitung / Image processing: Digital Imaging & Prepress, Mario Rott

Erschienen im / Published by:
VfmK Verlag für moderne Kunst GmbH
Schwedenplatz 2/24
1010 Wien / Vienna
hello@vfmk.org
www.vfmk.org

ISBN 978-3-903439-66-5

Vertrieb / Distribution
Europa / Europe: LKG, www.lkg-va.de
UK: Cornerhouse Publications, www.cornerhousepublications.org
USA: D.A.P., www.artbook.com

Bibliografische Information der Deutschen Nationalbibliothek: Die Deutsche Nationalbibliothek verzeichne diese Publikation in der Deutschen Nationalbibliografi detaillierte bibliografische Daten sind im Internet über dnb.de abrufbar. / Bibliographic information publishec by the Deutsche Nationalbibliothek: The Deutsche Nationalbibliothek lists this publication in the Deutsche Nationalbibliografie; detailed bibliographic data is ava lable on the Internet at dnb.de.

Textnachweis / **Text Credits**

Bildnachweis / **Image Credits**

Karo Akpokiere (S. / pp. 27, 29)
Alba Malika Belhadj Merzoug (S. / pp. 141, 143)
Lothar Baumgarten (S. / pp. 31, 33): Sammlung Genera Foundation – Dauerleihgabe am Museum der Moderne Salzburg / Generali Foundation Collection—Permanen Loan to the Museum der Moderne Salzburg; Bildrecht, Wien / Vienna
Danica Dakić / Bildrecht, Wien / Vienna (S. / pp. 35, 3
Forensic Architecture (S. / pp. 42–43)
Melanie Forsthuber (S. / pp. 145, 147)
Samuel Fosso und / and Jean Marc Patras, Paris (S. / pp. 45, 47, 49, 51)
Pia Geisreiter (S. / pp. 149, 151)
Charlotte Haslund-Christensen / Bildrecht, Wien / Vienna (S. / pp. 53, 55)
Magdalena Heller (S. / pp. 153, 155)
Hanna Imhoff (S. / pp. 157, 159)
Alfredo Jaar / Bildrecht, Wien / Vienna, und / and Galerie Hubert Winter, Wien / Vienna (S. / pp. 57, 59, 61, 63)
Voluspa Jarpa und / and mor charpentier, Paris (S. / pp. 65, 67)
Belinda Kazeem-Kamiński (S. / pp. 72–73)
Agnes Elena Kern (S. / pp. 161, 163)
Vera Kern (S. / pp. 165, 167)
Kevin Klinger (S. / pp. 169, 171)
Leonie Mirjam Lindinger (S. / pp. 173, 175)
Charlotte Pann (S. / pp. 178–179)
Adrian Piper (S. / pp. 82–83): Sammlung Generali Foundation – Dauerleihgabe am Museum der Moderne Salzburg / Generali Foundation Collection—Permanent Loan to the Museum der Moderne Salzburg
Lisl Ponger (S. / pp. 85, 87): Museum der Moderne Salzburg; Bildrecht, Wien / Vienna
Sabine Reisenbüchler (S. / pp. 181, 183)

a-Maria Schitter (S. / pp. 185, 187)
ulpting Feminism Reading Group (S. / pp. 189, 191)
s world is Ego No longer (S. / pp. 195, 197)
ra Walker, Sprüth Magers, London, und / and Sikkema
nkins & Co, New York (S. / pp. 92–93)
gelika Wienerroither (S. / pp. 199, 201)
dith Zaunschirm (S. / pp. 203, 205)
rija Živojinović (S. / pp. 207, 209)

tonachweis / Photo Credits
2022
ro Akpokiere (S. / p. 29)
ba Malika Belhadj Merzoug (S. / pp. 141, 143)
nica Dakić (S. / pp. 35, 37)
rensic Architecture (S. / p. 43)
muel Fosso (S. / pp. 45, 47, 49, 51)
a Geisreiter (S. / pp. 149, 151)
arlotte Haslund-Christensen (S. / pp. 53, 55)
agdalena Heller (S. / p. 153)
iner Iglar (S. / pp. 27, 42, 57, 59, 61, 63, 72, 73, 82, 87,
, 145, 147, 155, 159, 161, 167, 169, 185 oben / top, 195,
7, 201, 203, 205)
luspa Jarpa (S. / pp. 65, 67)
erner Kaligofsky / Bildrecht, Wien / Vienna (S. / p. 83)
nes Elena Kern (S. / p. 163)
ra Kern (S. / p. 165)
vin Klinger (S. / p. 171)
onie Mirjam Lindinger (S. / pp. 173, 175)
arlotte Pann (S. / pp. 178–179)
sl Ponger (S. / p. 87)
ario Punales (S. / pp. 31, 33)
abine Reisenbüchler (S. / pp. 181, 183)
a-Maria Schitter (S. / pp. 185 unten / bottom, 187)
culpting Feminism Reading Group (S. / pp. 189, 191)
ara Walker (S. / p. 92)
ngelika Wienerroither (S. / p. 199)
arija Živojinović (S. / pp. 207, 209)

eihgeber:innen der Ausstellung Teil I / enders to the Exhibition Part I:
aro Akpokiere, Hamburg
anica Dakić, Düsseldorf / Dusseldorf
ammlung Deutsche Bank, Frankfurt am Main
ara Walker)
orensic Architecture, London
ammlung Generali Foundation – Dauerleihgabe am
useum der Moderne Salzburg / Generali Foundation
ollection—Permanent Loan to the Museum der
oderne Salzburg (Lothar Baumgarten, Adrian Piper)
harlotte Haslund-Christensen, Kopenhagen /
openhagen
alerie Hubert Winter, Wien / Vienna (Alfredo Jaar)
elinda Kazeem-Kamiński, Wien / Vienna
or charpentier, Paris (Voluspa Jarpa)
Museum der Moderne Salzburg (Lisl Ponger)
Jean Marc Patras, Paris (Samuel Fosso)
Sprüth Magers, London, und / and Sikkema Jenkins & Co., New York (Kara Walker)

Leihgeber:innen der Ausstellung Teil II / Lenders to the Exhibition Part II:
Alba Malika Belhadj Merzoug, Melanie Forsthuber, Pia Geisreiter, Magdalena Heller, Hannah Imhoff, Agnes Elena Kern, Vera Kern, Kevin Klinger, Leonie Mirjam Lindinger, Charlotte Pann, Sabine Reisenbüchler, Eva-Maria Schitter, Sculpting Feminism Reading Group, this world is Ego No longer, Angelika Wienerroither, Judith Zaunschirm, Marija Živojinović

Generali Foundation
Kustodin, Leitung der Sammlung / Curator, Head of Collection: Doris Leutgeb
Kurator / Curator: Jürgen Tabor
Administration: Elisabeth Michl

Mitglieder / Members
Generali Versicherung AG
BAWAG P.S.K. Versicherung AG
Europäische Reiseversicherung AG
Apleona Real Estate AT GmbH

Präsidium / Board of Governors
Dietrich Karner, Präsident / President Generali Foundation
Gregor Pilgram, Vorstandsvorsitzender / Chairman Generali Versicherung AG

Vorstand / Managing Board
Axel Sima, Generali Versicherung AG
Erik Eybl, Generali Versicherung AG
Thorsten Sadowsky, Direktor / Director Museum der Moderne Salzburg

Kunstbeirat / Artistic Advisory Board
Johan Holten, Direktor / Director Kunsthalle Mannheim
Edelbert Köb, Kurator, Wien / Curator, Vienna
Chus Martínez, Leiterin des Institut Kunst Basel an der Fachhochschule Nordwestschweiz (FHNW) / Director of the Art Institute at the FHNW Academy of Art and Design, Basel

GENERALI

Museum der Moderne Salzburg
Direktor / Director: Thorsten Sadowsky
Kaufmännische Direktorin / Director of Administration and Finances: Friedrun Schwanzer
Direktionsbüro / Directors' Office: Helena Zellner
Public Relations und / and Marketing: Martin Riegler (Leitung / Head), Katharina Maximoff
Studienzentrum und Bibliothek / Study Center and Library: Stefanie Grünangerl
Besucherservice Visitor Services: Thomas Fenninger (Leitung / Head) und Team / and team
Technik / Technicians: Oliver Wacht (Leitung / Head), Patrick Gänser, Johann Gruber, Christian Hauer, Alija Salihovic

Ausstellungen und Sammlungen / Exhibitions and Collections:
Kuratorisches Team / Curatorial Team: Christina Penetsdorfer (Chefkuratorin / Chief Curator), Barbara Herzog (Sammlung und Bildarchiv / Collection and Picture Archive), Kerstin Stremmel (Fotografie und Medienkunst / Photography and Media Art), Andrea Lehner-Hagwood (Kuratorische Assistentin Fotografie und Medienkunst / Curatorial Assistant Photography and Media Art), Doris Leutgeb (Kustodin, Leitung Sam lung Generali Foundation / Curator, Head of Generali Foundation Collection), Lena Nievers (Sammlungsleite Moderne Kunst / Head of Collection Modern Art), Marijana Schneider (Zeitgenössische Kunst / Contemp rary Art), Jürgen Tabor (Sammlung Generali Foundatio Generali Foundation Collection), Tina Teufel (Zeitgenö sische Kunst / Contemporary Art)
Depotleitung und Registratur / Head of Art Storage ar Registrar: Annette Lill-Rastern
Registrarin / Registrar: Susanne Greimel
Restaurierung / Conservation: Desiree Rinne
Kunstvermittlung / Museum Education: Mirabelle Spreckelsen (Leitung / Head), Victoria Fahrengruber, Elisabeth Ihrenberger, Christine Fegerl, Magdalena Stieb, Cristina Struber, Theresa Weiss
Finanzen und Controlling / Finance and Controlling: Christine Latocha (Leitung / Head), Elke Fleischhacker Sarah Haas
Personal und Recht / Human Resources and Legal: Daniela Eibl
Beschaffung und Administration / Procurement and Administration: Roland Walchhofer (Leitung / Head), Dzemila Ibrahivomic, Claudia Tiefenbacher
Museumsshop / Museum Store: Sabine Stollberger (Leitung / Head), Nadja Leitner, Niklas Koschel, Julia Kronreif

Aufsichtsrat / Supervisory Board
Brigitta Pallauf (Vorsitzende / Chairwoman)
Simon Heilig-Hofbauer (Stv. Vorsitzender / Deputy)
Daniela Gutschi
Johannes Schwaninger

Das Museum der Moderne Salzburg wird durch Mittel des Landes Salzburg finanziert. / The Museum der Moderne Salzburg is sponsored with funds provided by the Province of Salzburg.

Museum der Moderne
Salzburg